Date Due

BIBLE TRANSLATION
AND
THE SPREAD OF THE CHURCH

STUDIES IN CHRISTIAN MISSION

GENERAL EDITOR
Marc R. Spindler (University of Leiden)

EDITORIAL BOARD
Jocelyn Murray (London)
Jean Pirotte (Université de Louvain)

VOLUME 2

BIBLE TRANSLATION
AND
THE SPREAD OF THE CHURCH

THE LAST 200 YEARS

EDITED BY

PHILIP C. STINE

SECOND IMPRESSION

E.J. BRILL

LEIDEN · NEW YORK · KÖLN

1992

This series offers a forum for scholarship on the history of Christian missionary movements world-wide, the dynamics of Christian witness and service in new surrounds, the transition from movements to churches, and the areas of cultural initiative or involvement of Christian bodies and individuals, such as education, health, community development, press, literature and art. Special attention is given to local initiative and leadership and to Christian missions from the Third World. Studies in the theories and paradigms of mission in their respective contexts and contributions to missiology as a theological discipline is a second focus of the series. Occasionally volumes will contain selected papers from outstanding missiologists and proceedings of significant conferences related to the themes of the series.

Enquiries regarding the submission of works for publication in the series may be directed to Professor Marc R. Spindler, IIMO, University of Leiden, Rapenburg 61, 2311 GJ Leiden, The Netherlands.

First impression 1990
Second impression 1992

The paper in this book meets the guidelines for permanence and durability of the Committee on Production Guidelines for Book Longevity of the Council on Library Resources.

Library of Congress Cataloging-in-Publication Data

Bible translation and the spread of the church: the last 200 years / edited by Philip C. Stine.
    p.   cm.—(Studies in Christian mission, ISSN 0924-9389; v. 2)
    Contains the major papers presented at the Center of Theological Inquiry, Princeton, N.J., October 29th-31st, 1988.
    Includes bibliographical references.
    ISBN 90-04-09331-1
    1. Bible—Versions—Congresses. 2. Bible—Translating—Congresses. 3. Missions—History—19th century—Congresses. 4. Missions—History—20th century—Congresses. I. Stine, Philip C., 1943- . II. Series.
BS454.B52   1990
220.3—dc20   90-46957
                                       CIP

ISSN   0924-9389
ISBN   90 04 09331 1

PRINTED IN THE NETHERLANDS

CONTENTS

INTRODUCTION

From the beginning of the Church, as it spread out from the Eastern Mediterranean, its expansion has been paralleled by Bible translation. Sometimes translation preceded and perhaps stimulated the planting of a new church; more often it followed. But translation into vernacular languages was, in most cases, so much a given, something that was simply understood as necessary to the life of the church, that it was rarely questioned. Most recently, the explosive church growth in Third World countries that began with the modern missionary movement of the last two hundred years brought with it a parallel mushrooming in the number of languages into which all or part of the Bible was translated.

One development which was at once an outgrowth of and a stimulus to this wave of new translations was the professionalization of Bible translation. Whereas translators have long known they needed good knowledge of the biblical languages and of exegetical methods and findings, until 50 years ago that was deemed qualification enough. But now few Bible translators come to their task without some training in theory and practice. The theories that modern translators follow incorporate work from a number of fields, among them linguistics, sociolinguistics and cultural anthropology, cognitive science and psychology, communication science, semiotics, and literary criticism. And thus translators are now more sensitive to cultural, sociological and psychological dynamics in the churches and societies where they are working than they were in the past.

The theological aspects of translation are also being considered. But although we may believe that theology can affect the kind of translation one prepares, and likewise the type of translation produced can affect the theology of a church, and although we may sense that a church develops faster and with a deeper faith if it has the Bible, and although we may recognize that introducing literacy will alter the world-view and cognitive processes of individuals, there has been no real effort to document these things or to study closely what has been wrought when the Bible has been translated.

Which is precisely why at the invitation of the United Bible Societies more than 50 churchmen and scholars, missiologists and scientists, met together from October 29th-31st, 1988, at the Center of Theological Inquiry in Princeton, New Jersey. What has Bible translation had to do with the growth of the Church over the last 200 years? How has it affected the theology of the new churches? Has it had any impact on the languages and cultures? What can we learn that will alter our goals and intentions for the future? These were among the questions the group sought to address.

This volume contains the major papers that were presented and discussed that weekend. Because most of them cover several interrelated subjects, they could be arranged in different ways. For example, Walls and Batalden are concerned with the context of translation, Arichea and Luzbetak with the process, and Sanneh, Whiteman, Escobar, Koyama, and Fick with the effects of translation.

But the arrangement in this volume recognizes instead the division between those papers which deal with theological issues and those concerned with cultural or political matters.

Lamin Sanneh's paper serves as an excellent introduction to the whole topic. He points out that Christianity was unique in turning its back on the geographical setting and language of its origin and in adapting instead "a multiplicity of geographical centers as its home", and indigenous languages through all cultures and languages. Sanneh studies both positive and negative effects of indigenizing the gospel through translation, and concludes that the process gave rise to a pluralism, which rather than weakening Christianity, became its source of strength since Christians are united not by cultural and linguistic similarities but by their common relationship in respect to God.

For Andrew Walls, translation of the Bible is parallel to and entirely dependent on the divine act of translation, the incarnation of Christ. As God in Christ became man, it was in a specific linguistic, historical, and cultural context, as is each Bible translation. Walls suggests that "a comparative history of translation would be an illuminating way of approaching the history of Christian mission". Two major models of Scripture use have been followed throughout history: that of Wulfila, who developed an orthography and translated the Bible into Gothic, and also trained an elite class to read it; that of Patrick, who required believers to use the Scriptures in Latin, not their vernaculars. For many centuries it was Patrick's pattern which prevailed, but in this last century the shift has been towards that of Wulfila.

Whereas Sanneh and Walls are concerned with the theological impetus and effects of translation, Daniel Arichea looks closely at theological questions that impinge on and affect the actual work of the translator. Whether to produce a formally equivalent translation, often called "literal", or an audience-centered one which is functionally equivalent is a profound theological decision, as are decisions on matters of text, canon, and exegesis. Arichea concludes that as we produce translations for specific audiences we are engaging in a theological task: translation is always interpretation.

In a detailed study of one particular political and cultural context of Bible translation, Stephen Batalden demonstrates that translators in Russian, in addition to considering the theological issues described by Arichea, would be inevitably engaged in political considerations. Decisions on text, canon, exegesis, type of language, type of translation—all are related to the matter of authority in the "highly structured Russian and Soviet politicized environment". The experience of the Bible Societies around the world would certainly confirm that the matter of authority has doomed more than one new translation, and studies of the forces that play in church and society should be taken very seriously before translation is attempted.

Samuel Escobar and Kosuke Koyama are concerned with the role that translation of the Scriptures has had in developing theologies in particular regions. Escobar, although speaking from a Latin American perspective, states a universal truth when he links the promise of a new indigenous theology to the availability of Scriptures in the vernacular language. Liberation theology, for example, represents "a return to the biblical sources of the Christian life, and a new reading of history". Among speakers of indigenous languages in Latin America, where translation of the Scriptures is only now taking place, what seems likely to emerge will be reflection by those churches on their identity, their future, and their liberation.

Koyama addresses the question of Asian theology, but argues that the only true indigenous theology is that of Jesus of Nazareth. "The Gospel must be accommodated to a given language in order to speak sensibly to the people in that culture". And thus for Westerners to use "indigenous theology" for African, Latin American and Asian theologies reflects a "Euro-centered parochialism". For him, the Bible is the literature wherein the languages of discontinuity and continuity are in dialogue in an effort to inspire humanity to free themselves from idolatry. A well-accommodated or contextualized theology must inspire us to demonstrate a self-giving love, so that "Bible translation is a participation in God's act of sharing God's indigenous glory with humanity".

Two papers deal specifically with cultural issues in translation. As Louis Luzbetak points out, translation is, after all, cross-cultural communication, and good translators will be able to listen to the cultures in which they are working. This sensitization requires that the translator understand 1) how culture is a design for living, a plan or a code for behavior; 2) how it is an integrated system of several subsystems operating simultaneously; and 3) how it is a dynamic, living organism, always acting and reacting.

If Luzbetak is concerned with the forces at play in a culture to which a translator must be sensitive, Darrell Whiteman ventures into largely unexplored terrain and wonders what evidence is there that Scripture translation has contributed to people's social and cultural development. It is a difficult quest, for it is not possible to isolate two societies where conditions are identical except for the factor of vernacular Scriptures. And further, anthropologists already biased against Christianity's influence on society have not isolated the particular effects Scripture translation may have had. Whiteman's response will surely have great importance for future research, however, as he elaborates a model of integral human development which permits Bible translation and many other factors to be measured and assessed as they affect development.

The challenge of the symposium was to understand better the correlation between Bible translation and the growth of the Church. At the last session, Ulrich Fick drew on the papers and discussions which had followed them to consider the future, and in fact, his paper could serve equally well as an introduction or as a conclusion to this volume. Fick points out that a distinct characteristic of the Bible which several papers illustrate is the diversity and yet unity. It is diverse because of its human element, as God reveals himself in human history, but its unity comes from the divine element, as all of it is part of a consistent revelation of God. If the Church of tomorrow is not to be fragmentized, and if it is to show that peoples of the world why they can be different and yet appreciate one another in unselfishness, then access to the Bible will be crucial.

Philip C. Stine

CONTRIBUTORS

Dr. Daniel C. Arichea, Jr., Philippines - UBS Translation Coordinator for the Asia-Pacific Region. Ph.D., Duke University. Professor of New Testament at Union Theological Seminary, Philippines until 1970, he has served since then as a UBS Translation Consultant in the Philippines and several other Southeast Asian countries, most notably Indonesia.

Dr. Stephen K. Batalden, USA - Associate Professor of History, Arizona State University. Ph.D., University of Minnesota. Has conducted research in Greece and the USSR and is a leading Western expert on the Orthodox churches in Eastern Europe, as well as Bible translations in those countries.

Dr. Samuel Escobar, Peru - Professor of Missiology at Eastern Baptist Theological Seminary, Philadelphia. Formerly Traveling Secretary and Associate General Secretary of the International Fellowship of Evangelical Students and General Director of the InterVarsity Christian Fellowship of Canada. Has taught in Canada, Colombia, Chile and the USA as well as in Peru, where he has also served as a pastor and been active in working for the human rights of victims of terrorism and oppression.

Dr. Ulrich Fick, Federal Republic of Germany - Former UBS General Secretary. Studied theology at Tübingen, Berlin and Bonn. Was involved in radio and television ministry for the Lutheran Church before becoming Program Director of Radio Voice of the Gospel in Addis Ababa. Served in numerous church and Bible Society positions in Germany before assuming his assignment as General Secretary in 1973, coordinating the work of more than 100 member societies and national offices which distribute Scriptures in over 180 countries. Has received honorary doctorates in Hungary and the Philippines.

Prof. Kosuke Koyama, Japan - John D. Rockefeller, Jr. Professor of Ecumenics and World Christianity, Union Theological Seminary, New York. After studies at Tokyo Union Theological Seminary, Drew and Princeton (Ph.D. thesis on Luther), Professor Koyama has taught in Thailand, New Zealand and the USA. He is widely acclaimed for the cross-cultural perspective he has brought to the study of theology.

Dr. Louis J. Luzbetak, S.V.D., USA - Ph.D., University of Fribourg in Anthropology, with linguistics and missiology as his minor fields. Currently in service with the Pontifical Council for Culture (Vatican). Formerly editor of *Anthropos*, President of Divine Word College, Epworth, Iowa, and Director of the Center for Applied Research in the Apostolate in Washington, D.C. Has taught anthropology at Catholic University of America, and linguistics at Georgetown, and has done research in New Guinea. Church mission has always been the focal point of his teaching and research.

Prof. Lamin Sanneh, The Gambia - Ph.D., University of London, African Islamic History. Is Professor of World Christianity at Yale University Divinity School. Prof. Sanneh is known for his studies of the indigenous character of the Christian faith and for his studies on the historical expansion and expression of Islam in Africa. He has studied and taught in Africa, Europe, the Middle East and North America.

Dr. Philip C. Stine, USA - UBS Translation Services Coordinator since 1984. Ph.D., University of Michigan. Formerly a UBS Translation Consultant and then Translation Coordinator for the Africa Region.

Prof. Andrew F. Walls, Scotland - Studied History and Theology at Oxford University. Served in Nigeria and Sierra Leone. He is Director of the Centre for the Study of Christianity in the Non-Western World, now located at the University of Edinburgh. For many years he has compiled the annual missiological bibliography for the *International Review of Mission*.

Dr. Darrell L. Whiteman, USA - Professor of Cultural Anthropology, E. Stanley Jones School of World Mission and Evangelism, Asbury Theological Seminary. Ph.D., Southern Illinois University. Dr. Whiteman has published widely on his research in the Solomon Islands, Australia and Papua New Guinea. He is the editor of *Missiology*.

LAMIN SANNEH

GOSPEL AND CULTURE:
RAMIFYING EFFECTS OF SCRIPTURAL TRANSLATION

A popular but erroneous view has been promoted in several quarters regarding the naturalness of separating gospel from culture, with the assumption that by that procedure Christians can get at the *gospel* pure and simple. However, this is no more possible than getting at the kernel of the onion without the peel. The *pure* gospel, stripped of all cultural entanglements, would evaporate in a vague abstraction, although if the gospel were without its own intrinsic power it would be nothing more than cultural ideology. If Christianity could be turned into a pure Platonic form, then it would be religion fit only for the elite, whereas if it was just a cultural disguise it would breed only manipulators. The real challenge is to identify this intrinsic power without neglecting the necessary cultural factor.

It is important to call attention to the fundamental character of Christianity as a force for cultural integration. Several paradoxes point to this fact. The first is that Christianity is almost unique among world religions for being peripheral in the place of its origin. Ever since Pentecost and the Antiochean breakthrough, Christianity has turned its back on Jerusalem and Bethlehem as secondary signposts, with the consequence of the religion becoming preponderant in regions once considered outside God's promises. The Christian religious psyche was purged of the "Promised Land" fixation, so that believers have almost to err to revert to any one center to the exclusion of others. The second paradox is that Christians are unique in abandoning the original language of Jesus and instead adopting Greek in its *Koine*, and Latin in its *vulgar* as the central media of the church.[1] Except in extremist sectarian groups, Christians never made the language of Jesus a requirement of faith or membership in the fellowship. It is this linguistic revolution which accounts for the entire New Testament canon being written in a language other than the one in which Jesus preached.[2] Thus it is that translation, and the cross-cultural implications related to it, came to be built into the very fabric of Christianity. Another striking paradox is the contention by Christians that God's eternal counsels are compatible with ordinary, everyday speech. This view cuts across the tendency in some parts of early Christianity to cast the religion into an elitist gnostic discourse.

---

[1] For a scrupulous account of the language issue in the Bible see Matthew Black, "The Biblical Languages", *The Cambridge History of the Bible: Vol. i: From the Beginnings to Jerome*, eds. P.R. Ackroyd and C.F. Evans, (Cambridge: Cambridge University Press, 1970, repr. 1988), pp. 1-29.

[2] Edward Gibbon writes, "The authentic histories of the actions of Christ were composed in the Greek language, at a considerable distance from Jerusalem, and after the Gentile converts were grown extremely numerous" (Gibbon, *Decline and Fall*, vol. i, 432).

Christianity in the mouth of Jesus was the divulging of the secret design of God,[3] and Christian faith the public attestation to that fact.

This view of religious language as belonging to the ordinary, commonplace world of men and women, and even of children,[4] is not necessarily shared by the other religious traditions which in fact are inclined to make a virtue of elitist secrecy, of a professional cultic language understandable only to the elite, initiated few. The Christian attitude to religious language places right at the heart of things the idea that people, especially ordinary people, should understand,[5] a view with momentous consequences for social and cultural awakening, with people feeling that the social enterprise as such is not

---

[3] Mk. iv:22; Lk. viii:17, xi:33; Jn. vii:4, xviii:20; W. Pannenburg, ed. *Revelation as History*, (New York: Macmillan, 1969), pp. 141ff.

[4] In his characteristically ebullient style, Erasmus (d. 1536) propounded this view in the context precisely of Scriptural translation. He wrote: "Indeed, I disagree very much with those who are unwilling that Holy Scripture, translated into the vulgar tongue, be read by the uneducated, as if Christ taught such intricate doctrines that they could scarcely be understood by very few theologians, or as if the strength of the Christian religion consisted in men's ignorance of it. The mysteries of kings, perhaps, are better concealed, but Christ wishes his mysteries published as openly as possible. I would that even the lowliest women read the Gospels and the Pauline Epistles. And I would that they were translated into all languages so that they could be read and understood by Scots and Irish but also by Turks and Saracens . . . Would that, as a result, the farmer sing some portion of them at the plow, the weaver hum parts of them to the movement of his shuttle, the traveller lighten the weariness of the journey with stories of this kind". Desiderius Erasmus, *Christian Humanism and the Reformation*, Selected Writings, with the Life of Erasmus by Beatus Rhenanus, ed., John C. Olin, New York: Harper Torchbooks, 96-97. See also Fr. Louis Bouyer, "Erasmus in Relation to the Medieval Biblical Tradition" in *The Cambridge History of the Bible, vol. ii: The West From the Fathers to the Reformation*, ed. G.W.H. Lampe, (Cambridge: Cambridge University Press, 1969, repr. 1988), pp. 492-505.

[5] In his study of the New Testament as enshrining the popular idiom of the age, Adolf Deissmann argued that the old literary style of classical Attic differed markedly from the New Testament style in its elaborate and cultivated refinement, whereas in the New Testament "the underground stream of the people's language springs up powerfully into the daylight". This prevented Christianity from becoming "a privileged esoteric affair of a small and exclusive upper class". Adolf Deissmann, *The New Testament in the Light of Modern Research: The Haskell Lectures, 1929*, (Garden City, NY: Doubleday, Doran & Co. Inc., 1929), p. 80. Deissmann continued, "Jesus spoke of the light and the candlestick, of the city on the hill, of father and child, bread and fish, egg and scorpion, of asking and giving, of seed and crop, of hunger and thirst. No long sentences, no speculative questions, transparent, pithy, plastic . . . The Gospel, because it was the message of God to humanity, could only reveal itself in the simplest of garments . . . Whoever has eyes to see can learn much from the linguistic facts which meet us in the New Testament. The linguistic estimation of the New Testament shows us that our Holy Book in its classical, creative period is in close contact with the middle and lower classes and in sharp contrast to the old artificial Atticistic culture which struggled for a new lease of life in the surrounding world. Had the Gospel leagued itself with this ancient culture from the beginning it would have endangered what is best in it, and, especially, its future as a message to humanity would have been impossible" (pp. 94, 105-6).

discontinuous with God's universal plan.[6] It is one of the great historical truths of our day that otherwise obscure tribes, without a claim to cosmopolitan attainment, should find in indigenous particularity the sole grounds for appeal to international recognition. It is the Christian promotion of this indigenous particularity with the vernacular translations of missions which laid the basis for the modern nationalist phenomenon.

A final paradox, with practical implications for ecumenical relations, is the universal phenomenon of Christians adopting names for themselves without the explicit warrant of the founder of the religion or of the New Testament itself. The proliferation of denominational names and religious orders is the staple of all Christianity, whether from the left and low, or the right and high. This again is in sharp contrast to the other major world religions, and especially with those religions that have a missionary tradition, such as Islam. The name "Muslim", for example, is shared by all the followers of Islam, whatever the real differences in culture, custom, history, language and nationality, with explicit Qur'ánic sanction for the rule.[7] Christians, on the other hand, identify themselves by a variety of religious labels, from Anglican to Zionist, with Methodists, Orthodox, Presbyterians and others making up the middle center. Instead of decrying this phenomenon, or applauding it in Islam, it is our duty to understand it within the general context of the *translatability* of Christianity.

In these factors of paradox lies the central issue concerning the relationship between gospel and culture. In many quarters people assume a position that gospel and culture would make a right combination in the Third World, but that the same combination in the West is wrong or harmful. Consequently Western Christian missions come in for severe criticism because they bring this harmful combination of gospel and Western culture into the Third World where they suppress indigenous expression. A logical position, however, should see that the successful Western cultural transformation of Christianity indicates a similar possibility for the Third World, and, conversely, that the harmful consequences of the cultural adaptation of Christianity in the West will in time extend to the Third World as well. This symmetrical argument brings us to what it is that

---

6 Commenting on the revolutionary implications of the vernacular Bible, the English historian, G.R. Elton, noted the role it regrettably afforded the common folk. G.R. Elton, *Reformation Europe: 1517-1559*, (Cleveland, Ohio: Meridian Histories of Modern Europe, 1964), 52. In the light of that sentiment, the following comment seems apt: 'The issue that frequently escapes the dragnet of the historian is the cumulative capital Christianity has derived from the common language of ordinary people. To the secular historian this fact has only political significance as a force for incitement; to the economic and social historian it is a fact that creates social mobility, and perhaps social tension. Yet to a Christian the confident adoption of vernacular speech as consecrated vessel places such adoption squarely at the heart of religious change, and thus at the heart of historical consciousness. The central and enduring character of Christian history is the rendering of God's eternal counsels into terms of everyday speech. By that path believers have come to stand before their God' (L. Sanneh, *Translating the Message: The Missionary Impact on Culture*, Maryknoll, NY: Orbis Books, 1989).

7 Qur'án xxii:77-78.

makes culture both a natural ally as well as a natural foe of the gospel. It does not really matter whether we are speaking of Western culture or Third World culture in this regard. In all situations the gospel seems to find its natural congruence within the cultural stream while at the same time encountering there its most serious obstacles. I should like to expound this theme in two complementary stages, first dealing with the positive aspect before turning to the negative. In the concluding stages of the paper I shall synthesize the positive and negative aspects and examine their theological significance. I should stress that my observations have the claim to nothing more than a preliminary and cursory exploration.

The Positive Force of Gospel and Culture

One of the most forceful presentations of the cultural basis of Christianity is the German scholar, Ernst Troeltsch, whose work, *The Absoluteness of Christianity*, has left an enduring impact on generations of scholars. Troeltsch's central argument is that the gospel and Western culture are indistinguishable to the extent that people cannot speak of the one without implying the other. Two pessimistic conclusions are drawn from this: first, that Christianity has become so culture-specific that it is incommunicable cross-culturally; and second, that non-Western converts face the doubly impossible burden of "westernization" and "christianization" simultaneously.

Troeltsch's position has been implicitly, but nevertheless seriously questioned by at least three contemporary Western scholars. The historian Arnold Toynbee, for example, has argued that the "westernization" of Christianity represents only an historical phase in the expansion of the religion. Taking the Hellenic transformation of the church as the Western paradigmatic shift, Toynbee pressed for a fresh view in which the Greek scientific metaphysic of the first four centuries of the church no longer holds sway for people today whose worldview may be different. For one thing, the cumulative scientific construction of the Universe today demands a shift of interpretation. For another the West itself is in process of being relativised by new forms of culture and civilization.[8] Toynbee's own views on decoupling Christianity from Western culture have not gone

---

[8] Arnold J. Toynbee, *An Historian's Approach to Religion*, (London and New York: Oxford University Press, 1956), pp. 129ff. See also his *Civilization on Trial*, (New York: Oxford University Press, 1948), and *Christianity Among the Religions of the World*, (New York: Charles Scribner's Sons, 1957). Toynbee wrote in that last title about the need "to purge our Christianity of its Western accessories", pointing to the admirable example set by Christian missionaries in seeking to divest Christianity of its Western cultural accretions (92-3). He said the tendency in the West to treat Christianity as inseparable from its culture is a form of reprehensible idolatry, a vice he believed Mussolini carried to its extreme when the latter called attention to what the Italian genius had done to Christianity which would have remained "a wretched little Oriental sect . . . far away in Palestine". The religion, Mussolini asserted, "was salvaged" by being carried to Rome where it had the fortune to become the universal Roman Catholic Church of which Italy had the honor to be the center.

uncriticised,[9] but few people can doubt the essential soundness of his reasoning that the West no longer holds a monopoly on God's design for the world. This same idea is forcefully expressed in the words of another Western scholar, R.G. Collingwood. He said that under the levelling impact of Christianity the West in its Greco-Roman manifestation ceased to be the center of the world, ushering in a Copernican revolution in which the universal historical process becomes everywhere and always of the same kind, which is "the general development of God's purpose for human life. The infusion of Christian ideas", he continues, "overcomes not only the characteristic humanism and the substantialism of Greco-Roman history, but also its particularism".[10] The third writer who also tried to place the West within a comparative worldwide Christian perspective is William Ernest Hocking. In a book he wrote on the theme of the emerging world culture,[11] Hocking approached the matter from the point of view not only of Western experience as an aspect of the diversity of human experience but of the relative status of Western institutions themselves. He focused in this sense on the intrinsically limited, rather than absolute, nature of the state as a safeguard for human freedom. Rare among Western philosophers in taking history seriously, Hocking confronted, without, however, resolving the question about the challenge of historical pluralism for what may be regarded as the theological core and essence of Christianity.[12] Similar rumblings concerning the

---

[9] The Oxford scholar, Albert Hourani, has done a stringent criticism of Toynbee's historical methodology as that impinges on Christianity. Albert Hourani, *Europe and the Middle East,* (Berkeley and Los Angeles: University of California Press, 1980), chapter 7, "Toynbee's Vision of History", 135-60.

[10] R.G. Collingwood, *The Idea of History,* (London and New York: Oxford University Press, 1946, repr. 1966), p. 49.

[11] William Ernest Hocking, *The Coming World Civilization,* (London: George Allen and Unwin, 1958). Hocking was also the author of a better known and controversial work, *Re-Thinking Missions,* (New York: Harper and Brothers, 1932), a work which was important in leading the Dutch theologian, Hendrick Kraemer, to produce his influential work, *The Christian Message in a Non-Christian World,* 1938.

[12] Hocking, *World Civilization,* 134ff. Hocking senses that particularity is indispensable to authentic Christian expression, but seems undecided about whether local grounding of the faith is unavoidably in conflict with universality. Taking Quakerism as an example, he said that few people will doubt that Quakerism has "best caught the genius of a particularity that is also universal" (p. 135). He then relates Quakerism to Catholicism, saying that they "together bear their partials of a total truth, which includes the truth of a continuing historical community of aggressive *caritas* at once material and spiritual" (p. 135). It is clear that Hocking is trying to juggle the interests of Christianity as a dynamic historical phenomenon alongside those of Christianity as a fixed dogmatic system, and then inferring from that tension a progressive element largely constituted as "internal advance in self-understanding". This way of dealing with the issue dissolves historical diversity into an idealist construction.

relative position of the West in world history can be discerned in the writings of Marshall Hodgson[13] and E.H. Carr,[14] to cite only two further examples.

The cultural formulation of religion, and of Christianity in particular, represents a formidable intellectual legacy in our world. Much of the confidence by which this legacy is promoted stems from the peculiar role of the church in promoting culture. The spectacular success with Latin, for example, shows the church as the preserver and guardian of the Western tradition.[15] In the Carolingian empire, to take a different example, Christianity fostered the use of the vernacular. A leading champion was Otfrid von Weissenburg, active between 863 and 871. Otfrid devoted himself to furthering the vernacular cause for both religious as well as secular purposes. He directed his attention to his learned contemporaries "who knew how to think and who can be encouraged through the vernacular to read more for themselves. Moreover, he combines learning with piety with great technical skill; something which no one had hitherto attempted in German on such a scale. Like the Heliand poet, Otfrid moved within the Germanic thought-world of warrior-ethos, loyalty and obedience, the lord-man relationship".[16] Some of Otfrid's pronouncements took the form of a manifesto to the vernacular. Furthermore, as Christopher Dawson has proved, even in the period of Latin hegemony Christianity in Northern Europe became the promoter of vernacular literature and languages.[17]

The early Christians were themselves in no doubt about the essential pluralism of the religion they propagated, and drew comfort from the thought. Justin Martyr (c.100-165 A.D.), for example, a Palestinian born of settlers in Neapolis (Nablus), remarked: "For there is not a single race of human beings, barbarians, Greeks, or whatever name you please to call them, nomads or vagrants or herdsmen living in tents, where prayers through the name of Jesus the Crucified are not offered up to the Father and Maker of the universe".[18] In his famous letter to the Emperor Trajan, Pliny the Younger alluded to the enormous social diversity existing within the Christian movement, making the religion extremely difficult to check in its spread and appeal. He also implies that

[13] Marshall G.S. Hodgson, "The Interrelations of Societies in History", *Comparative Studies Society and History*, v (1962-63), 227-250.

[14] E.H. Carr, *What is History?* New York: Alfred A. Knopf, 1962, repr. 1964, in particular chapter VI, "The Widening Horizon".

[15] See W.H. Frend, *The Rise of Christianity*, (Philadelphia: Fortress Press, 1984), p. 560.

[16] John Michael Wallace-Hadrill, *The Frankish Church*, (Oxford: Clarendon Press, 1983), p. 386.

[17] Christopher Dawson, *Religion and the Rise of Western Culture*, (London: Sheed and Ward, 1950), p. 115.

[18] J. Spencer Trimingham, *Christianity Among the Arabs in Pre-Islamic Times*, (London and New York: Longman, Beirut: Librairie du Liban, 1979), p. 94. Gibbon cites the same passage, *The Decline and Fall of the Roman Empire*, (New York: Modern Library), vol. i, p. 438.

Christian activity has acted to rejuvenate the older traditions, an important point to which I shall refer presently. He wrote despairingly,

> People of every age and rank and of both sexes will continue to be gravely imperilled. The contagion of that superstition has infected not only cities (*civitates*) but villages (*agros*) and hamlets; but it seems possible to check and correct it. It is clear, at least, that the temples which had been deserted are again frequented, and the sacred festivals long intermitted are revived. Sacrificial victims for which purchases have been rare are again in demand.[19]

Another early source, the anonymous *Epistle to Diognetus*, believed now to have been written not in 124 A.D. as generally claimed, but in the third century, takes a positive view of Christian cultural pluralism.

> The difference between Christians and the rest of mankind is not a matter of nationality, or of language, or customs. Christians do not live apart in separate cities of their own, speak any special dialect, nor practice any eccentric way of life . . . They pass their lives in whatever township—Greek or foreign—each man's lot has determined; and conform to ordinary local usage in their clothing, diet, and other habits . . . they are residents at home in their own countries . . . they take their full part as citizens . . . For them, any foreign country is a motherland, and any motherland is a foreign country.[20]

Ancient statecraft, in some contrast to present policy, saw cultural pluralism as a necessity for a strong and vigorous society, with Christianity as an engine for this. For example, when Hungary was transformed from "the Magyar robber state" "into the Apostolic Kingdom that was to be the eastern bulwark of Christendom", its founder, St. Stephen, seeking to emulate Rome whose greatness he attributed to its encouragement of pluralism, declared: *nam unius linguae, uniusque moris regnum imbecile et fragilum* ("for weak and fragile is a kingdom with one language and custom").[21] There may, of course, be the usual

---

[19] Moses Hadas, tr. and ed., *A History of Rome: From Its Origins to 529 A.D. as Told by the Roman Historians*, (New York: Doubleday Anchor Books, 1956), p. 131. Also *The Letters of Pliny the Younger*, tr. & ed. Betty Radice, (New York: Penguin Books, 1969, repr. 1985), pp. 293-95.

[20] *Early Christian Writings: The Apostolic Fathers*, tr. & ed. Maxwell Staniforth, (New York: Penguin Books, 1968, repr. 1982), pp. 176-77.

[21] Dawson, *Western Culture*, 137. Dawson's own views on Christianity and culture have come under attack. Commenting on the ideas which Dawson presented in his book, *Beyond Politics*, T.S. Eliot took him to task for saying that the extent of Christians creating culture should be limited to participation in a voluntary organization of culture, which in a democratic society is the political party. T.S. Eliot, *Christianity and Culture: The Idea of a Christian Society and Notes Towards the Definition of Culture*, (New York and London: Harcourt Brace Jovanovich, 1968), pp. 59-61. Eliot's own proposals smack too much of the

Constantinian peril in coopting Christianity as an accoutrement of state policy, in Hungary or anywhere else, but the issue here is Christianity as a positive force for an invigorated pluralist culture. It is the opposite of the popular notion of Christianity as ruthless cultural iconoclasm. This introduces the second, negative stage of the relationship of gospel and culture.

The Negative Force of Gospel and Culture

In his majestic work on the Roman Empire, the 18th century historian, Edward Gibbon, formulated the thesis, now congenially implanted in the Western liberal temper, that Christianity dealt a mortal blow to the empire by introducing endemic provincialism and fostering stubborn congregational particularism at the local level.[22] Gibbon goes on further to impute subversive motives to Christian attitudes towards the empire, saying that Christians considered "every disaster that happened to the empire as an infallible symptom of an expiring world".[23] He made colorful assertions about Christianity as the enemy of enlightened progress, saying that culture in its noble rebirth must discard the religion as the butterfly with the chrysalis. Sir James Frazer, who in anthropological science belonged to the Intellectualist School, picked up these views and embellished them with a wealth of ethnographic detail, using evidence of Christianity's open frontiers with Paganism as signs of a shared irrational defect.[24] In Frazer's evolutionary model magic, religion and science followed each other in an ascending, superseding order,[25] with the religious gadfly destined for extinction in the evolutionary process as such. There are innumerable variations on this theme, with Edmund Leach, another British anthropologist, calling for the overthrow of religion and the full emancipation of human beings from the fetters of dogma.[26]

In a curious way this negative view of Christianity was gratuitously promoted by Christian scholars themselves, even though for them the focus is on the power of Christianity to succeed where others failed, or were thought to be failing. An eloquent proponent of this view of Christianity is the German scholar, Ulhorn. Writing in 1882, he postulated: "Had the stream of new life

status-quo in some enlightened reincarnation to be a meaningful prescription.

[22] Edward Gibbon, *The Decline and Fall of the Roman Empire*, (New York: Modern Library, N.D.), 3 vols, vol. i, pp. 671-726.

[23] Gibbon, *Decline and Fall*, vol. i, 405-6.

[24] James Frazer, *The Golden Bough: Part IV: Adonis, Attis, Osiris: Studies in the History of Oriental Religion*, 3rd edition, (London: Macmillan & Co., 1914), pp. 300-301.

[25] For a rigorous critique of Frazer and other evolutionary theorists, see Sir Edward Evans-Pritchard, *Theories of Primitive Religion*, (London and New York: Oxford University Press, 1965).

[26] See, for example, his 1967 BBC Reith Lectures, *A Runaway World?* (London: BBC Publications, 1968).

issuing from Christ encountered ancient life when the latter was still unbroken, it would have recoiled impotent from the shock. But ancient life had by this time begun to break up; its solid foundations had begun to weaken . . . "[27] This became the thundering theme in Eric Dodds' influential book,[28] which elicited a counter-rejoinder in an edited work.[29] Dodds' main argument was that "For the people of the Empire it was a time of increasing insecurity and misery; for the Church it was a time of relative freedom from persecution, of steady numerical growth, and above all of swift intellectual advance".[30] The basic outline of Christianity under this negative thesis is that cultural opportunism enabled the new religion to profit from the crisis and misfortune whose causes lay outside the religion. Dodds put it in sensational terms as follows:

> From a world so impoverished intellectually, so insecure materially, so filled with fear and hatred as the world of the third century, any path that promised escape must have attracted serious minds. Many besides Plotinus must have given a new meaning to the words of Agamemnon in Homer, "Let us flee to our own country". That advice might stand as a motto for the whole period.[31]

In his magisterial study, Kenneth Scott Latourette advances an identical argument. "Had Christianity been born in a vigorous young culture whose adherents were confident of its virtues", he hypothesized, "it might have met a different fate".[32] However, in their different ways these writers base their reasoning on evidence which is by no means unequivocal. For example, Latourette, scrupulous to the hilt, admits that Christianity had encountered a vigorous Neoplatonism which "had the endorsement of a much larger proportion of the upper classes than did the eventual victor".[33] For his part, Gibbon signalled the conversion of people from what he called "the advantages of natural endowment or fortune".[34] As demonstrated in the works of Augustine, Christianity gave evidence of having encountered a massive cultural and

---

[27] Ulhorn, *Die christliche Liebesthätigkeit in der altern Kirche* , p. 37, cited in Adolf von Harnack, *The Mission and Expansion of Christianity*, New York: 1908, 2 vols., vol. i, 22n.

[28] Eric R. Dodds, *Pagan and Christian in an Age of Anxiety*, (New York: W.W. Norton, 1970).

[29] Robert C. Smith and John Lounibos, eds., *Pagan and Christian Anxiety: A Response to E.R. Dodds,* (Lanham, MD: University Press of America, 1984).

[30] Dodds, *Pagan and Christian*, 106.

[31] Dodds, *Pagan and Christian*, 100-101.

[32] Kenneth Scott Latourette, *A History of the Expansion of Christianity,* vol. i, (New York: Harper and Brothers, 1937), pp. 163-64.

[33] Latourette, *Expansion*, i, 164.

[34] Gibbon, *Decline and Fall*, vol. i, 440-441.

intellectual tradition in the Greco-Roman world, an encounter bearing the hallmark of challenge rather than opportunism.[35]

We can evaluate the arguments of the negative impact of Christianity on culture by saying that the religion in its spread seems to encourage local revitalization. This does not contradict the views of someone like Gibbon; it merely calls into question his operative assumption about culture and civilization being synonymous, with Christians showing a contempt for both by their misguided faith in immortality.[36] However, local revitalization, especially in the form of organized community life and responsibility, may sometimes come into conflict with the structures of centralized control. If that is what Christianity has meant in the Greco-Roman world, then the Christian conflict with the Empire should be assessed differently rather than in terms of the alleged anarchy of Pietism.

As I have tried to show, Gibbon shares his negative evaluation with many of those who wish to paint a more positive picture of Christianity but who nevertheless assume that Christian universality is compromised by local particularity. Hocking, for example, was disinclined to see anything of much value in the "localization" of Christianity, so that when he considered Western Christianity he baulked at the notion on the grounds of the Western component being evidence of too "local" an adaptation. His words bear citing in full:

> Western religion has, for over three centuries, had the unique advantage of constant intercourse with a science and philosophical activity independent of itself, and yet relevant to its being. Largely through this free intercourse it has moved toward solving insights which, made part of its own vital impulse, promise to give it curative impact on any modern society. Yet this whole historic process, and its involvement in western culture, may tend to localize it. And if Christianity as a whole is distinctively western, its significance for world civilization is—I will not say nullified from the start, but discounted.[37]

The fact of the matter is that the localization of Christianity is an essential part of the nature of the religion, and that without that concrete, historical grounding Christianity becomes nothing but a fragile, elusive abstraction, salt without its saltness. This is the problem which dogs all attempts at defining the core of the gospel as a pure dogmatic system without regard to the concrete lives of men and women who call themselves Christian. And it is precisely the historical concreteness of Christianity which makes cross-cultural mutuality possible and meaningful. A sort of "United Nations" of the essence of Christianity presumes the existence of "individual nations" of Christian particularity to give it

---

[35] Augustine, *Confessions*, Penguin Books, viii, 2, 4, 5. *City of God,* (New York: Penguin Books, 1972), Box X, pp. 371-426.

[36] Gibbon, *Decline and Fall*, vol. i, 402.

[37] Hocking, *World Civilization*, 80.

substance and credibility. World solidarity and national particularity are not necessarily in conflict. Rather, it is the respective ideologies these forms breed which make them problematic both in their separateness and in their combination. The Christian perspective on this matter may help resolve enduring difficulties in the relationship between the universal and the particular, and hence between gospel and culture.

The Theological Foundations of Culture[38]

In the heated and sophisticated discussion about religion and culture, there is a recurrent idea that religious truth is inseparable from culture, not just in the fortuitous way culture entangles religion but in the fundamental sense that the cultural configuration of religion is also its final and essential form. In this view cultural markers in the religious life not only signify religious reality but also constitute the reality itself. There is, however, something of a jump, or at any rate awkward transition, at this point, for it is contended that while definitive of religion, nevertheless religious traditions are themselves cultural refractions of God who can enter the human stream only through them. Thus on one hand God and culture are fused and, on the other, they are differentiated, a position that threatens both religion and culture with collapse into tautology, and almost certainly creates a strained ambiguity as follows: the relationship between religious persons from different traditions and God is *significantly* the same on the level of meaning, though on the level of *representation* the relationship is different because of the variety of cultural signs by which the relationship is signified.

This argument, or a species of it, has been so powerfully advanced in recent years[39] that intelligent Christians find themselves swept by its force. This argument promotes a certain type of contradiction in taking as real ideal notions and their cultural configuration, so that cultural perceptions become theological conceptions, qualitative analogies turn into literal facts, and representation becomes identity. However, the real issue is whether cultural forms can be *both* a point of reference for God *and* be themselves what they stand for; that is to say, whether forms of representation can change to become themselves the subject they represent.[40] It seems reasonable to say that cultural formulations of

---

[38] This section of the paper draws on an earlier paper of mine, "Pluralism, Mission and Christian Commitment: Conflict or Convergence?" *Theology Today*, April 1988.

[39] John Hick promotes a version, perhaps more subtle and refined than many, of this view of religion and culture. John Hick, *Problems of Religious Pluralism*, (New York: St. Martin's Press, 1985).

[40] The great 19th century Sankritist and historian of religion, Max Müller, referring to this phenomenon, once spoke of religion as "a disease of language", a phrase which haunted him in later years. Müller meant by that the tendency of metaphorical language employed in

God are possible because God is available in the first place as a model, rather than that culture feeds on itself to produce a sacral mode as self-reward. However we look at it, the mountain can scarcely worship the mouse of its own labor.[41]

Religious people can respond that while they employ culture to represent the divine being to themselves, the divine being thus conceived may not be identified with certain cultural manifestations to the exclusion of others, so that a partial cultural representation would not be made into a comprehensive criterion of God. The Christian position, or at least the portion that I understand, allows cultural access and utilization without making end and means identical.

In the detailed specific responses religious people make, it can be said that God is connected to culture, but, in the general scheme of salvation history, God is connected to culture not as a figure of identity but as part of the overall plan to bring everything under subjection to Christ.

This may sound at once threatening and inconclusive, threatening because it rejects cultural systems as in any sense definitive of truth, and inconclusive because it perceives culture as inseparable from the truth.

However, we can reply that the truth of God is finally destroyed if it becomes absolutely synonymous with corresponding cultural forms ("Think not what you can do for God but what God can do for you"). The fundamental question, then, is whether the truth of God has as well to be capable of being conceived beyond cultural systems if it is to amount to anything more than ethnocentrism, though if it bypassed such systems altogether it would be nothing more (or less) than subjective abstraction.

Both extremes are avoided by the cross-cultural exposition of the message, so that cultural forms are upheld in their plural diversity without being absolutized in their unique particularity. The great historical forms of culture are thus consummated through the refining milieu of common ethical

---

a religious context to harden and obscure the original and concrete experience and its attributes which gave the initial impetus. For example, the striking idea that a memorable event once occurred at dawn may come down in metaphorical language as: "Apollo loved Daphne; Daphne fled before him and was changed into a laurel tree". In this account Apollo is a solar deity, and Daphne, the Greek for a laurel tree, was dawn. The story then unpacks as the sun chasing away dawn. It is called the Solar Myth. The process at work here, according to Müller, is the personification as deities the experience and its attributes. Thus *nomina* became *numina*. Or, to take another example, the king dying in a Western battle may become mythologised as the symbol of the sun setting in the West, whereas Apollo killing the python comes out as the allegory of summer driving out the winter. Müller believed, therefore, that philology (he was professor of Comparative Philology at Oxford) would be the instrument needed to remedy the defect of religious language. It sounds unconvincingly as if the disease and its cure are the same. For an evaluation of Müller see Evans-Pritchard, *Theories*, 1965, and also the same writer's posthumous work, *A History of Anthropological Thought*, ed. André Singer, (New York: Basic Books, Inc., 1981). On the general matter of religion as a cultural system, see the chapter by that title in Clifford Geertz, *The Interpretation of Cultures*, (New York: Basic Books, 1973).

41 This matter of not confusing cause and consequence and of separating cart from horse is expounded by G.K. Chesterton in his short essay, "The Priest of Spring", G.K. Chesterton, *Stories, Essays and Poems*, no. 913, (London: Everyman's Library, 1935, repr. 1965).

accountability. From the perspective of the Gospel historical forms become more than disconnected episodes; they become coherent links in the chain that binds us into communities.

This is the *instrumental* view which Christianity in its worldwide expansion ✓ has come to take of culture. It grows out of the Christian view of who and what God is, and its effect has been to endow the religion with a pluralist culture at the heart of the gospel.

It is important to spell out what is the particular, peculiar Christian understanding of culture, and do this from the perspective of the New Testament. The primitive Christians inherited from Judaism the Law and the synagogue as the exclusive standards of religious truth. However, from their understanding of the life and work of Christ, they came to a fresh view concerning God's impartial action in all cultures. The watershed for this new understanding was Pentecost which set a seal on mother tongues as sufficient, autonomous channels of access to God,[42] a piece of cultural innovation which enabled the religion to adopt the multiplicity of geographical centers as its home. Christians continued to cherish their Judaic roots in the context of growing pluralism within the church, a pluralism at the core of which is the principle that no culture is the exclusive norm of truth and that, similarly, no culture is inherently unclean in the eyes of God. So Jews, Gentiles, barbarians, Scythians, Cypriots, Arabs, Goths, Ethiopians, Copts among others, were all to be found within the fellowship. In time too, numerous intellectual streams discharged their share into the church, so that Aquinas could speak of the great advantage that accrued to the church from the fact that the Fathers and early apologists had been pagans. The confident adoption, and fundamental adaptation, of *Gnostic* materials shows the pluralist character of early Christian thought. These were among the repercussions which stemmed from the original Christian assumption that the gospel may be translated out of Galilean Aramaic and Hebrew into country (*Koine*) Greek, so that, as I observed at the beginning of this paper, most of the first converts had ✓ no living knowledge of the primary language of preaching of Jesus. Clearly the early Christians understood that the language issue may be detached from the question of faithfulness to the message of Jesus Christ, and that gives us an important clue about culture as *instrumental*.

Two major consequences for the religious status of culture may be characterized as, first, the *relativization* of all cultural arrangements, and, second, the *de-stigmatization* of all Gentile or taboo cultures. That was how such taboo cultures, regarded through time and eternity as outside the pale of salvation, came to qualify as among the firstfruits of God's measureless bounty. These two consequences became the heritage that opened the way for teeming pluralism in the community, with Christians drawing on a complex assortment of cultural materials to define and undefine themselves, something which has relevance for issues of denominational identity. Thus in the early centuries the new religion moved forward like an oriental caravanserai, with its complex baggage of exotic

---

[42] Acts ii:6,8,11.

teachings, baffling mysteries, colourful sounds and an eclectic ethical code. In the jumble and tumble of social encounter, Christians spoke a bewildering variety of languages, with the new experience sometimes exciting bursts of separatist fervour. In this respect, at least, Christianity was a major cultural as well as religious revolution whose force has endured into our own time. Its basic outline is extremely simple: from the point of view of God's "plan of salvation", all cultures are equally valid, if equally inadequate.

It is pertinent to ask what sustained this important change, and what its lessons are for Christians today. If Pentecost was the monument to the salvific potential of mother tongues, then St Paul was the pre-eminent person who carved his name on that monument. Paul understood completely the specific and general implications of Pentecost, and was equally prepared to stake his reputation on what Pentecost stood for. The effect of the gospel, Paul affirms, was to *de-stigmatize* the culture and the people associated with it: Jews, Gentiles, Barbarians and provincials all now stand on an equal footing under God's salvific purpose. Judgement had come upon the world, upon the Jew first, but also upon the Gentile, to wit, that the terms of one people's self-understanding, though invaluable for knowing God's intentions, are not, however, the absolute or exclusive norm for others. And so those matters, such as dietary regulations, circumcision and holy days, which are central to Jewish particularity, should nevertheless not be constituted into a principle of exclusion from, or participation in the fellowship.[43] Similarly, Gentiles are under notice not to make an exclusive norm of their own cultural particularity, that is to say, not to reduce religion to cultural ideology and thus indulge in self-absolutization.[44] Essentially, Paul says, nothing is unclean in itself,[45] or, to put it in contemporary language, sacrality is not intrinsic to culture or nature but is something with which the religious person invests cultural or natural objects, when they become religious subjects. Paul instead urged the believers to respect cultural practices *for the sake of each other* because of the God who gives them all things. God in Jesus Christ, the Apostle teaches, affirms our particularity in all its forms. But there is a major, fundamental qualification, namely, that form of cultural particularity which absolutizes and thus excludes is itself *excluded*. Ethnic individuality, yes, but ethnic divinization, no.

It is from this position that Paul builds the majestic structure of Christian pluralism in Romans xii and 1 Corinthians xii. Christianity thus came to adopt a plurality of cultures as natural extensions of the religious proclamation without surrendering the *instrumental* view of culture. This is both a simple and delicate matter. Culture, however lofty or privileged, remains in the Pauline

---

43 Rom xiv:5-23.

44 Rom. iii:9; xi:22; Gal. iii:28-29.

45 Rom. xiv:14. Also 1 Cor. vii:18-20 where the Apostle attempts specifically to *relativize* circumcision, seeking neither to *ban* it nor to *enjoin* it. It introduces a fundamental qualification into the Apostle's exhortation to *keep the commandments of God* (second half of verse 19) if those commandments included observance of circumcision.

account an instrument and channel under God's undivided sovereignty. Yet that sovereignty, being *one*, is itself mediated to us through the *many* bottlenecks of culture.[46] Thus Christians hallow culture by the paradox of denying its intrinsic sacrality, and elevate it by opposing its idolization. It is part of the Pauline achievement that it enables us in this way to reconcile the *One* and the *Many*.

The Christian encounter with culture has provided us with the first rigorous, not to say modern, critique of culture, and that legacy, whatever its chequered history, has endured through the centuries. The religious form of the issue helped summarize in an acute way the sickness that had eaten away at the foundations of Greco-Roman society, and now threatens our own. That religious form of the problem was: if new converts to the church are required to pass the test of Gentile cultural attainment, then, Paul insists, what distinguishes that from the test the Jerusalem church for its part applied to Gentile converts themselves?[47] In other words, does not the relative value of culture remain the *same* even when, and especially since, the circumstances are *different*? And should not Christians advocate cultural *differences* where at the same time they are committed to theological *consistency*? That, it seems, is the only way to uphold *contingency* alongside *consistency*, of the *general* with the *specific*.

Paul's insight on this issue is to my mind decisive for all subsequent engagement with the question. He formulated pluralism as the necessary outworking of the religion he believed Jesus preached. This pluralism was rooted for Paul in the *Gentile breakthrough*. Paul's view is that God does not absolutize any culture, whatever the esteem of that culture. Furthermore, Paul believed that all cultures have cast upon them the breath of God's favour, thus cleansing them of all stigma of inferiority and untouchability. These two ideas constitute what we may regard as the insipient *radical pluralism* of Pauline thought. When he stressed faith over against works, Paul was intending to enunciate the inclusive principle of God's right and freedom to choose us without regard to our cultural trophies. Faith as the absolute gift of a loving, gracious God,[48] is the relativizing leaven in culture. Western psychology and its theological variants have unjustifiably subjectivized the issue, pitting inward assurance against social engagement, with the tendency to reduce religion to what Flannery O'Connor

---

46 This idea brings to mind the words of the contemporary song: *We are the forest of ten thousand seeds in shades of green that hold the sun. With mingled roots our limbs together lean; We are the many and the one.* Words by Caroline McDade.

47 Galatians ii:11-14.

48 See the splendid and still relevant study of C.H. Dodd, *The Meaning of Paul for Today*, (London: Fontana Books, 1964), p. 80. See also J. Christian Beker, *Paul the Apostle: The Triumph of God in Life and Thought*, Philadelphia: Fortress Press, 1980. It may well be that the *Epistle of James*, with its hard-knocking pronouncements about muscular Christianity, develops this theme of faith and works as not being in conflict with each other, especially when the faith of Abraham is reckoned by the Epistle as an example of works (James ii:21). But it is not necessary to plunge into this matter here, with all its intricate and elaborate treatment in erudite writings.

has called "sweet invention".[49] In fact, Paul desired above all to safeguard the cultural particularity (not *particularism*) of Jew as Jew and Gentile as Gentile, while challenging both Jew and Gentile to find in Jesus Christ their respective true affirmation.

Paul's legacy to the church includes this exacting vigilance over the doublesidedness of culture. Christian life is indelibly marked by the stamp of culture, while Christian sources also instruct a penultimate status for culture. In the final analysis the church must utter the prophetic word in culture, and sometimes even against it. Paul could with justice be seen as a cultural iconoclast in his defiance of idolatrous tendencies in culture, but he cannot be regarded as a cultural cynic, for in his view God's purposes are mediated through the particularity of cultural streams.

Vernacular Languages and Cultures under the Gospel

With the modern missionary enterprise we come upon spectacular examples of cultural pluralism in the church.[50] To begin with, vernacular translations of the Bible began with the adoption of indigenous terms, concepts, customs and idioms for the central categories of Christianity. Secondly, vernacular criteria began to determine what is or what is not a successful translation, with indigenous experts rapidly moving to challenge Western interpretations of Christianity.[51] Thirdly, the employment of the vernacular led to a proliferation of languages into which the Scriptures were translated.[52] Fourthly, in numerous significant cases missionary translations were the first attempt to write down the language. Where this was the case Christian translators have had to produce vernacular alphabets, grammars, dictionaries and vocabularies of the language, supplementing these with compilations of proverbs, idioms, axioms, ethnographic materials, and accounts of local religions, customary practice and law, history and political institutions. Such a detailed and scrupulous inventory of the vernacular culture triggered unimaginable consequences in the wider society, resulting almost everywhere in arousing deep loyalties towards the

---

[49] Flannery O'Connor, *The Habit of Being,* (New York: Farrar, Straus, Giroux, 1979), p. 479.

[50] In his summary of the cultural and linguistic impact of the Bible, Eric Fenn points out the indigenizing potential of Scriptural translation. Eric Fenn, "The Bible and the Missionary", *The Cambridge History of the Bible, vol. iii: The West From the Reformation to the Present Day,* ed. S.L. Greenslade, (Cambridge: Cambridge University Press, 1963, repr. 1988), pp. 383-407.

[51] A recent example of this shift of interpretation is given in Vincent Donovan, *Christianity Rediscovered,* (Maryknoll, NY: Orbis Books, 1983).

[52] In 1984 more than 1,800 languages were involved in some form of Bible translating. In Africa alone some 522 languages were involved, with complete Bibles available in over 100 languages. *Scriptures of the World,* (London, New York and Stuttgart: United Bible Societies).

indigenous cause. Often that was the seedbed of nationalism. It is impossible to ✓ over-estimate the revolutionary impact of Christian translation on hitherto illiterate societies and their now new encounter with the West. In addition, to bring this list to its final stage, there was a theological truth implicit in all this enterprise, and that concerns God's prevenient grace which preceded the missionary and by which missionaries themselves proceeded to adopt existing forms and usage *as if God was their hidden life.*

It is clear that missionary translators saw a natural congruence between indigenous cultures and the gospel, with the diversity and plurality of those cultures justifying commitment to the particularity and specificity of cultural materials. Not only individual languages, but also minute dialectical differences were noted and preserved in translations.[53] Mission seems to press to its logical conclusion the premise of the universal admissibility of all cultures in the general sweep of God's "plan of salvation", eager to witness to God in the words and names of other people's choosing.

Concerning the role of language, it is important to hold in our mind that in traditional societies language and culture are closely intertwined, and that in religion both are promoted in an integrated, dynamic way. Therefore missionary translations appealed to the very roots of these societies, touching the springs of life and imagination in real, enduring ways. Perhaps it was to this phenomenon that Pliny the Younger referred in his letter to the Emperor Trajan, namely, that Christian renewal also transforms while stimulating older habits and attitudes. Whatever the case, it would be appropriate to conclude this section of the paper with a closer clarification of the vernacular issue in Christian missionary translation, and do this in two interconnected stages. The first concerns the *instrumental* view of culture, and, in particular, the question of language and its relationship to religion and culture in traditional societies. The second has to do with the question of the particular and the universal, of the general and the specific, of truth as *One* and of culture as *Many* in its diverse manifestations and contingencies, and how in the final analysis that impinges on the theme of gospel and culture.

With vernacular translation, missionaries introduced a new level of complexity into Christian usage. In the multi-lingual setting of tribal societies, concepts of God resonated with ancient usage, with refinements taking place in incidents of ritual observance and customary practice. Often it is not the jealous God of Calvinistic clericalism that translators had adopted, or thought they were adopting, for the vernacular Scriptures, but the polyonymous deity of the tribe, resplendent with theophorous titles. Furthermore, the very pluralism in vernacular translation created increased local awareness and forced practical comparisons across tribal boundaries, showing how the "God and Father of the Lord Jesus Christ" of apostolic preaching came to be invested with a plurality of

---

53 In the Chinese translations, for example, some 47 versions were employed by missionaries, with eight additional ones in Taiwan. *Scriptures of the World*, map 15. A similar detailed attention was given to Arabic and its local variants.

names, none of which excludes the others. This theological inclusiveness had its counterpart in the social sphere where in many places inter-ethnic encounter became possible for the first time outside the constraints of tribal blood-feud and fratricidal grudge.[54]

In turning to the second part of our analysis I should like to recapitulate at the same time the problem of the *One* and the *Many*, of the particular and the universal. It is clear that in employing vernacular languages for translation, missionaries saw these languages as more than arbitrary devices. On the contrary, they saw them as endowed with divine significance, so that they may substitute completely for the language of revelation. The fact that all languages are, for the purposes of Christian translation, interchangeable, makes them *instrumental*, so that in their very differences they all serve an identical purpose. A certain general view came to undergird and persist in the plurality of languages, with the important point that vernacular particularity is compatible, rather than in conflict with such a general idea. Languages were seen as the *Many* contingent refractions in which the *One* God was mediated, so that particular cultural descriptions of God might convey in concrete terms the truth of God without that in any way excluding other cultural descriptions.

The question then arises as to whether what is said in any language totally exhausts the meaning of God, or whether languages, any or some languages, have to be augmented to improve their intrinsic capacity. As an alternative view, it may be maintained that language, indeed all languages, are inherently inadequate and that religious truth ultimately, if not immediately, transcends human words. This view has respectable advocates in many sections of Christianity, although the question for us is its implication for the culture that is thus transcended. Whatever the case, so far as the history of mission is concerned, such a transcendent view of religious truth does not seem to have induced in missionaries an indifference to culture. In that sense we are back to the question regarding the intrinsic adequacy of language. The missionary view was that all languages may be regarded as complete autonomous systems, and that purer forms of the language, however puzzling and unfamiliar, served best the purposes of translation. So linguistic investigations were mounted to erect as authentic an indigenous system through which God might be mediated with all the nuances and specificity of cultural originality.

A working principle of language and culture was implied in this procedure. Missionaries were confident that once they made a successful conjunction between a linguistic symbol and what it brings to mind, then the religious process could commence meaningfully, and we can say that much of what has been said against missionaries overlooks this vernacular confidence of theirs.

Three theoretical notions may be identified in their operational view of language and culture. The *first* is that language furnishes *elliptical* statements

---

[54] Aspects of this social and theological inclusiveness are treated in the article of the present writer, "Christian Missions and the Western Guilt Complex", *Christian Century* 8, April, 1987.

which enable people to define instrumental relationships, and in religious language elliptical statements refer to those things in which God reveals himself, especially as effects. The *second* is that language enables people to make *symbolical* statements to the effect that what in itself is not God but represents God to certain persons is in fact God for those persons in those contexts. That is to say, such language or symbols achieve the end of directing attention to the symbolic character of an object to the exclusion of whatever other qualities language or symbols may possess in another context. Two brief examples may suffice. Kissing the crucifix was considered an act of reverence by early Catholic missionaries, whereas in certain parts of Africa kissing as such was considered an act of defilement, repugnant to the instinct of the people. To take a second example, for a mystical religious group the bat is considered a symbol of initiation and divine wisdom, and occurs as such on the coronation robe of King Roger of Sicily. Yet in the different context of popular Western culture the bat is a symbol of ill-omen. The two contexts share in common a recognition of the categories of divine wisdom and ill-omen, but they employ contrasting cultural symbols to *signify* this. The *third* is when language encourages the use of *figures of identity* so that a close enough relationship is conceived between the thing spoken of with what it is said to be, with the result that virtual metamorphosis, a symbolic mutation, takes place. This clearly happens in most cultures: the sound and tones of Hebrew, Arabic and Sanskrit, for example, are in their respective religious contexts the embodiment of the divine or ultimate reality, while in certain sections of Christianity the bread and wine of the communion are the transubstantiated body and blood of Jesus Christ. Among the Yoruba of West Africa the *orita*, the auspicious crossroad, is a symbol of power, while for the Nuer rain, thunder, lightning, sun and moon, as well as consecrated cattle are not God exactly, but *gaat Kwoth*, "children of God" and so on. However, a missionary tradition like Christianity has to face the challenge of recasting symbols in terms meaningful to target audiences. Bread and wine in China or Japan,[55] for example, would have a vastly different understanding, if they have any at all, while the Good Shepherd theme would confound rather than enlighten both an Eskimo congregation, and, as Nida and Reyburn have suggested, the pig-keeping communities of Polynesia.[56] Furthermore, a missionary Christianity would have to make room for new cultural symbols, such as the Peace Pipe of the Lakota Indians,[57] the Wisdom Fire of the Cherokee

---

[55] For a detailed account of this issue in Japan see Masao Takenaka, *Rice Christians*, and for China see George Minamiki, S.J., *The Chinese Rites Controversy: From Its Beginning to Modern Times*, (Chicago: Loyola University Press).

[56] Eugene A. Nida and William D. Reyburn, *Meaning Across Cultures*, (Maryknoll, NY: Orbis Books, 1981).

[57] See Paul B. Steinmetz, S.J.: *Pipe, Bible and Peyote among the Oglala Lakota*, Stockholm Studies in Comparative Religion, (Stockholm: University of Stockholm, 1980).

Indians[58] and the communal medicine and riverain oracles of African religions. [59] Making room for these new cultural materials also requires relativizing them so they do not become new sources of ideology themselves.[60]

It is this incredible complexity that Christianity encountered, and in fact promoted, in its non-Western expansion. The specificity of vernacular usage was reflected in indigenous names for God and in idiomatic forms grounded in local life and experience. Missionary translators tried to get at authentic local forms and in the process documented the result of their investigations, giving meticulous accounts of procedures and principles of research which went far beyond the narrow issue of Bible use. Such a detailed attention to indigenous particularity fostered unprecedented cultural pluralism within the general scheme of world Christianity. For example, indigenous hymns, prayers and invocations, heavily freighted with older religious attitudes, sentiments and ideas, were now transcribed and incorporated into Christian use where ecumenical interest gave them international range.

In turns out, then, that missionary translation expanded and enriched Christian religious repertoire, and it did this by eschewing uniformity as its norm. The operational view of language in Christian translation assumed a close relationship between language and the God spoken of, so that in any cultural representation God can be detached in the mind from the things said to be Him, even if these peculiar cultural forms, be they the Peace Pipe, the bread and wine, the Wisdom Fire, the *orita*, or what have you, cannot in those specific situations be so easily detached from the idea of God as such. This gave culture and language a penultimate character, allowing them to be viewed in their *instrumental* particularity.[61] In insisting on particularity, for example, Christian missionaries did not wish to imply that God is other than what He is, but that in particular cultural contexts and circumstances God has definite, particular qualities and attributes which do not belong to Him in other contexts and circumstances. It is not that these qualities and attributes are incompatible with

---

[58] Dhyani Ywahoo, *Voices of our Ancestors: Cherokee Teachings from the Wisdom Fire*, (Boston and London: Shambhala Publications, 1987).

[59] E.E. Evans-Pritchard: *Witchcraft, Oracles and Magic among the Azande*, (Oxford: Clarendon Press, 1937, revised abridged edition, 1976). Also Michael C. Kirwen: *The Missionary and the Diviner: Contending Theologies of Christian and African Religions*, (Maryknoll, NY: Orbis Books, 1987).

[60] Commenting on this matter, Gordon Kaufman affirms: "If indigenization were to mean that the idea of God became so completely adapted to the concepts and norms and practices of a new culture that it no longer could serve as a radical standard of criticism for that culture . . . full indigenization of the idea of God would be its destruction. For the concept of *One* who is at once truly absolute and truly human is never completely 'at home' in the relativities and imperfections . . . of any culture . . .". Gordon D. Kaufman, "Theological Method and Indigenization: Six Theses", in Samuel Amirtham, ed., *A Vision for Man: Essays on Faith, Theology and Society*, (Madras: Christian Literature Society), 1978, p. 59.

[61] A kindred theme is treated in Aubrey R. Johnson, *The One and the Many in the Israelite Conception of God*, (Cardiff: University of Wales Press, 1961), pp. 14, 15-16, etc.

God generally defined, but that something more, in respect to the pool of qualities and attributes, is added by each particular context.[62] Those qualities and attributes become the modes and individual ways in which God becomes real for particular people in particular situations and circumstances even though those situations and circumstances by their nature do not repeat themselves for everyone anywhere else or to the same degree. The Psalmist may declare that God is a shield or a rock, or Luther that God is a might fortress and bulwark, or a Western existentialist liberal that God is the God of feeling without any of them excluding other descriptions of God, such as the dewynosed One of a cattle-owning culture, the One of the sacred stake of a pigherding people, the nimble-footed One of the sacred dance, and the longnecked One of a hunting group. Furthermore, this rule makes it possible not only to approach God as the *One* and the *Many*, but allows for indefinite polarities in descriptions of God. As such, apparently contradictory things may equally validly be said of God, such as that God gives life and that God takes life, that God creates and that He destroys, guides and leads astray, fills us with abundance and afflicts us with adversity at the same time, brings terrifying judgment upon us and also surrounds us with tender care and love, strikes us blind but also unseals the eyes of understanding, and so on. As such the Nuer speak of God being in the new moon and in the hurricane.[63] In this way the totality and range of human experience can be postulated of God's infinite manifestations, refractions and visitations without courting the awkward rationalist nemesis of admitting God on the explicable but not the inexplicable side of life.[64]

On the cultural level a similar plurality and polarity is possible from this approach. The context of Western mission provides as good an example as any. Between Europeans and native populations, on the one hand, and, on the other, among tribal groupings themselves, there are differences on the cultural and linguistic level. These differences are unique and particular even though all these *many* groups represent the *one* idea of humanity. What unites them, however, is more than a question of species but their common *relationship* in respect to God. For this reason the cultural signs and symbols which *differentiate* them in their respective particularities *unite* them in relation to God. It is God as this third term who thus truthfully unites what cultural forms properly differentiate.

---

62 Something like this idea may offer an escape hatch for Hocking who writes wistfully about the bewildering religious pluralism in Protestant Christianity. "My own feeling about the multiplicity of sects is that most of them that have become a factor in contemporary society have had some reason for existence; most "reforms" have been needed. But that function of reform should be a function provided for within the church, not calling for schism, but for self-searching and reconception, in the persuasion that variety of expression which is not hostile to the essence may contribute to the life of the church" (Hocking, *World Civilization*, 134).

63 See Sir Edward Evans-Pritchard, *Nuer Religion*, (New York: Oxford University Press, 1956).

64 See, for example, Isaiah ix:21; Rev. ii:8ff; Deut. xxix:1-5.

Consequently Christian commitment to this God has necessarily involved commitment also to cultural forms in their essentially radical pluralism.

In conclusion, no discussion of this topic is complete without more than a polite nod in the direction of H. Richard Niebuhr whose work more than a generation ago set the pace for us.[65] Niebuhr cuts through the liberal cultural transformation of Christianity into an enlightened, humanizing but essentially this-worldly philosophy, with social belief and action replacing human sinfulness, spiritual reality and eternal judgment. In taking up cudgels on behalf of a threatened and waning orthodoxy, Niebuhr was responding to particular cultural pressures in his day and age. Thus neither in his methodology and language nor in his general conclusions did Niebuhr propose something which his contemporaries would not have recognized as natural developments from the stock and branch of Western culture. And that made him a powerfully effective voice for his time and circumstance. Nevertheless, Niebuhr was not concerned with the worldwide phenomenon of Christian cultural practices where he would have seen the outlines of fresh permutations and new combinations emerging under explicit Christian aegis. It is reasonable to speculate that such evidence might have affected his work in a different direction.

At any rate his concern for not reducing Christ into a mere cultural protagonist is a valid one, although in this paper I have tried to advance *different* grounds for making the *same* distinction. The conclusion I have reached, therefore, is a slightly modified version of his own formulations. I am concerned not only to safeguard the authority of Christ but the authenticity of culture as well. The connection between Christ and culture, to stick to the Niebuhrian formulation, is much closer than either what Niebuhr calls the "conversionist" or the "dualist" position, and more susceptible to cultural manipulation than the liberals might think. It is thus pertinent to observe that it is not only religious sensibility which leads Christians to distinguish between Christ and culture, it is sensibility also for what promotes authentic culture. When we conceive the matter in these terms, so that the *One* gospel becomes meaningfully mediated through the *Many* refractions of culture and historical contingency, and reflect on what Paul has to say on the issue, then the Apostle emerges with new significance. Such a view of gospel and culture blunts considerably his sharp dualist tone. The incipient *radical pluralism* we have identified in Paul helps us

---

65 H. Richard Niebuhr, *Christ and Culture*, (New York: Harper Colophon Books, 1975, first published 1951). Compare also the same author's *Radical Monotheism and Western Culture*, the Montgomery Lectures of 1957, (New York: Harper & Brothers, 1960). In *Radical Monotheism* Niebuhr argues that the central conflict in Western culture is between monotheist faith and henotheism, especially nationalism. He distinguishes between monotheist faith and religious faith, saying the faith present in religious loyalty is the same as that present in other forms of faith commitment in the secular sphere. The conflict arises between the two types of faith, Niebuhr argues, because henotheism makes a finite society the object of trust and loyalty. In a different connection, but still related to the issue of radical pluralism and religious integrity, Gordon Kaufman has written about the radical effects of the principle of God's absoluteness. "God is the great relativizer of all false absolutes", he writes (Kaufman, "Theological Method and Indigenization", p. 58).

to moderate any endemic conflict between gospel and culture. For instance, when he admonishes the believers not to allow the rules of food to destroy the work of God,[66] Paul is not proposing that eating and praying are in conflict, or even that the one is done from a lower motive and the other from a higher one, but that God and food in any exclusivist combination nourish neither spirit nor body. It is the worst form of addiction, and it is not only Christians, but especially Christians, who deserve better. So Christian pluralism in its uncompromising, rigorous form, is not only a committed state of mind with regard to God's *Oneness* in sovereignty and power, but a committed style of living with respect to the *many*-sidedness of culture. In that convergence we may find strength for the critical relationship between the gospel and the contending cultural ideologies of our time.

[66] Rom. xiv:15,20.

ANDREW F. WALLS

THE TRANSLATION PRINCIPLE IN CHRISTIAN HISTORY

Translation and Incarnation

Politics is the art of the possible; translation is the art of the impossible. Exact transmission of meaning from one linguistic medium to another is continually hampered not only by structural and cultural difference; the words of the receptor language are pre-loaded, and the old cargo drags the new into areas uncharted in the source language. In the end the translator has simply to do his best and take risks in a high risk business.

In the light of the frustrations inherent in the translation process, it is the more astonishing that God chose translation as his mode of action for the salvation of humanity. Christian faith rests on a divine act of translation: "the Word became flesh, and dwelt among us".[1] Any confidence we have in the translatability of the Bible rests on that prior act of translation. There is a history of translation of the Bible because there was a translation of the Word into flesh.

In the other great faiths of the world, salvation does not depend on translation in this way. India has long known faith in the divine presence in the universe, and faith in the divine saving intervention in the universe. But if, as is characteristic of old India, salvation lies in attaining or realizing identity with the divine, no act of divine translation takes place. Meaning is not actually transferred from the divine to the human sphere, for the human sphere has no permanent significance, or, indeed, reality; the phenomenal world is just what Hindu sages have long said it is, illusion, *maya*.

Even Judaism and Islam, which come from the same Semitic matrix as Christianity, and share the Christian characterization of God's manward activity as speech, do not represent it as *translated* speech. In Islamic faith God speaks to mankind calling to obedience. The sign of that speech is the Qur'an, the direct speech of God, delivered in Arabic at the chosen time through God's chosen Apostle, unaltered and unalterably fixed in heaven for ever. In prophetic faiths God speaks to humanity; in Christian faith, God becomes human. This conviction conditions the Christian attitude even to prophetic speech. Though the earliest Church was Jewish and retained the Jewish Scriptures, the Christian approach to the Bible is not identical with the historic understanding of the Torah. The Christian Scriptures are not the Torah with an updating supplement. The translation of the speech of God, not just into human speech but into humanity, implies a different type of encounter with the divine. Much misunderstanding in Christian-Muslim relations has occurred from the

---

[1] John 1.14.

assumption that the Bible and Qur'an have analogous status in the respective faiths. But the true Christian analogy with the Qur'an is not the Bible, but Christ. Christ for Christians, the Qur'an for Muslims, is the Eternal Word of God; but Christ is Word Translated. That fact is the sign that the contingent Scriptures (also describable as Word of God), unlike the Qur'an, may and should constantly be translated.

Incarnation is translation. When God in Christ became man, Divinity was✓ translated into humanity, as though humanity were a receptor language. Here was a clear statement of what would otherwise be veiled in obscurity or uncertainty, the statement "This is what God is like".

But language is specific to a people or an area. No-one speaks generalized "language"; it is necessary to speak a particular language. Similarly, when ✓ Divinity was translated into Humanity he did not become generalized humanity. He became *a person* in a particular locality and in a particular ethnic group, at a particular place and time. The translation of God into humanity, whereby the sense and meaning of God was transferred, was effected under very culture-specific conditions.

The implications of this broaden if we take the Johannine symbol of the Word made flesh along with the Pauline symbol of the Second Adam, the Ephesian theme of the multi-ethnic New Humanity which reaches its full stature in Christ, and with Paul's concern for Christ to be formed in the newly founded Gentile churches.[2] It appears that Christ, God's translated speech, is re-translated from the Palestinian Jewish original. The words of the Great Commission require that the various nations are to be made disciples of Christ.[3] In other words, national distinctives, the things that mark out each nation, the shared consciousness and shared traditions, and shared mental processes and patterns of relationship, are within the scope of discipleship. Christ can become visible within the very things which constitute nationality. The first divine act of translation into humanity thus gives rise to a constant succession of new translations. Christian diversity is the necessary product of the Incarnation.

Further, as Christian faith is about translation, it is about conversion. There is a real parallel between these processes. Translation involves the attempt to express the meaning of the source from the resources of, and within the working system of the receptor language. Something new is brought into the language, but that new element can only be comprehended by means of and in terms of the pre-existing language and its conventions. In the process that language and its system is effectively expanded, put to new use; but the translated element from the source language has also, in a sense, been expanded by translation; the receptor language has a dynamic of its own and takes the new material to realms it never touched in the source language. Similarly, conversion implies the use of existing structures, the "turning" of those structures to new directions, the

---

2 Cf., e.g. Rom 5.12-6.14; 1 Cor 15.20-28; Eph 2.11-22, 21.7-16; Gal 4.19.

3 Mt 28.19: Note that it is the *nations*, not some people within the nations, who are to be discipled.

application of new material and standards to a system of thought and conduct already in place and functioning. It is not about substitution, the replacement of something old by something new, but about transformation; the turning of the already existing to new account.

Thus in the Incarnation, the Word becomes flesh, but not *simply* flesh; Christian faith is not about a theophany or an avatar, the appearance of divinity on the human scene. The Word was made *man*. To continue the linguistic analogy, Christ was not simply a loanword adopted into the vocabulary of humanity; he was fully translated, taken into the functional system of the language, into the fullest reaches of personality, experience and social relationship. The proper human response to the divine act of translation is conversion: the opening up of the functioning system of personality, intellect, emotions, relationship to the new meaning, to the expression of Christ. Following on the original act of translation in Jesus of Nazareth are countless re-translations into the thought forms and cultures of the different societies into which Christ is brought as conversion takes place. Conversion is not the substitution of something new for something old (in the great act of translation into humanity, Christ added nothing to the humanity made in God's image); nor the addition of something new to something old (in the the great act of translation, Christ took nothing *from* humanity). Conversion is the turning, the re-orientation, of every aspect of humanity—culture-specific humanity—to God. For Christ was the full expression of God in human medium. Of its nature, then, conversion is not a single aoristic act, but a process. It has a beginning; we cannot presume to posit an end.

Bible translation as a process is thus both a reflection of the central act on which the Christian faith depends and a concretization of the commission which Christ gave his disciples. Perhaps no other specific activity more clearly represents the mission of the Church.

The parallel of Scripture and Incarnation is suggested in the opening words of the Epistle to the Hebrews on the relation between the partial, episodic, occasional words of God spoken through the prophets and the complete and integrated Word spoken all at once in the Son.[4] The issues and problems of Bible translation are the issues and problems of Incarnation. The struggle to present writings embedded in languages and cultures alien to the present situation of every people is validated by the act which translated God into the medium of humanity. As the Incarnation took place in the terms of a particular social context, so translation uses the terms and relations of a specific context. Bible translation aims at releasing the word about Christ so that it can reach all aspects of a specific linguistic and cultural context, so that Christ can live within that context, in the persons of his followers, as thoroughly at home as he once did in the culture of first century Jewish Palestine. We may take it that the endemic hazards and problems of translation are a necessary part of the process of Christian mission. Key words or concepts without an obvious equivalent in the

---

4 Heb. 1.1-2.

receptor language, central Biblical images rooted in the soil or history of the Middle East or the usages of the Roman Empire, the shift of meaning in apparently corresponding words, the luggage that receptor language terms carry with them—these are the means by which the word about Christ is applied to the *distinctives* of a culture, and thus to its commanding heights. New translations, by taking the word about Christ into a new area, applying it to new situations, have the potential actually to reshape and expand the Christian faith. Instead of defining a universal "safe area" where certain lines of thought are prescribed and others proscribed or ignored (the natural outcome of a once-for-all, untranslatable authority), translatability of the Scriptures potentially starts *inter*actions of the word about Christ with new areas of thought and custom. Again the contrast with the Qur'anic Word is manifest.

In this respect translation resembles conversion; indeed, it is a working model of conversion, a turning of the processes of language (with the thought of which that language is the vehicle and the traditions of which it is the deposit) towards Christ. And like conversion, it has a beginning but no end. However effective the impact, it is never good enough; and as social life and language change, so must translation. The principle of translation is the principle of revision.

There is one exception to the revision principle. The translations of Christ that take place as believers within different cultures respond to him are *re*translations. These incarnations of Christ are contingent on that first Incarnation with its firm anchorage in time and space, its "crucified under Pontius Pilate". Similarly, Biblical translation is re-translation, with the original always at hand. The various translations can always be compared, not only with the original, but with other translations made from the same original. Though each act of translation, like each process of conversion, takes the original into new territory and potentially expands it, the absence of a family resemblance among the products would properly give rise to suspicion. Diversity arising from the penetration of new culture complexes is not incompatible with coherence arising from the fact that the various translations have been made from a common original. And in this, too, Biblical translation mirrors Christian mission. It is not possible to have too much of the localizing and indigenizing principle which makes the faith thoroughly at home, nor too much of that universalizing principle which is in constant tension with it, and which links that local community with its "domestic" expression of faith in the same Christ of Christians of other times and places. It is possible only to have too little of either.

Perhaps a comparative history of translation would be an illuminating way of approaching the history of Christian mission, and to Christian expansion—not only in the geographical and statistical sense of the spread of the Church, but the dynamic expansion of the influence of Christ within the Church that comes from attempts at the radical application of his mind within particular cultures. What follows must of necessity be restricted to some early examples which illustrate the theme.

Translation and the Cultural Transformation of Christianity

The translation principle was at work even in Christianity's ante-natal period. At least by the second century before the Christian era, the Jewish Scriptures were being turned into Greek. It is significant both that the traditional Jewish story about the origin of the Septuagint translation ascribed to that translation a missionary purpose, and that the reality of its origin probably has little to do with any Jewish mission to the Gentiles. The likely origin of the Septuagint lies in the fact that Greek was fast becoming the first language of so many Jews in Alexandria and other extra-Palestinian Jewish communities; it was, in fact, a Jewish vernacular translation. Nevertheless, the generally accepted account came to be that Ptolemy Philadelphus, King of Egypt, a Gentile who had conceived an abundant veneration for the Scriptures, had sought the translation, and that God had rewarded him and demonstrated the divine approval of the undertaking by means of a signal miracle. The translation of the Scriptures into Greek is seen in these stories as being as manifestly the work of God as the tables given to Moses on Sinai.

That earliest translation committee must remain the envy of all its successors. Although it consisted of seventy (-two) translators, the work was complete in seventy-two days. Still more remarkably, the learned Alexandrine Jew Philo, living early in the first Christian century, tells us that versions, prepared individually, were word for word identical, "as though dictated to each by an invisible prompter". And he goes on:

> Who does not know that every language, and Greek especially, abounds in terms, and that the same thought can be put in many shapes by changing single words and whole phrases . . .? This was not the case, we are told, with this law of ours, but the Greek words used corresponded literally with the Chaldean [i.e. Hebrew], exactly suited to the things they indicated . . . The clearest proof of this is that, if [Hebrews] have learned Greek, or Greeks [Hebrew] and read both versions, the [Hebrew] and the translation, they regard these with awe and reverence as sisters, or rather as one and the same, both in matter and words, and speak of the authors not as translators, but as prophets and priests of the mysteries, whose sincerity and singleness of thought has enabled them to go hand in hand with the purest of spirits, the spirit of Moses.[5]

There is no doubting Philo's sincerity in these convictions (though there is more than a little whether he knew any Hebrew). But one cannot read him long before realizing how steeped is this Jewish Alexandrine in Plato, and how well

---

5 Philo, *Life of Moses* 2.26-42 for this story and quotation (translation by F.H. Colson and G.H. Whittaker in the Loeb edition). The earlier and better known account is in the *Letter of Aristeas*.

acquainted with Stoic writers. If for him Moses is the purest of spirits, Athens as much as Sinai has set and shaped his mind. In other words, even among Jews the field of reference of the Scriptures has been extended, and Moses and the prophets given new intellectual company. Philo can use them as authoritative when he explores the thought world of the host community of Alexandria whose speech and much of whose education he shares. The most precious possession of his people, the Torah, becomes *nomos*, or rather *The Nomos* in Greek, and Greek-speaking Jews (who have themselves to deal with Alexandrian law, and with Roman law) find themselves with a contribution to the Platonic and Stoic debates on the nature of law, which could never have arisen without the translation of the Scriptures. And Philo's Hellenistic surroundings have taught him that Greeks stumble at questions about the nature of reality because they were unaware of what every Jewish child knew from infancy, the activity of the sovereign God in creation. He knew also that they often could not hear the plain words of the prophets about God stretching out the heavens like a curtain, because of questions which could occupy no one brought up solely in Hebrew learning. The phenomenal universe is material, and hence alien to Spirit: how can Pure Spirit be responsible for matter? Philo—following a line developed by other Greek-speaking Jews before him[6]—finds a key to such Greek questions within the Scriptures themselves. The key lay not indeed in the affirmations of Deutero-Isaiah about the creator, nor primarily within the creation narratives of Genesis (though he noted how God "spoke" there), but in the Book of Proverbs, in the passages personifying wisdom or showing God's use of "wisdom" in His creation. Gradually the widely canvassed Greek idea of Word/Reason (*logos*) coalesces with the Biblical theme of wisdom, until Philo can present *Logos* as a sort of shock absorber between the transcendent God and His creation. "To his Word, chief messenger, highest in age and honour", says Philo, "the Father of all has given the special prerogative, to stand on the border and separate the creative from the Creator".[7] The *Logos* thus becomes the point at which human contact is possible with the Sovereign Lord. By the use of the Jewish Scriptures in an essentially Greek philosophic discourse, the transcendent God, the God of Israel, is introduced into the heart of thoroughly Greek questions. Greek thinkers using only Greek resources would have left the God-factor on the periphery of those questions; devout Jews using only untranslated Scriptures would have dismissed the questions themselves as so much Gentile profanity. No wonder Philo rejoiced in the story of Ptolemy Philadelphus and the Septuagint. In due time countless Christians were to follow his path.

Early Christianity was thus already touched by the translation principle. Not even Jewish Palestine could be culturally and linguistically sealed off from the Hellenistic world; and the very words of Jesus come to us in Greek dress. The radical Stephen slashes at the heart of traditional Judaic religiosity about the

---

6 Most obviously in the *Book of Wisdom* (e.g. ch. 7) belonging to the previous century.

7 Philo, *Who is the heir of divine things?* 205.5, translation of Colson and Whittaker in Loeb.

Temple with the sabre of the Septuagint;[8] and the process which called the Septuagint into being is given Gospel authentication as the Pentecost crowd of Dispersion Jews hear the wonderful works of God, not in the sacred language of the Temple liturgy (the object of their pilgrimage), but in the languages of the various nations that were their real mother tongues.[9]

The time came when traditional Judaism rejected the Septuagint; most probably because the Christians had got hold of it. More literal translations, such as those of Symmachus and Theodotion, were used when Greek was absolutely necessary. In due time there was a retreat from translation altogether. The delighted legends of the miraculous origin of the Septuagint gave place to grudging recognition of the event as an exception to the general rule, a sign for the particular benefit of Ptolemy Philadelphus rather than a pointer to the salvation of the world.[10] Eventually we reach the bald statement that the Torah cannot be turned into Greek, an absolutism that Islam was later to echo.[11] But by this time the Septuagint was afloat in the world under new colours, in the care of Christianity that was now as overwhelmingly Hellenistic and Greek speaking as it had once been overwhelmingly Jewish. And it was to aid in a variety of ways in the application to Hellenistic culture of the Christ event. That application was to take Christian faith into a vast complex of ideas, principles and relationships, to seek their subjection to Christ.

The cultural translation of Christianity gave the Scriptures a new status and purpose. They were no longer ethnically Jewish; their field of application was universal. Justin tells how, when he had tried all the philosophical schools and found himself as far as ever from the true end of philosophy, the vision of God, he met an old man who urged him to read the Jewish prophets—"more ancient than all those who are esteemed philosophers . . . who . . . foretold what would come to pass, even what is now coming to pass".[12] Justin took the advice, and it led him to Christ. His contemporary Tatian similarly testifies:

> Some barbaric writings came into my hands which were too old for Greek ideas and too divine for Greek errors. These I was led to trust, owing to their very simplicity of expression and the unstudied character of their authors, owing to their intelligible descriptions of creation, their foreknowledge of the future, the excellence of their precepts and the fact

---

[8] Acts 7.2-53. Cf. Acts 15.16ff, where the argument of James the Just turns on the Septuagint text.

[9] Acts 2.11.

[10] *Megillah* 9 a quotes Rabbi Judah as indicating that only the Pentateuch can be translated into Greek, because of the precedent of King Ptolemy.

[11] *Sepher Torah* 1.8, "Seventy elders wrote the Law in Greek for King Ptolemy, and that day was as bad for Israel as the day in which they made the calf, for the Law could not be translated corresponding to all requirements" (translation, C.K. Barrett, *The New Testament Background*, London, 1956, p. 213).

[12] Justin, *Dialogue with Trypho*, 7.

of their embracing the universe under the sole rule of God . . . They furnish us . . . with something which had been received but which, thanks to error, had been lost.[13]

Both Justin and Tatian, well versed in conventional philosophy, are impressed by the antiquity of the Jewish Scriptures, which they knew only because of the Septuagint, by their predictive content (related directly to the person of Christ) and their relevance to the most urgent questions of intellectual discourse. The fact was that the Septuagint was the only alternative literature in the Greek world which could claim comparable antiquity with the Greek corpus. That antiquity of the literature used by the Christians was important: the world view of Hellenistic civilization rested on the conviction that every important question had been canvassed; in itself Christianity thus stood condemned by its very novelty. The demonstration therefore that the Christians had writings older than Socrates, that Moses wrote before Plato, nay (as the boldest apologists could assert) Plato got some of his best passages from Isaiah, was a major apologetic consideration.

By their translation into Greek and use by converted Hellenistic Gentiles, the Hebrew Scriptures took on a new purpose and were applied within a new universe of thought. They became an authoritative sourcebook for Greek Christians seeking to build a coherent world view. The Greek translation of the Scriptures may have been necessary in various ways to the Dispersion Jewish scholar Philo, the Hellenistic Jewish Christian Stephen, the ambicultural missionary rabbi Paul, but each of them could claim another history and another spiritual homeland. Justin and Origen had no such other home; the Scriptures in Greek were necessary to them for the building of a cultural and intellectual house that they could recognize as home. They could neither wholly abandon the Hellenistic world of their inheritance, nor leave it in the form it had for their unreconstructed contemporaries. Justin, the eclectic philosopher, continues as a teacher of philosophy from his conversion to his martyrdom; for Christianity is simply divine philosophy, leading (as in Plato's teaching true philosophy does) to the vision of God. The Scriptures—including (and in some ways, because of their antiquity, especially) the Jewish Scriptures—provide him with an authoritative text for the radical criticism of his heritage. That his heritage was corrupted and full of demonic things he had no doubt. But there was truth there too. There had been Greeks before Christ like Socrates, who had rejected the false gods and suffered for it. Surely such as Socrates had spoken according to *Logos*, reason? And if they did, must not this reason of theirs come from the source of all reason, the *Logos*, the Divine Son of the Father?[14] And so the daring *Logos* symbol taken by the Fourth Evangelist, already foreshadowed by Philo, appears in a new context and with a differently freighted significance. The *Logos* of the Fourth Gospel may not be the *Logos* of Philo's liminal shock-absorber; its most important component may well be the active Hebrew *Dabhar Yahweh*, the Word

---

13 Tatian, *Oration* 29.

14 Justin, *1 Apology* 46.

of the Lord. But it is the *Dabhar Yahweh* translated, and translated into a medium where the term is already loaded, and in a setting in which much of the original significance can probably not be heard. The load in the translation propels it towards Justin, who, with other early Hellenistic Christian writers takes it further into realms which neither Philo nor the Fourth Evangelist reached. It becomes an indispensable tool by which to bring Christ into contact with the Greek heritage; and Christ becomes its criterion of truth. The prior loading of the word *Logos* may have meant that Greeks who spoke no Hebrew (that is, nearly all of them) missed many important things about the *Logos* as the active Word of God, but it did not mislead them about their salvation. Indeed, it enabled them to see that salvation.

But the loading of words is not a one-directional process. We have only to think of a still more daring piece of translation risked quite informally by Jewish Christians in the first recorded sustained encounter between the word about Christ and Greek-speaking pagans. According to the Book of Acts unnamed believers originating from Cyprus and Cyrene spoke to Greeks in Antioch about "the Lord Jesus".[15] In all previous proclamations, Jesus had been presented as the Messiah, the Saviour of Israel. In this new, Hellenistic-pagan context, he is given the title *Kyrios*, the title Hellenistic pagans gave to their cult divinities. One might have expected (did any of their more cautious contemporaries predict?) that the result would be the recognition of the Lord Jesus as one more cult divinity alongside the Lord Serapis or the Lord Osiris. The major reason this did not happen was undoubtedly that those pagans who responded were brought into a community where the Septuagint was constantly read, and the Biblical associations of *Kyrios* penetrated their minds and attached themselves to the cult divinity title. But in the first encounter, the loading of *Kyrios* with the cult divinity idea was vital. It is doubtful whether unacculturated pagans in the Antiochene world could have understood the significance of Jesus in any other way. None of us can take in a new idea except in terms of the ideas we already have. Once implanted, however, this understanding of the word received a set of controls from its new biblical frame of reference. In time much of the original loading of the word disappeared altogether.

Another feature of the Septuagint took on a new significance as that translation progressed under Christian auspices towards the heart of Hellenistic culture. In the Hebrew text of the Old Testament, of course, the divine name is represented by the Tetragrammaton, for in the Old Testament God has a personal name. But centuries of Jewish reverence did not allow that name to be pronounced, and in the Septuagint that reverence is given concrete form. The Tetragrammaton is replaced by *Kyrios*. God in the Septuagint has no name.[16]

---

15 Acts 11.20.

16 *Kyrios*, of course, appears in the Septuagint as the title of the Sovereign God, but this would not be an aspect which a pagan was likely to seize on; nor is it likely that these early Gentile Christians, who in the opening chapters of Acts present Jesus to Jews as Messiah, sought to present him to Gentiles as the God of Abraham, the Creator and Lawgiver.

This sharpened the confrontation of early Christianity with the popular religion of the Greco-Roman world. God was *not* Zeus/Jupiter, or Saturn/Kronos, or any amalgam of the gods. He was *ho Theos, the* God, over and against them all. If this gave force to the rejection of the gods of popular religion it also lubricated the connexion of Christianity with that indigenous philosophical tradition which also had rejected popular religion, which had spoken of the ultimate principally in abstract terms or in negatives. That connection was to have momentous consequences for the whole of Western theology.

Altogether the effect of that first pre-Christian translation was crucial for the development of an indigenous Hellenistic Christianity. But it was also exemplary for the whole history of Gentile Christianity, a direction indicator for the encounter of many peoples in their subsequent interaction with the Christian faith. Many of the issues that have occurred since in or as a result of the work of Bible translation are foreshadowed in that first great movement of cross-cultural Christian diffusion. Hellenistic people could not be converted without the conversion of the whole universe of Greek thought. That universe was the construction of centuries. There was no question of its being abandoned or substituted—no such option really existed. There was no alternative for Hellenistic Christians but the conversion of Hellenistic culture itself, the steady application of Christ and the word about Christ to its processes and priorities—another work of centuries. In that process the existence of the Septuagint was critical. The New Testament, itself partly a work of translation into Greek from a Jewish medium and conveyed through Jewish minds, could hardly have had the radical effect it did except for its association with the Greek translation of the ancient Jewish literature, the alternative classical corpus.

Oral Recital in a Literary Culture

The Greco-Roman world had an established literary culture, a large literate community and a widespread and efficient mechanism for book production. Christian literature came to a market and to reading habits already shaped by the uses of non-Christian literature. It developed, however, some uses of its own.

The old man who told Justin to read the Hebrew prophets clearly assumed that he would be able to get access to them and to the Gospels. And Justin himself, explaining to a Greek audience (in a book, of course, which he clearly hopes non-Christians will read) what it is that Christians actually do in their meetings, explains that the memoirs of the apostles and the writings of the prophets are read for as long as time permits.[17] (There are indications in early Christian literature that this was often quite a long time.) The Church's Scriptures are those read in Church, and it was this public reading of Scripture, a natural continuation of synagogue practice, which must have been normative for

17 Justin, *1 Apology*, 67.

most members of the early Christian communities. The practice was maintained by the earliest Christian communities outside the Greek world. The oldest surviving document of North African Christianity records the trial of a group of Christians on 17 July 180. The accused have a box which they say contains The Books, and the letters of Paul, a righteous man.[18] Since the record is in Latin, the books presumably represent an early vernacular translation. In the Great Persecution a hundred and twenty years later, in the same part of Latin-speaking Africa, the magistrates were carrying out a Government order that all Christian books should be confiscated. The Mayor tells the bishop to hand over the writings of the law and "anything else you have", but search reveals only one large volume; the clergy say the readers have the rest. Examination of the readers' houses produces four books from one, two from another, none from a third.[19] In other words, a few years before Constantine's accession the fundamental importance of the books for the vitality of Christianity is recognized even by the Government. But the books are primarily for *public* reading; even the clergy do not possess their own copies. Books belong to congregations, and there is an order of ministry specially responsible for their care and for public reading. Even in this literary culture, the process of communication for most Christians was essentially oral, and its auditorium was the regular worship of the Church. And as literary compositions, the pre-Vulgate Latin translations do not even read well; they bear all the marks of later "missionary" translations. The young Augustine, a Latin-speaking African who found Greek heavy going, turned from them in disgust, as unworthy of comparison with Cicero. The Latin Scriptures may, of course, have sounded better in public recital; as it was, the mature Augustine found a theological rationale in their "lowliness".[20]

Christianity and Northern Oral Culture

In its next great cross-cultural diffusion of Christianity, a faith which had made its home in a long-established literary culture with a Mediterranean history and priorities, had to make terms with the world-views of the disintegrating tribes, settled or semi-settled marauders and peasant cultivators who bordered the Roman Empire and brought about its gradual dissolution. Among the new Christians there was no indigenous literary culture, no large literate community and no market-oriented book production.

Nor was there any over-arching missionary strategy for the evangelization of the West. The conversion of the West took place as a result of a variety of disparate initiatives from Church authorities (most famously Pope Gregory the

---

[18] *Acts of the Scillitan Martyrs.*

[19] *Gesta apud Zenophilum* (Text in *Corpus Scriptorum Ecclesiasticorum Latinorum* 26, 186-188).

[20] Augustine, *Confessions* 3.9, "My swelling pride shrank from their lowliness, now could my sharp wit pierce the interior thereof" (Pusey's translation).

Great), political expansionists (most notoriously Charlemagne) and a stream of inspired ascetics (of whom Celtic Christianity produced a prodigious number). Amid centuries of muddled response, and a linguistic situation in constant flux, it is not surprising that there were different attitudes to translation. For our present purposes two contrasting examples must suffice. They are not exactly contemporary, but the conditions in which they worked were broadly parallel and the central figures themselves had much in common.

Ulfilas, or Wulfila as he was among his own people, was Gothic by birth though descended from Christian captives taken from Asia Minor. He was the leading figure in the Gothic Christian community which emerged from these captives from the Hellenistic-Roman world, and spoke both Greek and Gothic. Not surprisingly, he was Arian, for this would be the natural expression of the Christianity of his origins. At the age of 30 he was consecrated Bishop of the Goths, at that time living beyond the fringe of the Roman Empire. His vigorous evangelism was only too successful, and he and many of his people eventually moved to form a Gothic enclave within the Empire. With the complex history of the Visigoths we are not here concerned, nor with the precise part which Wulfila played in their conversion. There seems no reason to doubt the stories which credit him with bringing to birth a complete translation of the Bible into Gothic; complete, that is, apart from the Books of Kings, which he is said to have left aside because his people needed no more instruction as to warfare. Before he could produce his translation he had to design an alphabet for Gothic.[21]

In other words, Wulfila is an early example of what was to be a regular feature of the later missionary movement. He was the creator of literature within a culture otherwise entirely oral. Once created, it had to be sustained, which meant the creation of a literate class (there was no hope for many years to come of a literate *community*). The natural model was the Hellenistic one, of an educated clergy, with a rank of readers who might graduate to higher things.

The Goths became a Christian people, spread out over a vast area. They impinged more and more on the Empire, and the time came when the Goths provided the Emperor. And throughout Gothdom, in and beyond the Empire, Wulfila's version of the Scriptures was read. It is the sole monument of Gothic literature. Not only was it the beginning of Gothic literature: it *is* Gothic literature. Though Wulfila was an Arian, and though the Goths were long Arian, there is nothing particularly Arian about it. But then, no characteristically Gothic theology has come down to us. When Gothic Arians discussed theology with Greek Nicenes, they presumably did so on Greek ground, with Greek intellectual weapons and bilingual texts; and the distinguished historian of the Visigoths has raised the question whether Wulfila did his people the best service by placing their access to Scripture in a vernacular which no non-mother tongue

---

21 For Wulfila (floruit 340-370) there is a brief life by his pupil Auxentius and references in Philostorgius (*Ecclesiastical History* 2.5) and other 5th century writers. See G.W.S. Fridrichsen, *The Gothic Version of the Gospels*, Oxford, 1926 and *The Gothic Version of the Epistles*, Oxford, 1936.

speaker had reason to learn. Alas that we do not know more of the life and thought of those early Gothic Christians who filled up the ranks of the laity and spoke no Greek or Latin.

A century after Wulfila, at the other end of Europe, Patrick began his strange career. There are parallels between them; Patrick, though not Irish by birth, was British and Celtic-speaking. He came from the Romanized Christian population left demoralized in Britain after the Roman Empire decided to reduce its overseas commitments. He spoke and wrote Latin too, though probably not as well as Wulfila, and he had no Greek, in which Wulfila was fluent. He first went to Ireland as a captive, just as Wulfila's forbears had gone to Gothdom; was a slave there, came there to a deep experience of God, escaped and later returned as a missionary. Ireland, unlike his homeland, had never been part of the Roman Empire, and lacked such characteristic Roman features as towns and administrative centers. Patrick, a Celt himself, shared the Celtic view of a universe packed with potentially hostile powers, which he confronted with the name of Christ. He did not behave like a Roman bishop; he travelled as the Irish kings did, and Irish ecclesiastical organization was in Roman terms distinctly odd. He lamented his crude Latin and his ignorance of Greek; more polished Gallo-Latin Christians over the water raised their eyebrows at his rusticity and at an early sin which impeded his ordination, and may have found it hard to cope with a man who had quite such vivid experiences of the devil jumping on to his chest.[22]

Patrick, like Wulfila, needed to produce a class of readers and Scripture experts. Like Wulfila, he had to start by producing a small literate community, and we are told that he regularly taught alphabets. But these were *Latin* alphabets. Patrick, with all his closeness to Celtic life and thought, attempted no vernacularization of Scripture. Indeed—though he was clearly a Celtic preacher of immense power and presence—when he uses a Scripture passage almost as a curse on a chief who has kidnapped Christian women, he writes as though it will have special force in Latin.[23] He raised a group of followers who wrote better Latin than himself, who composed beautiful Latin hymns (not to mention beautiful Celtic ones), who produced books of unrivalled artistry, who set Ireland in the mainstream of Western culture, and made it a nation of scholars.

Patrick, rather than Wulfila, represents the dominant practice of this, the third phase of Christian expansion, at least as far as Western Europe is concerned.[24] The acculturative process which the evangelization hastened had the

---

[22] Patrick (? c. 390-? c. 460) is his own biographer. The references here are to his remarkable *Confession*.

[23] Patrick, *Letter to Coroticus* 20: "These are not my words, that I have presented in Latin, but those of God, of the apostles and prophets who never lied".

[24] Eastern Christianity followed a different path, though even here we see the growth of "special languages" such as Church Slavonic as well as genuine vernacularization. For the most remarkable incident cf. A.P. Vlasto, "The Mission of S.S. Cyril and Methodios and its aftermath in Central Europe", in G.J. Cuming, *The Mission of the Church and the*

effect of taking the consciousness of the peoples of the north and west beyond locality and the kinship group which had traditionally bounded their societies. Eventually it was to lead to the concept of Christendom, the territorial Empire of Christ. The existence of a common language for Scripture, liturgy and learning was a powerful factor in this. "At the present time", says Bede in 731 A.D., "there are in Britain, in harmony with the five books of the divine law, five languages and four nations—English, British, Scots, and Picts. Each of these have their own language; but all are united in their study of God's truth by the fifth—Latin—which has become a common medium through the study of the scriptures".25 The Church saved Latin, as it was to save or strengthen many languages in centuries to come through making them the vehicle of the Christian Scriptures and of Christian worship. But it was not Latin as a vernacular language that was saved; Latin emerged as a "special" language for Christians, the universal language of that literate class of Christians who conducted the liturgy and publicly read the Scriptures. It had other important effects also, besides uniting the disparate peoples of the Empire of Christ in a common Christian culture. It gave them a shared past by connecting their local and national story with that of the Christian Roman Empire and of the early Church; it gave them a shared intellectual heritage by connecting them with the history and literature of old Rome.26 In the first Christian encounter with the Hellenistic world we are immediately conscious of the process of evangelization by translation. In the encounter with the northern peoples the process of evangelization by supplementation is often more obvious. The language of Scripture is less the motor for the penetration of an established culture than the vehicle for the appropriation and expression of a new identity.

But this is only part of the story. Vernacular exposition of the Scriptures remained an important duty as it had been for Patrick. The Anglo-Saxon missionary Boniface, serving under Frankish auspices in territory coming under Frankish control, insisted that the renunciation of the devil required by the baptismal vow should be explained in the vernacular, but the baptismal formula itself delivered in Latin.27 Here is an early distinction between what demands the believer's comprehension and active participation and the representative acts of the Church which are safest and strongest in the special language of the Church. And as vernacular languages themselves became written languages, vernacular translations naturally appeared as an adjunct to the official Church versions. Bede, most Roman in obedience yet most English in outlook, was at the time of

Propagation of the Faith, (Cambridge, 1970), pp. 1-16.

25 Bede, *Ecclesiastical History* 1.1 (Translation of L. Sherley Price).

26 The Gallo-Roman bishop, Gregory of Tours, seamlessly joins history from the Fall to Clerment Ferrand via Jerusalem and Rome in his *History of the Franks* see I.1.

27 cf. J.M. Wallace-Hadrill, *The Frankish Church*. Oxford, 1963:377-389.

his death preparing a translation of John's Gospel into the speech of Northumbria.[28]

The vernacular principle received its most rigorous assertion in the sixteenth century. Protestantism is essentially Northern vernacular Christianity. Its very diversity is related to the diversity of the local settings; it is Christianity translated, not only into local languages but into the local cultural settings of Northern Europe. It is probably no accident, as Fernand Braudel points out, that the line between Catholic and Protestant Europe so closely follows the line between the true provinces of the Roman Empire and the areas in which Roman rule was temporary, peripheral or absent.[29] The principal exception is Ireland—Patrick's Ireland.

The period which produced this spectacular demonstration of the vernacular principle also saw two other developments with far-reaching consequences. One was technological: the development of printing made possible the widespread ownership of copies of the Scriptures. This opened the way for private, individual study to supplement public reading in the congregation. For many more Christians than formerly, private rather than public reading became the principal and most potent form of encounter with Scripture. The changes involved in moving from an oral to a literary relationship with Scripture, and from a communal to an individual one, require more consideration than can be given here. Perhaps the change of relationship assisted Christian penetration of Western culture in which individualization was becoming increasingly important.

The other critical development was the beginning of the next phase of Christian cross-cultural diffusion. It was eventually to lead to the situation in which we now stand, the passing of the Christian center of gravity from the West to the South, as Christian recession in Europe accompanied massive Christian adhesion in Latin America, Sub-Saharan Africa, the South Pacific and a few areas of Asia.

The new era was to demonstrate all the translation questions of the earlier encounters of Christian faith with other cultures. The way of Wulfila and the way of Patrick are both evident in that era, and the distinction is not simply that between "Protestant" and "Catholic" approaches. Early Protestant history in West Africa raised the question for a time (a very short time!) whether a vigorous English-speaking African Church would not render African languages unnecessary,[30] and today one may well wonder whether English has not simply taken over from Latin as the special international language of theology. William Smalley has drawn attention to the phenomenon of language hierarchies, in

---

28 Cuthbert, *Life of Bede*, ad fin.

29 F. Braudel, *Civilization and Capitalism*, Vol. 3: *The Perspective of the World*, English Translation London, 1984, p. 66.

30 Andrew F. Walls, "Black Europeans, White Africans . . ." in D. Baker, ed., *Religious Motivation: Biographical and Sociological Problems for the Church Historian*, Oxford, 1978, 339-368.

which people use different languages for different purposes; including sacred purposes.[31] The relevance of this to the history of Christian expansion deserves further exploration.

In the latest phase of Christian expansion Wulfila has overtaken Patrick as in the previous one Patrick overtook Wulfila. Both now assume mass readerships rather than seminal literate classes, since both now have the capacity to provide copies of the Scriptures in numbers. (Both must also take account of the extent to which oral cultures remain oral, and respond to Scripture orally, even when they possess a literature.) The measure of their effectiveness is how far the Word once more recognizably takes flesh in the cultures in which they work, and people behold *His* glory under human conditions.

[31] E.g. W.A. Smalley, "Thailand's hierarchy of multilingualism", *Language Sciences* 10,2 (1988).

DANIEL C. ARICHEA

THEOLOGY AND TRANSLATION:
THE IMPLICATIONS OF CERTAIN THEOLOGICAL ISSUES TO THE TRANSLATION TASK

Introduction

The Bible is many things, but a very important part of its nature as a book is that it is primarily a theological document. If this is so, then the task of translating the Bible is necessarily a theological task, and anyone engaged in Bible translation should, by necessity, be concerned with theological issues primarily as they relate to translation itself.

This paper is an attempt to address several theological issues which are deemed pertinent to Scripture translation. Among the questions that form a background of this discussion are: What do we translate? How do we translate? Why do we translate? Is there any theological basis for the task of Bible translation, and particularly for the whole Bible Society program of producing audience-centered translations of the Scriptures through the application of dynamic or functional equivalence translation principles?

I welcome this opportunity of sharing these ideas with this forum which is composed mainly of non-Bible Society people, in order to benefit from the results of meaningful dialogue. All of us, I am sure, are interested in the task of translating the Scriptures and communicating the biblical message clearly for our time.

I. What are We Translating?: The Problem of Text and Canon

One primary question that has direct relevance to the translation task is: what is the object of translation? What do we translate? It is easy enough to say that we translate the Bible, but what in fact is the Bible that is to be translated? What are its perimeters in terms of form and content? To ask these questions is necessarily to go into the areas of *text* and *canon*.

A. Text

One of the most important concerns in the translation task has to do with determining and defining the biblical text. Translators are of course told that the object of translation is the Hebrew text of the Old Testament and the Greek texts of the New Testament and the Deuterocanon/Apocrypha. But many translators have no idea about the complexities involved in determining a reliable and accurate biblical text.

What affirmations can we make regarding the relation of the text to the translation task?

1. *First of all, textual studies will always be of great significance to the translation process.*

Eugene Nida is certainly right when he writes that "a translation can never really be better than its textual base, for the underlying text is where all biblical scholarship begins".[1]

One cannot consider the question of text without mentioning with a deep sense of gratitude the tremendous efforts, both past and present, which have been exerted in the reconstruction of the biblical text. Textual criticism has indeed done and continues to do a great service to biblical studies in general, and to the translation task in particular.

Since the text is of vital importance in the translation task, it is no surprise that the Bible Societies have always been and continue to be interested in textual studies. It is also in this area that the Bible Societies have clearly demonstrated their dependence on the resources of biblical scholarship. The UBS Greek New Testament and the recently concluded *Hebrew Old Testament Text Project* (*HOTTP*) are indications of the Bible Society's concern for the biblical text and its willingness to seek the help of the most competent biblical scholars in order to make available to translators the results of textual scholarship. And this cooperation is going to continue, I am sure, because textual criticism remains a continuing concern: there is always need for study and evaluation of past, present and future evidences, particularly in the light of new textual discoveries and new insights into the textual process.

2. *For the translation process, the most helpful textual decisions are those which are based on critical, literary and linguistic principles.*

Insofar as textual matters are concerned, the Bible should be regarded like any other book, and its textual development treated like that of any other writing. To put it negatively, textual conclusions should never be based on *a priori* theological assertions regarding the Bible and the textual process. As an example, we can cite the recent resurgence of interest in the majority text.[2] An

---

1 Eugene A. Nida, "Quality in Translation", *The Bible Translator* 33-3, July 1982, 329-332. 329.

2 The majority text is defended by many conservative scholars. Among them are Jacob Van Bruggen, *The Ancient Text of the New Testament*, (Winnipeg: Premier Printing Ltd., 1976) and also *The Future of the Bible*, (New York: Nelson, n.d.). The position of providence with regard to the majority text is examined in Harry A. Sturz, *The Byzantine Text Type and New Testament Textual Criticism*, and D.A. Carson, *The King James Version*

examination of recent publications on this matter tends to show that the majority text is often defended not primarily on textual/critical grounds but on theological grounds (e.g. God's providential care over the text). There is a real danger here of elevating the biblical text to a super-human or non-human level and hence not subject to critical scientific rules. And when theological considerations play a decisive role in determining the text which is the object of the translation task, producing quality translations becomes doubly difficult if not impossible.

3. There is a need of making textual information accessible to the translator.

There are of course a lot of published materials on textual studies, but most of these are very technical and beyond the grasp of many translators in the field. There is a constant need of producing much simpler publications, in order to enable translators, especially non-biblical specialists, to grasp not only the importance of the text, but also the whole matter of textual criticism.

Three publications may be mentioned. First, *The Greek New Testament* published by the United Bible Societies attempts to help translators in the evaluation of textual problems by providing a graded evaluation for textual variants which are cited.[3]

Secondly, Bruce M. Metzger's *A Textual Commentary on the Greek New Testament*[4] explains in detail and in non-technical language the textual decisions made in the *GNT*. This is an indispensable tool for anyone who wants to make full use of the *GNT* critical apparatus.

Thirdly, *The Text of the New Testament* by Kurt and Barbara Aland[5] which includes an introductory manual to the *GNT* and the Nestle-Aland *Greek New Testament*, and a chapter introducing the whole practice of New Testament textual criticism.

There are also scholarly editions being planned for many Asian languages, and once published, these will be very helpful to translators as well as to pastors and theological students.

Debate, (Grand Rapids, Michigan: Baker Book House Co., 1979). An attempt to prove the provenance of the majority text scientifically is in William Pickering, *The Identity of the New Testament Text,* (Nelson, 1977). For a criticism of his position, see Carson, op. cit.

3 Kurt Aland writes that this feature was "insisted upon by Eugene A. Nida against the whole editorial committee, if I may speak out of school, and in retrospect I believe he was right" (*The Text of the New Testament,* Leiden, E.J. Brill, 1987, p.44).

4 London: United Bible Societies, 1971.

5 See Note 2.

B. *Canon*:

Whereas text deals with the wording of what we are translating, canon deals with the form and boundaries of the text. The text is necessarily related to the formation of the canon and to individual books within it. There have been various efforts to define more clearly the stages of canon formation, and in fact many of these stages have been positively identified. For example, the *HOTTP* has identified four phases in the development of the Hebrew text, namely, (1) oral or written literary products in forms as close as possible to those originally produced; (2) the earliest form or forms of the text which can be determined by the application of techniques of textual analysis to existing textual evidence; (3) the consonantal text as authorized by Jewish scholars shortly after A.D. 70, also known as the Proto-Masoretic text; and (4) the Masoretic text, as determined by the Massoretes in the 9th and 10th centuries A.D.[6]

The relationship between text and canon is discussed at length by Brevard Childs and James Sanders in three recent publications.[7] Childs restates the goal of textual criticism as the recovery of the canonical text rather than the Urtext. The canonical text for both the Old and the New Testaments is that which the believing communities have accepted as Scripture and which has attained a state of stability. For Childs, the canonical shape has great significance, and it is the canon which is the context of both textual and hermeneutical endeavors.[8]

---

[6] Another example of an attempt to identify stages of formation is found in Joseph Fitzmyer's Commentary on Luke (*Anchor Bible*, Volume 28). Fitzmyer writes: "Various stages of the gospel tradition are invoked at times to explain one aspect or other of the Lukan story of Jesus. Stage I of the gospel tradition is concerned with what the historical Jesus of Nazareth did and said; Stage II with what was preached and proclaimed about him after the resurrection; and Stage III with what NT writers decided to put in writing concerning him. What immediately confronts the reader of the Lucan Gospel is a form of Stage III of that tradition. It is the result of literary composition, based on material inherited by the author from Stage I and II and fashioned by him into a synthesis, an interpretation of the Christ-event . . . The primary concern of this commentary is to interpret the Lucan form of Stage III; how has Luke presented Jesus in his two-volume work, especially in its first part, the Gospel . . . " (v. VIII).

[7] Brevard Childs, *Introduction to the Old Testament as Scripture*, Philadelphia: Fortress Press, 1979, especially pp. 84-106. Also *The New Testament As Canon: An Introduction*, (Philadelphia: Fortress Press, 1985). The volume by James A. Sanders is *From Sacred Story to Sacred Text*, (Philadelphia: Fortress Press, 1987).

[8] According to Childs, the goal of textual criticism is not the recovery of the Urtext, but "the recovery and understanding of the canonical text" (*Old Testament as Scripture*, p. 96). The canonical text "denotes that official Hebrew text of the Jewish community which had reached a point of stabilization in the first century A.D., thus all but ending its long history of fluidity" (p. 100). While Childs does not identify the canonical text with the Masoretic text, yet he clearly implies that the two are virtually identical. For example, while he recognizes that the stabilized text is only a consonantal text, yet he goes on to say that "the vowel points served to preserve and register the oral tradition of how the text was to be read and did not function as a critical or innovative grammatical enterprise." (p. 98). Moreover, even when a part of the canonical text is obviously defective, Childs still insists

A related but somewhat different position is put forward by James Sanders.[9] While putting to question the aim of textual criticism as getting back to the original text, he nevertheless prefers as the main object of textual criticism not a stabilized text which has removed all ambiguities and problems, but a text representing an earlier stage characterized by fluidity and greater variety. As far as the Old Testament is concerned, even the Masoretes were not so much interested in getting back to an *ipsissima verba* of the biblical text or to completely standardizing the text as to preserve a text with its own particularities, peculiarities, and even anomalies. The Masoretes "have preserved for us a pluralistic text that has remarkably resisted assimilations and homogenization of readings". As such, "they have richly enhanced the pluralism of the Bible by their care for the text and by their preserving the multiple possibilities".[10] Sanders regards this pluralistic nature of the text as the proper object of canonical criticism and other critical studies:

> Perhaps revival of a pluralistic sense of canon and of a deep appreciation of the pluralistic texts that have been entrusted to us from many generations and of their functions through the ages in the believing communities that have passed them on, may allow us to perceive a more limited and yet greater value of the tools of biblical criticism developed and honed over the past three centuries.[11]

that it is this mutilated text which is the object of textual study. Discussing I Samuel 1.24, in which there is an obvious error, Childs writes,

> The canonical approach to this text would assess the effect of this mechanical error in the MT in relation to its earlier and apparently original reading in the other text families. In addition, it would attempt to assess the range of interpretation possible for this mutilated MT text . . . Within the fixed parameters of a canonical corpus the method seeks to determine how the meaning of a given passage, even if damaged, was influenced by its relation to other canonical passages (p. 105).

In *The New Testament as Canon*, Childs puts to question the traditional understanding of the goal of New Testament textual criticism which is "to present exactly the original words of the New Testament, so far as they can now be determined from surviving documents." Instead, the goal of textual criticism is "to recover the New Testament text which reflects the true apostolic witness found in the church's scripture". And since the Greek text was stabilized in the *koine*, textual criticism should help us recover a text which represents the last stages of stabilized *koine* tradition. He writes, "Working within the initial context of the textus receptus, the text critic enters into a process of searching for the best received, that is, canonical text". He then gives this summary statement: "The canonical model of textual criticism proposes a continuing search in discerning the best received text which moves from the outer parameters of the common church tradition found in the textus receptus to the inner judgment respecting its purity". This sounds simple enough, but I must confess I don't exactly know what it means!

9 Sanders, *From Sacred Story*, p. 145.

10 Ibid., p. 146.

11 Ibid., p. 147.

These ideas of Childs and Sanders, together with the whole matter of canon (or canonical) criticism, accent for us the following questions: (1) What stage of formation of the biblical books and of the canonical corpus itself is the object of the translation task? (2) How important is it to distinguish between individual biblical books and compilations of these books? (3) What is the place of textual criticism in the canonical process? To answer these questions, there is need to discuss first of all the individual books within the canon, and secondly, the canon as a whole.

1. Individual Books within the Canon

With regard to individual books within the canon, what stage of the canonical process should be considered as the object of the translation task? Definitely it is not the period of oral tradition which represents the first stage in the text formation process; neither is it the stage when these traditions were initially put into writing. Is it then the book as originally composed by an author with the use of sources both oral and written? Or is it the book as it has undergone changes through the hands of various redactors? While all of these stages are important, yet the primary object of the translation task is a further stage: when a particular book is accepted as Scripture by the believing community. This is perhaps identical with the second phase (the accepted texts) of the four-stage history of the Hebrew text which has been identified by the *HOTTP*. It is of course possible that the shape of the book in this second stage is the same as its shape when it was included in an approved list, although it is quite likely that some changes were made before it reached this final stage.

To make this clear, let us give a few examples: a.) As far as the Gospels are concerned, the object of translation is not a Proto-Luke, or an Urtext of Mark, or a reconstructed Aramaic text of the teachings of Jesus. We translate the Gospels as we have received them, i.e. as they were shaped when they became accepted as Scripture by the early believing communities. b.) In the light of internal evidence, it is quite likely that the Corinthian correspondence consists of at least four letters; this has significance for the task of interpretation, but as far as translation is concerned, the Corinthian correspondence is translated as two letters, since this is the shape it had when it was accepted as Scripture by the believing community. c.) While the findings of critical scholarship may support the position that the book of Isaiah is composed of at least two, and perhaps three parts, representing different historical contexts, yet in the translation task, the book of Isaiah is considered as a unity, although the different historical contexts may be explained in an introduction or in appropriate notes.

But what about *specific textual problems* within individual books within the canon? Does the fixing of the canonical form of a book include the resolution of all textual problems within it? Or is there ground for the position that even after the canonical shape of a particular book is fixed there is still fluidity in specific parts particularly insofar as actual wordings of the text are concerned? This is where Sanders' ideas regarding the fluidity and pluralistic nature of the canon are significant. The establishment of a canon does not deter or diminish critical analysis of the text; it should in fact enhance creative and critical study of the text. If this is so, then canonical and textual studies go together, since discrepancies and latent possibilities within the canon are and continue to be legitimate concerns of textual and critical studies.

A further point needs to be made, namely, that it is important to respect the integrity of individual books within the canon. Childs' idea of doing theology in a canonical context seems to have limited application insofar as the translation task is concerned. In translation, taking every book separately and translating the best text and analyzing every text in the light of its immediate and wider context within the book is still the most useful and perhaps the only valid stance insofar as producing accurate translations is concerned.

2. The Canon as a Whole

This matter of canonical shape also has relevance for the whole canon and its relation to the translation task.

a. *The order of books within the canon*. That there is meaning in the ordering of the canon is asserted by many scholars. For example, Sanders has proposed that the Torah should be understood as the "hermeneutical construct" of the rest of the Old Testament.[12] Shepherd suggests a similar position with regard to the Gospels in relation to the New Testament.[13] There are also scholars who hold to

---

[12] See Sanders, *Torah and Canon* , also Sheppard "Canonization", pp. 26f: "For classical Judaism as well as its roots in the pre-exilic period, the term Torah designated both the first collection of five biblical books and the Scriptures as a whole. Moreover, the term functioned as a hermeneutical idiom or construct which designated the subject matter of both the first part and the whole of Scripture". See also Wright, *The OT and Theology*, (New York: 1969, p. 180).

[13] So Sheppard writes, "If 'Torah' became for Judaism the main rubric to describe the authoritative revelation in Scripture, 'Gospel' became the Christian counterpart . . . Moreover, the potention of letting the theological views of a later period help define the meaning of earlier traditions is built similarly into the shape of the Hebrew Bible and the New Testament. In the former, the prophets, whose books often predate the present Torah, are nonetheless put after the Torah as though they are commentary on it. So in the New Testament, the letters of Paul which were written before are placed after the Gospels as theological commentary on the same subject. If the prophets are for Judaism in the shadow of the Torah, so Paul's letters are placed in subordination to the rendering of the gospel through the narratives about Jesus" ("Canonization", p. 30). For a dissenting opinion, see W. Marxsen, pp. 30f. While Marxsen admits that the NT canon 'has all the appearance of a planned arrangement,' he however underplays the theological significance of the canonical arrangement. He writes, "The sequence in the NT is simply an ordering according to literary genre and provides no hint about dates. One could ask if literary genre is also a major factor in the transfer of Daniel from the Writings to the Prophets in the Christian re-arrangement of the Jewish Canon".

the view that the differences in the ordering of the canon has theological significance.[14]

We have to recognize, of course, that there is a great deal of subjectivity involved in this matter, especially since there are different orderings of the canon. However, in view of the possibility of theological motifs in the canonical order, it is important that such orderings are respected in the translation task. Any attempt to reorganize the books for one reason or another should be resisted, since it would undermine the possible purposiveness of the canonical order.[15]

b. *The importance of the whole canon.* There is another aspect that the canon reminds us of, and it is that the Bible Society movement is committed to the whole canon, and not only parts of it. This has traditionally meant the Old Testament and the New Testament. But since the Bible Societies now include the Roman Catholic Church and the Orthodox churches as part of their constituencies, then it is imperative to include the Apocrypha/Deuterocanon as part of Bible Society concerns on the principle of meeting the needs of the total Christian community. The practice of providing only the Old Testament and the New Testament can be justified only as long as the Bible Society movement is regarded as strictly a Protestant one. However, the moment it is recognized that the Bible Society movement works with all churches and confessions, including the Roman Catholic Church and the various Orthodox churches, then to provide these Christian groups with what they regard as the whole canon is not only possible but also necessary.

This commitment to the whole canon also puts to question the practice of translating just the New Testament or parts of it. The aim of the Bible Societies should be to provide their constituencies with the complete Scriptures. Sometimes, of course, for various reasons, it is more practical to have an abridged Old Testament, or for a Readers Digest type of abridged Bible, but

---

14 Robert P. Caroll has observed that for the Jew the Bible ends with a note about the building of the temple (II Chronicles 36.22-23), whereas for the Christian the OT ends with the promise of the coming Elijah who will prepare the people for the day of Yahweh (Malachi 4.5-6). Caroll writes, "These different endings . . . epitomize in a number of ways certain essential features of and differences between Judaism and Christianity". (Robert P. Caroll, "Canonical Criticism: A Recent Trend in Biblical Studies?" *The Expository Times*, Vol. 92, No. 3, December 1980, 73-78, 76).

15 An example of a rearrangement in terms of chronology is William Barclay, *The New Testament* (2 Volumes), Colins, 1968. In an attempt to minimize if not remove anti-Jewish polemic in the Gospels, Norman Beck proposes a reordering of the New Testament: "The time has come for us to reverse the sequence of Matthew and Mark in our New Testament editions so that Mark will be read more frequently and so that the chronological and theological development from Mark to Matthew will be more clearly seen. Luke-Acts can be placed together next, followed by the Fourth Gospel, the Johannine epistles, and the Apocalypse. 2 Peter should be the concluding document of the New Testament collection, as it is in this study". (*Mature Christianity*, London: Associated University Press, 1985, p. 145).

providing the Christian community with the whole canon should be the ideal goal. This is the significance of "Bible" in every society's name.

This does not of course mean that a translation of the whole canon would be provided for every language. Considering the number of languages in the world and the resources of the Bible Societies, that would indeed be an impossible task. However, there are ways of providing a remedy for this situation. Sometimes the provision of the whole canon can be satisfied through some other translation which are usable to a given constituency. This is true of smaller language groups which have access to and can easily use a complete translation in a larger language. Be that as it may, the principle is still valid that the Bible Societies, whenever possible, should provide a language constituency with what they acknowledge as the whole canon of Scripture.

II. What Kind of Book are We Translating: The Nature of the Bible as Sacred Literature

The first part of this paper dealt with the text which has to be translated, together with the scope of the translation task. In this second part, we want to ask the question: what kind of book are we translating? To ask this question is to go into the subject of the nature of the Bible and its authority, together with theological justification for the translation task. What is so special about this book that we have to go through considerable effort to have it translated in various languages all over the world? Are there valid theological reasons for the various translations that are currently produced by the Bible Societies, e.g. common language texts, New Reader Scriptures, Scriptures in comics form, audio Scriptures, etc.?

The nature of the Bible can be discussed in many ways. In this paper, we want to focus on the nature of the Bible as both a literary and a theological book. As the former, it is comparable to any other secular writing; as the latter, it is often invested with special characteristics worthy only of God. And certainly, Patrick Miller is right when he talks of the "tension between the Bible as historical document and the Bible as living word: it is the tension between the Bible as a written record out of the history or Israel and the early church (fully comparable to many other such records) and the Bible as the Word of God that transcends the temporal context out of which it rose without ever being divorced from its original shaping".[16]

What are the implications of these assertions for the study of the Bible and the translation task?

---

[16] Patrick D. Miller, Jr. "The Translation Task", *Theology Today* 53 (January 1987), 540-545, 542.

A. *The Bible as a Literary Composition: the Importance of Scholarship*

First of all then, the Bible is a literary book and therefore a result of human effort. This is an inevitable conclusion when the nature of the Bible as written literature is taken seriously. From the human point of view, the Bible is no different from any other human literature. It contains only human words. It is influenced by the prevalent culture of its day. The different writings within it are bound by the literary conventions of their own time and utilize literary genres which were in current use. While the temporal, geographical and cultural boundaries contained in the Bible are much wider and broader than those in most other ancient books, this does not diminish the character of the Bible as a product of human activity.[17]

The Bible is indeed a human book, and no theological assertions can deny or undermine this fact. To be sure there are theological arguments put forth to explain the necessity of the Bible taking the form of a human book,[18] but even though such arguments may be valid, in the end we have to admit that these are in the area of faith and not of sight; these are confessions of faith rather than conclusions of scholarship. However, the character of the Bible as a human book is both an assumption and a conclusion of scholarship, and any statement of faith about the Bible has to take seriously this humanness. To put it another

---

[17] Cf. Henry P. Hamann, *The Bible between Fundamentalism and Philosophy*, p. 54: "Everything about the Bible shows its humanity: the origin and genesis of the individual writings; the collection of the various and very different compositions into one definitive library; the transmission of the text to various writings down through the centuries; and the translations of the original languages".

[18] Cf. Vawter, *Inspiration*, p. 169: "God has infused into it His word, not by depriving it of anything human but rather by utilizing all of its many and diverse human qualities. He has accommodated Himself to the ways of man; not an ideal, unhistorical man, but man in his only historical *condition*, precisely the man who needs to hear the *saving* word of God. This is the man we find in the Bible, and thus the word has come to him". Likewise Barr, *The Bible in the Modern World*, pp. 20-21: "The person of Christ, as understood in traditional christology, is taken as an analogy. He is both truly God and truly man; and correspondingly the Bible is both Word of God and Word of Man . . . The entire Bible is human word, subject to the strains, weaknesses and errors of any human product . . . But the entire Bible is also a divine Word; it has something to say that does not arise from human culture and is immanent within it . . ." Also Berkouwer, *Holy Scripture*, p. 200: "Just as the incarnation of Christ demands that it be searched after to the depths of humiliation and in all its weakness and revilement, so the writing of God's Word, the revelation of God invites us also to recognize in Scripture that weak and humble aspect, the form of a servant . . . Christ carried a cross, and a servant is not greater than his master. Scripture is the maid servant of Christ. She shares his revilement". So also Achtemeier, *Inspiration*, p. 95: "We never confront God in Scripture except as he speaks within human forms and human history. The Word of God in Scripture is not delivered in a timeless and absolute form, unaffected by contemporary cultural and linguistic realities . . . God has become a wholly historical figure . . . To make of Scripture something more supernatural and timeless than God's own self-revelation in his Son is surely to withdraw oneself from a serious consideration of the intention of Scripture".

way, any statement of faith about the Bible which has no room for its character as the product of human efforts must be regarded with caution if not skepticism.

What are the implications of the human character of Scripture to the task of translation?

1. *Treating the Bible as human composition makes possible the task of translation, together with interpretation and proclamation.*

Having lived and worked in Indonesia for 13 years, I am very much aware of the Islamic attitude towards the Qur'an: since it is regarded as a book that came down from heaven in its present form, it is therefore not possible to translate it. Not that there are no existing translations of the Qur'an, but most of these translations are labeled commentaries rather than translations.

A similar attitude towards the Bible is found in the Christian community. There are many Christians for whom "the human aspect of Holy Scripture lost all constitutive meaning and became blurred through the overwhelming divine reality of God's speaking".[19] In many parts of the world, the Bible as the Word of God is identified with a particular translation; in such cases, further translation becomes an almost impossible endeavor.

It has also been noted that when the divine origin and character of the Bible is emphasized at the expense of the human, then interpretation is de-emphasized. biblical exposition consists mainly of quoting passages of Scriptures, and any passage which needs further elaboration is explained by the use of other Scripture citations.

It may be mentioned that every time we encourage in any way the idea that reading the Bible is sufficient in itself without the necessity of interpretation or proclamation, then we are participating in minimizing the character of the Bible as human literature and overemphasizing its divine character.

It is for this reason that the traditional Bible Society position of printing Biblical texts without note or comment is counter-productive. The practice of including various readers helps in Bible Society publications is a most welcome development, since these notes provide help in the understanding and meaningful interpretation of Scripture, and at the same time contribute to the dismantling of the myth that reading the biblical text is all that is needed.

Finally, we should also disclaim the position that translations are sufficient in themselves. A translation does (or should) make the biblical message clear, but it does more than that: it also presents the biblical text in such a way as to make appropriation of its message a real possibility. Ideally, translation should not close the text but open it up for meaningful interpretation and proclamation. A good translation is an indispensable tool for responsible hermeneutics.

---

[19] Berkouwer, *Holy Scripture*, p. 25.

2. The human character of the Bible makes it possible to do justice to its diversity.

One of the characteristics of the Bible as a human book is that of its rich diversity which is eloquently displayed in the Bible's use of various literary genres, the presence of different styles of writing, the variation in details, and finally and most importantly, the diversity in theological positions. Diversity within Scripture is considered by many to be a serious liability which lessens the Bible's authority and trustworthiness. Therefore attempts have been made either to minimize the diverse elements in Scripture, or else to deny their existence altogether.

There is room, however, for a more healthy and positive attitude towards diversity in Scripture.[20] For one thing, diversity within Scripture enriches our understanding of God and his acts within the world.[21] Diversity also gives us an understanding of how the community of faith responded to the challenges that it faced. Different situations entailed different responses, but more importantly, the same situation gave rise to diverse responses due to divergent perspectives. This understanding of diversity also allows the biblical material to become a model for the church of today in responding to the challenges of its own day and time.

How should translation deal with this diversity within Scripture? There seems to be no alternative but to be faithful to this diversity. No attempt should be made to harmonize the varying details within the biblical material. The rich diversity in *literary forms* which characterizes the biblical writings should be reflected in translations. However, this does not mean that biblical forms should be slavishly retained; it does mean that serious effort should be made to discover in the receptor language literary forms which have functional similarities with the literary forms contained in the biblical text; it is these functionally equivalent forms in the receptor language which are appropriate vehicles of the meaning and intention of the biblical text.

Furthermore, the diversity in *style* should also be reflected in our translations. Anyone reading the Greek New Testament will notice very quickly the varying styles of different books, as for example, the Gospels compared with the Letters. The tendency of modern translations, however, is to flatten out the whole Bible, so that the resulting product reflects only one style, thus giving the impression that the Bible is written by one person. There needs to be more concerted efforts to discover styles in the receptor language which are

---

[20] This more healthy attitude is accented by two recent books: James Dunn, *The Unity and Diversity of the New Testament*, (Philadelphia: Westminster, 1977), and Paul Hanson, *The Diversity of Scripture*, (Philadelphia: Fortress, 1982).

[21] Hanson writes (*Diversity*, p. 11), "The Bible itself contains the most lucid illustrations we possess of the manner in which the diversity in tradition can foster an understanding of reality and the ultimate grounding of reality in God which, far from threatening to undermine faith in the God of the Bible, actually fosters a more profound understanding of the activities of that God in the world".

functionally equivalent to the styles within the biblical record, and to employ these equivalent styles in the actual task of translation.

A more difficult problem, and in the end more rewarding, is that of *theological diversity* within the biblical corpus. The diversity in Scripture is not limited to minor details or to style and literary genre; there is also diversity of theological understanding. James Dunn points out that only as the full diversity of the New Testament canon is recognized can the New Testament function as canon. To absolutize one position within the New Testament is either to deny the validity of other New Testament positions or at least make these positions secondary and insignificant. For example, to make absolute the system of church polity and government found in the Pastorals is tantamount to not doing justice to the diversity of church organizations that are reflected in the total New Testament record.

The tendency of most Christians, both as individuals and as groups, is to be theologically monolithic, and this tendency is usually justified by an appeal to the canon, or at least a part of it. But this usually means absolutizing one aspect of the canon, or in the least giving primary importance to that aspect of the canon which somehow agrees with a person's theological disposition. A good example of this is the evangelism-social action dichotomy. By overemphasizing the evangelistic function of the canon, the aspects which deal with concerns for society and its problems are often minimized if not neglected altogether. In the same vein, emphasis on the social relevance of the Gospel often results in the neglect of the evangelistic function of the canon.

Greater awareness and deeper appreciation of the rich variety of theological positions and responses within the canon would lead us to a stance of openness and tolerance of the views of others who base their positions equally from the canon. This does not mean that there is no room for commitment. Commitment is indeed important, but it should always be characterized by openness and tolerance, and informed with the awareness that any human stance can never be absolute but always subject to human limitations in terms of both perspectives and goals.

This leads us to ask what the implications are for our work in translation as well as in the Bible Society movement in general. We in the Bible Societies need to reexamine our strategy to see whether we are really taking full advantage of this diversity in our programs. In our desire to be faithful to this diversity, we of course need continuing dialogue with the rest of the Christian community, and especially with those engaged in scholarly pursuits. In this area as well as in others, The Bible Society movement in general, and the translation task in particular, need to pay attention to developments in biblical scholarship and make use of the results in the most effective way possible.

3. Finally, the human character of the Bible makes it possible and necessary to analyze it like any other book.

One of the effects of over-emphasizing the divine character of the Bible is that applying modern scholarly methods in the analysis of the biblical material is often viewed with suspicion. There are even some who assert that there is a unique way of analyzing the Bible and therefore it should not be treated like any other book.[22]

Insofar as the translation task is concerned, it has to be affirmed that the Bible needs to be studied and analyzed using all the available tools of scholarship. As Brueggemann puts it, "Scholarship discipline invites us to view the text as an 'it', as an object we control and and explain".[23] Sandra Schneiders talks about the scholar's job as distancing the text from the modern reader: "The primary characteristics of the text insofar as they determine the work of the scholar are its objectivity and the distance separating the reader from the text. The interpreter must bridge the gap but not suppress the distance".[24] She writes further:

> The primary concern of the critical scholar is with what might be called the "original" meaning of the text, what the text meant (or probably meant) in its own historical/cultural setting and original language. The scholar wants to explain the text, how it came to be, what and who produced it, how it 'makes sense' as a text, what it says. The scholar's

---

[22] See e.g. Hill, *The King James Version Defended*, (De Moines, Iowa: The Christian Research Press, 1973). A few quotations will make clear Hill's position: "If the doctrine of the divine inspiration of the NT is a true doctrine, then NT textual criticism is different from the textual criticism of ordinary books" (p.2). "The consistently Christian method interprets the materials of NT textual criticism in accordance with the doctrines of the divine inspiration and providential preservation of the Scriptures. The naturalistic method interprets these same materials in accordance with its own doctrine that the NT is nothing more than a human book" (p.3). This approach toward the Bible is sometimes spoken of as "faith without scholarship" (Chinn, Douglas S. and Robert C. Newman, *Interdisciplinary Biblical Research Institute*, Report No. 3, 1979, pp. 36-7).

[23] Walter Brueggemann and Hans Wolff, *The Vitality of Old Testament Traditions*, p. 20. Cf. this quotation from Bird: "We encounter it (the Bible) as a fully human work, having no special language or logic of its own, existing in no special world of its own. Thus its message and meaning must be sought in the same way and with the same tools as any other work of literature or written communication. This demands knowledge of the languages in which it is written, recognition of literary forms, sensitivity to changing mood and contexts, and attention to author and audience as well as occasion and purpose of writing" (Phyllis A. Bird, *The Bible as the Church's Book*, Philadelphia: The Westminster Press, 1982, p. 71).

[24] Sandra Schneiders, "Church and Biblical Scholarship in Dialogue", *Theology Today* 42, October 1985, 353-358, 354.

primary task is to maintain the distance between ancient text and modern reader.[25]

We therefore have to affirm the relevance and in fact the indispensability of scholarship in the task of analyzing the biblical text with the aim in view of ascertaining its meaning, purpose, and intent. And scholarship is not limited to strictly biblical pursuits, but also includes linguistic studies as well as other scholarly disciplines that contribute to better understanding and appreciation of the biblical material. The production of quality translations is simply impossible without the aid of all the scholarly resources which are the product of long and serious endeavors to objectively analyze the biblical text in its ancient setting and in the process help in discovering and clarifying its text, structure, meaning, intention, and purpose. Modern biblical scholarship in its various manifestations is still the best way, if not the only way, to discover the world of the Bible, to uncover the layers of meaning within the biblical material, and as a result opens it up for meaningful translation.

In view of the above, the involvement of the United Bible Societies in these descriptive endeavors needs to be encouraged and enhanced. We should continue to make use of the results of modern critical scholarship, and at the same time participate in these endeavors, especially as we realize that we have significant contributions to share primarily in the area of translation as meaningful communication of the biblical message.

B. The Bible as a Theological Book: The Importance of Theology

After stressing the importance of the human character of the Bible, and the necessity of utilizing the tools of scholarship in biblical analysis, we have to stress anew the nature of the Bible as sacred literature, that is, a book which contains faith statements about God: his acts in history, his will for people, and his purpose for all of creation. The expression "faith statements" should be stressed, for whatever else can be said of the Bible, it must be finally stated that it primarily contains confessions of faith of various believing communities as they were faced with specific challenges and situations, and as they tried to discover the will of God in these situations.[26]

---

25 Ibid., 355. Schneider writes further: "In this work, the exegete renders a very important service, not only to other scholars but to the church as well; for unless the text remains truly 'other,' in some sense strange and alien to us, it will not be able truly to speak to us, to be genuinely revelatory for us".

26 This is stressed by Walter Brueggemann, in *The Vitality of Old Testament Tradition*. Taking his cue from Von Rad, Brueggemann asserts the theological motifs in the preservation and writing of the Pentateuchal stories: "The people pass the stories on, not because they are interesting lore, but because they bear a message having to do with the life and identity of the community" (Brueggemann, p. 26). What is said of the Pentateuch can, of course, be said of the whole biblical corpus.

Unless analysis of the Bible takes into account and touches upon its theological nature and content, such analysis should be considered as incomplete and insufficient.

1. The Inspiration of Scripture

A very important aspect of the Bible as theological literature is its quality as inspired by God. There has always been and will continue to be a lively interest in the doctrine of inspiration. Although this doctrine is understood and promulgated in various ways, nevertheless it is generally recognized that some kind of doctrine of inspiration is important, because it underscores the special nature of the Bible as Christian Scripture. Paul Achtemeier puts it this way:

> What is at stake in that doctrine is nothing less than the question of the importance of the Bible as the source for Christian belief and action. However one may want to conceive of that inspiration, it points to the belief on the part of the church that there is a unique linkage between God's communication with humankind and that specific collection of literature . . . Unless that Bible can in some way claim a unique status and authority in its content and intention, the Christian faith becomes . . . a human attempt to solve human problems, suffering from the delusion that it represents something more.[27]

But the Bible is not simply a record of affirmations of faith; rather, the affirmations recorded in the Bible are meant to be normative, hence authoritative for the communities to which these are addressed. (So Brueggemann, p. 30: The Hexateuch "is a normative statement created by Israel's best theologians to give expression to what everyone ought to believe which means not what they always do believe, but what they agree is the measure of authentic faith".) What this means is that the biblical books even before they were included in a list called "canon" already contained the element of normativeness and were therefore intended to be authoritative for the communities to which they were addressed. It was through these books that the communities defined their identity and measured their faith.

It does not mean of course that biblical writers/redactors, editors were consciously writing canonical literature. What they were doing was simply expressing what they considered to be God's will for a particular community, but without any thought of such written material being used by any other community, much less being handed down from generation to generation until the present day. I am sure Biblical writers did not have any idea that for years and years afterwards their writings would be scrutinized, dissected, translated, analyzed, and subjected to varying degrees of use and abuse. They had no idea their writings would be put together under one cover and termed "canonical", "Word of God", "inerrant", "infallible", and considered the absolute rule of faith and practice for all time to come. And I think we do the Biblical writers a grave injustice if we treat their writings as normative Scripture without taking into consideration the complex history by which these writings finally came to be known as the Christian Bible, the collection of writings which are canonical, authoritative and normative for the Christian Church.

[27] *The Inspiration of Scripture*, p. 13, Vawter makes the same point: "Sacred Scripture is a unique literature and when all is said and done, that is the essential point that the doctrine of inspiration has tried to register" (*Biblical Inspiration*, p. 158). Barr also writes, "If we use

Our aim in this paper is not to present a thorough and comprehensive discussion of the doctrine of inspiration, a task which is impossible anyway, considering the extent of the literature on the subject and the divergent positions of various segments of the Christian community. The most we can do is to attempt to relate inspiration to translation. With this purpose in mind, we make the following assertions:

a. *A doctrine of verbal inspiration is counter productive in the translation task especially when it is linked closely with inerrancy and infallibility.*[28]

These last two are not in themselves biblical terms but are widely used especially among certain Christian groups. The logic of the argument which relates these three concepts together seems to be: the Bible is inspired, therefore it is infallible and inerrant.[29]

the term 'inspiration', the result is that we emphasize the origin of the Bible. It comes from God, and this differentiates it from other writings which are the work of men" (*The Bible in Modern World*, p. 13).

[28] The position of inerrantists is set out in many publications among which are the following:

James Montgomery Boice, ed., 1978. *The Foundation of Biblical Authority*, Grand Rapids, MI: Zondervan.

———. 1977. *Does Inerrancy Matter?*, Oakland, CA: International Council on Biblical Inerrancy.

Harold Lindsell. 1976. *The Battle for the Bible*, Grand Rapids, MI: Zondervan.

———. 1977. *God's Incomparable Word*, Minneapolis, MN: World Wide Publications.

———. 1979. *The Bible in the Balance* Grand Rapids, MI: Zondervan.

Included in this last volume is "The Chicago Statement on Biblical Inerrancy".

[29] For example, Lindsell: "We need to remember that biblical inspiration precedes inerrancy and has a dynamic relationship to it. We do not believe the Bible is inspired because it is inerrant. We believe it to be inerrant because it is inspired—inspired by the God of all truth" (*The Bible in the Balance*, p. 46). Then he adds, "But today's problem is that some who claim to believe in the inspiration of the Bible refuse to believe in its inerrancy".

A comment by Gerald T. Sheppard, himself of evangelical background, is worth noting: "I have always found it strange that the highest affirmations of Scripture among competing evangelicals are two almost synonymous, double negatives. I begin to suspect that the real difference between . . . infallibility . . . and . . . inerrancy . . . is more sociological and political than it is theological" ("Recovering the Natural Sense", in *Theology Today*, 38-3, October 1981, 330-337, 333).

Such a position can become a hindrance to the translation task. For one thing, it can and does lead to attempts at harmonization of the biblical text. ①
When inerrancy seems to be contradicted by the text, should translators translate in order to be true to the doctrine of inerrancy, or should they translate the text as it is, regardless of whether it proves or disproves inerrancy? Often, when the former course is followed, there are adjustments made in the translation in order to allow for possible harmonization of the passages in question. An example of this is how the Living Bible translates Luke 24.20a, which in the RSV is translated "Then he led them out as far as Bethany". In the light of the information in Acts 1.12 that the Ascension took place at the Mount of Olives, the Living Bible attempts to harmonize the two accounts by translating Luke 24.20 as: "Then Jesus led them out along the road to Bethany", and with a note which reads: "Implied. Bethany was a mile or so away across the valley on the Mount of Olives".

In this regard, it is possible that one reason for the preference of the majority text is its tendency to harmonize parallel passages and to correct information that is suspect insofar as factual accuracy is concerned. An example of this is Mark 1.2, where "Isaiah the prophet" is changed to "the prophets", which fits the composite nature of the quotation which follows.

Another aspect of verbal inspiration which has less than positive results is ②
its tendency to identify the Word of God with particular words. This has sometimes resulted in some translations being identified with the Word of God, an occurrence which is present not only in the English-speaking world, but in other parts of the world as well. Words used in these translations are understood as inspired by God and therefore have become sacred, and should not under any circumstances be changed in the translation. Thus in the island of Samoa, people will continue to read *areto* (from Greek *artos*) in the Bible, despite the fact that *flawa* is now the common word for bread. This understanding of inspiration therefore encourages literal and formal translations, that is, translations which reproduce very closely the formal features of the biblical text.[30]

---

[30] See, e.g. Van Bruggen's strong endorsement of formal correspondent translation in *The Future of the Bible*, (New York: Nelson). The NIV and the Living Bible seem to deny what is being said here, but a closer examination of these translations reveal that many formal features of the Biblical material are retained. For both translations, the following features are present:

a. Keeping the order of verses intact and not telescoping verses together.

b. Not omitting any verses, even those which are considered by textual criticism as obvious additions.

c. Limiting restructuring to linguistic features.

d. Retaining traditional biblical-theological vocabulary, such as blood, redemption, Son of Man, etc.

e. As much as possible, retaining the form of favorite passages, e.g. Psalms 23, John 3.16, Genesis 1.1, John 1.1, etc.

f. And, with regard to the NIV, the retention of the complicated structures of the biblical material, which makes the NIV sound like a modern KJV, even though as a whole it is more dynamic than the RSV.

It seems clear then that verbal inspiration as a presupposition for translation can become a hindrance rather than an aid in the production of translations that are faithful to the meaning and intention of the biblical text.[31]

b. *There is need for the doctrine of inspiration to be informed by modern critical scholarship.*

It is unfortunate that many people who hold to the traditional notions of inspiration and equate it with infallibility and inerrancy tend to ignore or deny the validity of the findings of modern biblical scholarship. For example, Harold Lindsell defends the unity of the book of Isaiah on the basis of John 12.38 where Isaiah 53.1 is quoted and Isaiah the prophet is explicitly mentioned as the author. So he concludes: "If the critics are right, then John is wrong. And if John is wrong, then the Scriptures are not infallible".[32]

For Lindsell, therefore, any critical opinion regarding the book of Isaiah is completely ignored. Instead, the Gospel of John is made the authority on the authorship and composition of the book of Isaiah, a subject matter which I am sure is completely foreign to the Gospel's concern.

Despite this, it is very heartening to note that many modern day scholars, including some who openly profess to belong to the conservative or evangelical camp, are allowing the doctrine of inspiration which they hold to be informed by the findings of critical biblical studies.

c. *Inspiration should be relevant to the whole process of the formation of any given biblical book and even of the whole canon.*

To take seriously the history of the formation of individual books and of the canon is to take into consideration the various stages through which the biblical material went before it reached the written stage which we now have. The traditional views on inspiration usually assume a very simple view of authorship, i.e. that every book of the Bible is written by one author who wrote the book at a certain time. Furthermore, it is assumed that the written stage is

---

[31] Nevertheless, it is right to ask with Berkouwer, "Is it possible to understand verbal inspiration in any other way than as 'mechanical dictation'? And why do some continue to use the term 'verbal inspiration' while nonetheless sharply opposing any mechanical view?" (*Holy Scripture*, p. 158).

[32] Harold Lindsell, *The Battle for the Bible*, 101-102. Lindsell writes further: "The precision of the Greek in John's Gospel is such that no reasonable exegesis can avoid the conclusion that John believed Isaiah 53 was written by the historical person called Isaiah. So even if one were to claim that all of Isaiah is the Word of God, but deny that Isaiah wrote the entire prophecy, then the result is to call into question the truth of what John wrote when he stated that Isaiah authored chapter 53".

the first stage in the formation of Scripture. In most cases it is also assumed that the biblical author was conscious of writing Holy Scripture.

The fact of the matter, however, is that the formation of the individual books and of the whole canonical corpus is indeed complex and complicated. Furthermore, it is generally agreed that many if not most of the books within the canon are of composite authorship, and that in many cases, it is difficult, in fact impossible to identify who the author is.[33] If this be the case, then, it is legitimate to ask who indeed is the "inspired" author of a biblical book. To the assertion that it is the person who put this into writing who is the inspired author, Vawter contends,

> Could this history really be ignored in the pursuit of a concept of an inspired word? It was conceivable that the final 'author' might have had the very least to do in the process from which a given text has emerged.[34]

Achtemeier also writes:

> To put the total weight of inspiration on that final individual who sets down the results of a long process of formulation and reformulation . . . is to make a mockery of the intimate relationship between Scripture and community . . .[35]

It seems better therefore to relate inspiration to the whole process of the formation of the biblical books and of the whole canon, and not to an individual who plays a role in the process, or a particular stage in the process.[36]

d. *A more helpful model for the translation task is a functional understanding of inspiration.*

---

[33] Achtemeier relates this to the communal nature of Scripture: "The anonymity of Scripture may thus be tied to the fact that its production is far more a community act than an individual one, and may indeed bear witness that inspiration is to be understood in a broader sense than simply as an inspired individual producing an inspired book" (Paul Achtemeier, *The Inspiration of Scripture*, pp. 117-118).

[34] Vawter, p. 88.

[35] Achtemeier, *The Inspiration of Scripture*, pp. 133f.

[36] *The Inspiration of Scripture*, p. 134. Barr makes the same point when he locates inspiration in the history of God's people: "It must mean the inspiration not of writers of books, but of the tradition of the believing community, out of which scripture was eventually formed. It must mean that God was with his people in ancient times, in his Spirit, so that their responses to him were in adequate measure true and valid responses, which thus formed some sort of index to his nature and activity" (Barr, *Scope and Authority*, p. 124. See also *The Bible in the Modern World*, pp. 17f.).

It is indeed significant that in the key verse for the inspiration of Scripture, II Timothy 3.16, inspiration is closely linked to specific functions of Scripture, such as soteriological, catechetical, apologetic and ethical. From this it can be deduced that inspiration should be related to the various functions of Scripture understood as sacred literature, and not to other matters which are outside these legitimate functions.

An aspect of the functional approach to inspiration is the recognition that somehow inspiration is related to the way the biblical material was used in the community of faith. The inspiration of Scripture can be spoken of as a faith claim which arises out of the appropriation of these materials by the Christian community. In the process, some writings came to be valued more than others because of their function and value within the community of faith. It could be that in these writings, the Christian community saw how these human words were being used by God as instruments for his divine purposes.[37] It could be that through these writings they experienced the power and truth of the Spirit of Christ.[38] It could be that they found in these writings a message which had the power to transform their lives through the power of the Holy Spirit.[39] In other words, through these writings more than others, the community heard God speaking to them, showing them his will in their concrete and particular situations and giving them paradigms on how they should as God's people respond creatively and relevantly to these situations. In this case therefore, as Achtemeier puts it, inspiration is not simply an *a priori* assumption but an *a posteriori* discovery.[40]

e. Related to the functional approach is an understanding of inspiration which links it to revelation and communication.

That is to say that when we talk of the Bible as the inspired Word of God, we understand the Bible to be the means by which God reveals himself to the world,

---

37 Cf. H. Ridderbos, *Studies in Scripture and its Authority*, pp. 25f.

38 Thomas Hoffman, "Inspiration", in *Catholic Biblical Quarterly* 44-3, July 1982, 450-469.

39 Achtemeier, *Inspiration*, p. 160.

40 *Inspiration*, 135-136. Achtemeier writes further: "Just an the canon resulted only after some centuries of experience with a variety of Christian writings, which determined some to be more valuable than others, so the traditions that compose the various books, the situations that called them forth, and the respondents who shaped them at the various stages were evaluated in the experience of the community of faith. In that experience, some traditions were found to be of more value and were included in the ongoing traditions of the community" (136).

One should not, however, relate inspiration directly to the formation of the canon. Leiman's discussion regarding inspiration and canonization is relevant at this point, see *The Canonization of Hebrew Scripture*, (Hamden, CT: Archon Books, 1976).

and by which God communicates himself and his will to humankind. In other words, the Bible is and becomes God's Word to the world.

There is a sense in which one can say that the Bible is the Word of God, that this is part of its intrinsic quality. Such a statement is of course a statement of faith. Furthermore, such a confession of faith is directly connected with the appropriation of the Bible within the community of faith. In other words, as already mentioned, the church came to confess the Bible as the Word of God because it found the Bible functioning as Word of God in its own life. While future generations, including our own, can accept this confession of faith, yet such a confession does not really mean very much until like the early church and the generations that followed, we too can discover in our own use of the Bible that it too functions as Word of God in our own lives individually and collectively. And here again, we make another faith assertion, namely, that it is by the work of the Holy Spirit that we are able to appropriate the biblical message, understand it properly, and apply it relevantly to our own situation. This, it must be reiterated, is a faith assertion.

If inspiration then can be interpreted as related to the work of the Holy Spirit in enabling God's message to be proclaimed, heard, understood, and appropriated, then it is not possible to limit inspiration to authors or manuscripts, or even to the written corpus which we now call the Bible. Vawter has a relevant quotation in this regard:

> If the role of the word in the Church was to be seen less as archival testimony and more as the continuing presence of the Spirit . . . then the inspirational process itself ought to be considered not as merely terminating in a literary text but as touching also the later reader and hearer of the word. For word is not properly word, not the means of communication and revelation, until it has been taken in, until the process of communication is thereby completed. When we are dealing with an inspired word, then, inspiration should be regarded as proper to every stage of such communication.[41]

If Vawter is right, and I think he is, then inspiration is a process, a continuing activity, with a past, a present, and a future dimension. Inspiration is closely linked to the whole process of communicating God's message. This means that any and every stage that can be identified in the formation of the Bible is considered as participating in the inspiration process. Furthermore, this process also includes every attempt to make the message properly understood and relevantly appropriated. This would mean that within this process are included the tasks of interpretation and proclamation. But more importantly, any attempt to make this message clear and understandable to specific audiences through the task of translation should also be understood as part of the inspiration process. And this is one place where we can find theological justification for

---

[41] Vawter, *Biblical Inspiration*, p. 79.

meaning-centered and audience-sensitive translations, e.g. the use of dynamic equivalent translation principles, and the resulting products such as common language translations, New Reader Scriptures, comics, audio Scriptures, translation for the handicap, Children's Scriptures, and others which are aimed primarily at meeting the needs of specific audiences. And when we engage in such activities, we are also being faithful to the nature of the biblical material, to its particularity and concreteness in relation to specific audiences.

C. The Search for Balance: The Relation between Scholarship and Theology

In the previous discussion, we have stressed the nature of the Bible as both human composition and sacred literature. Both of these aspects are equally important and should therefore be taken seriously in the translation task.

This leads us to the whole subject of what the task of biblical scholarship is in relation to the nature of the Bible as a sacred literature. What indeed is the relationship between the descriptive and the theological tasks, that is, between analyzing the Bible as literature and regarding the Bible as normative for Christian faith and life?

First of all, there are some who maintain a rigid division between the descriptive and the theological tasks, with the latter being assigned to theologians, preachers and ordinary biblical readers, and the former to biblical scholars.[42]

This emphasis on the descriptive task in biblical scholarship is exemplified in the articles which are read in scholarly conventions and which find their way into learned biblical journals. Of this, Hanson writes: "One need only read the titles of papers at the professional meetings to see to what ends scholars go to avoid treatment of the theological meaning of a biblical text".[43]

But secondly, there are some who advocate a close relationship between the descriptive and the theological tasks. As Childs puts it, "Bible and theology belong together, both on the descriptive and constructive levels".[44] The descriptive task is recognized as only the first step in the study of the biblical

[42] A good example of this position is found in Krister Stendahl, "Biblical Theology, Contemporary", in The IDB, I, pp. 418-432. For a critique of this position, see James Smart, *The Past, Present and Future of Biblical Theology* , pp. 42f. Smart writes, "The sharp distinction such as Stendahl makes between the meaning then and the meaning now is a treacherous one. The scholar . . . has no access to the original meaning unless the text has some meaning for him now. Exegesis is a dialogue between the Then and the Now in which the student must be trained if he is not to find himself as a preacher with the biblical text too distant from him for him to hear what it is saying now" (p. 43). See also Blenkinsopp, *Prophecy and Canon*, where he criticizes this excessive emphasis on the original meaning of texts. (pp. 9f.).

[43] Hanson, "The Responsibility of Biblical Theology to the Communities of Faith", *Theology Today*, 37-1, 39-50, 41.

[44] *Biblical Theology in Crisis*, p. 26.

text. A necessary second step is to bridge the gap between the then and the now, to make the so-called hermeneutical jump from the world of the Bible to the world of today.[45] As John Goldingay puts it,

> We can in fact only rightly hear the Bible's message as we do bridge the gap between its world and ours. Appreciating its meaning in its own day, even 'objectively', cannot be a cool, 'academic' . . . exercise. We may only be able to do so in the act of working out and preaching the equivalent . . . message today. Thus exegesis and exposition are interwoven after all.[46]

Sandra Schneiders makes a similar point. While recognizing the differences between the scholar and the informed believers in their attitude toward the biblical text, she nevertheless stresses that their roles are complementary to each other:

> The academy and the church need each other in the work of biblical interpretation. Their roles are different but not contradictory because their concerns with the text, though diverse, are complementary. The basic difference is that, whereas the scholar is largely absorbed by the problematic of distance between ancient text and present interpretive context, the believer is primarily concerned with the nearness, the intimacy with the self-revealing God, which the text mediates . . . All scholarly work on the biblical text, at least when carried out by the religiously committed Christian, must aim beyond its primary task of explanation toward genuine and transforming understanding. The final goal of biblical scholarship is the same as that of believing contemplation: that the text become, in and for our time, Word of God in the church of Jesus Christ.[47]

Maintaining a healthy balance between the descriptive and the theological tasks is of an ideal to be aimed for. It is not a matter of affirming the priority of the descriptive over the theological or vice versa, but it is making sure that these two aspects of biblical interpretation are related to each other. How often has it been that the descriptive task is carried out without any sensitivity to the theological implications of the results of its investigation. On the other hand, it is also true that many theological discussions, even those that are characterized

---

45 Steinmitz, p. 37, also Smart, *The Past, Present and Future of Biblical Theology*, p. 60: "The historical operation is only the first half of exegesis, and if it is not to be destructive, has to be combined with theological penetration which discovers in the text the element that makes that author's witness alive and meaningful for the person of today".

46 "Expounding the New Testament", in *New Testament Interpretation*, p. 352, see also Ralph Martin, "Approaches to New Testament Exegesis", in pp. 220-251. Martin examines in this article the various approaches in bridging the gap between the "then" and the "now".

47 Schneiders, op. cit., 358.

as Bible-oriented ones, often have no relation to or even are against the very spirit of the biblical text.

Having said that, one must go on and stress the necessity and in fact the indispensability of the theological task even in the area of translation. James Smart describes biblical theology as "an aspect of biblical interpretation which is as indispensable as the linguistic, literary, and historical if the Scriptures are to be heard in the church and the world".[48]

What is the extent of the theological task and how should it be carried out? What James Barr asks about the biblical scholar is also relevant for those of us in Bible translation: "How far must he think and work, and how far does he think and work, in terms that are really theological?"[49] He distinguishes between a statement like "We believe that God is X" and "This or that biblical writer said, or thought, that God is X". He writes,

> The first is a statement of personal faith, or a statement of the church's faith; it is a theological statement in the strict sense. The second is a descriptive statement: perhaps historical, perhaps structural, perhaps falling under some other category, but in any case a descriptive statement. The first is a statement which, however closely related to evidence, is not merely an interpretation of evidence; its logic is not

---

[48] James Smart laments this failure in the following quotation: "The general failure of both biblical science and the church to face squarely the hermeneutical problem has created a serious hiatus between the two contexts in which the Bible is interpreted, the university and the theological seminaries on the one hand and the Christian congregation on the other. University had seminary are likely to be dominated by the historical interest and, even where the theological concern is present, the complexity of biblical scholarship has become so great that often when the student has been introduced to the languages, the literary and historical problems, the cultural and religious milieus of biblical times and a general survey of the religious developments, there is little time or interest remaining for theological questions. But when the graduate becomes pastor of a congregation, what was most important in seminary is now least important and what was least considered there is now a matter of life or death for his ministry. Consistently for years there has been an underestimating of the distance between these two contexts in which the Bible is interpreted, as though it were a very short and easy step the seminary graduate has to take from the one to the other and should be able to make it quite effectively on his own. The distance is greatest when the biblical scientist insists that his task as historian is purely descriptive with responsibility only to make clear what the text originally meant. He sends his students out ill- equipped for the tasks of ministry. Scholars and churchmen must come awake to the fact that some of the most capable students of the Bible in university and seminary have not been making that journey very successfully from school to church, from fact to faith, from historical record to sermon text, from cultural artifact to Christian revelation. They seem to get lost or delayed somewhere in between. And a year later, or two or ten years later, the Bible from which they are preaching to their congregation is not at all the Bible with which they graduated from seminary. Too late and unprepared they encountered the basic hermeneutical problem and either retreated into an evasive conservative stance or took something more readily usable than Scripture as the basis of their preaching". For a positive regard for the pre-critical understanding of Scripture, see Steinmetz, "The Superiority of Pre-Critical Exegesis", *Theology Today*, 37-1, April 1980, 27-38.

[49] *Scope and Authority*, p. 21.

exhaustively explained by stating the evidence to which it may relate itself. The second is an interpretation of given evidence.[50]

Can we also ask of the translation task along these terms? If our job is primarily descriptive, then we should understand ourselves not as theologians in any sense, but as technicians. Questions which are strictly theological in nature, such as "What is the authority of the Bible for today?" need not be our concern. Instead, we should be concentrating on questions like "What does the Bible, or this or that biblical book say about the authority of the Bible?"

Anderson writes the following about biblical scholars:

> Scholars demonstrate their scholarship by concentrating on technical problems, often talking among themselves in an esoteric language that outsiders cannot understand. Few there are who want to undertake the formidable task of trying to grasp the totality of Scripture as a coherent whole and hence to become biblical theologians who endeavor to speak to the church.[51]

Perhaps we should also ask whether the Bible Societies are producing biblical theologians who can "speak to the church", and whether in fact the churches want the Bible Societies to do so. Is the very nature of the Bible Societies as servants of all the churches influencing in some way their theological stance, both in their attitude and participation in the theological task?

One thing is at least clear, and that is, an important part of our theological task is producing translations that reflect clearly the nature of the Bible as a theological book which was relevant to communities in the past and which is and can still be relevant for today. Translation is definitely a very important way of incarnating the Word of God in the world, because the message becomes alive and understandable, and thus opens up the possibility of incarnating the biblical message in the life of people and society.

Let me briefly give three examples of how theology is taken seriously in the translation task.

The first example has to do with the translation of technical theological terminology in the Bible. The traditional way of dealing with these terms is to translate them literally, and on a one-to-one correspondence. Thus *dikaiosune* is always "righteousness", *charis* is always "grace", *basileia tou theou* is always "kingdom of God", and so on. This practice creates at least two problems. For one thing, these terms are very hard to understand. For another thing, many of these terms have multiple meanings in the biblical material and it is very difficult, in fact at times impossible for the ordinary biblical reader (and for the unordinary as well?) to determine what a technical term would mean in a particular context.

---

50 Ibid, p. 22.

51 *The Bible in the Church Today*, p. 2.

That is why it is so exciting to translate using the principles of dynamic equivalence, where it is possible to render technical terms according to their meanings in specific contexts. Thus in the Good News Bible, *dikaiosune theou* is translated in Matthew 6.33 as "what God requires", but in Romans 1.17 as "God puts people right with himself". The German common language translation translates *basileia tou theou* in a dynamic and creative way. Many translations have dealt with the richness of terms like *irene, doxa, charis, pistis* etc., and have unlocked the mysteries of these terms in the printed text. And the translation task can do much more in this area in order to share the theological richness of the Bible with ordinary readers.

The second example has to do with relating the translation task to significant movements within the church and society, such as human rights, liberation movements, feminism, etc. To what extent should we allow the translation task to be informed and influenced by these developments?

Let me first all reassert a key principle in translation which I am sure we all adhere to, and that is, faithfulness to the meaning and function of the biblical text is still the most important measure of the quality of any translation. But having said that, I should go on and say that there are certain non-translational (can we say "theological"?) issues which can and should influence the translation task. If, in dialogue with these non-translational issues, we become conscious of certain adjustments which can be made in the translation without compromising exegetical or linguistic principles, then by all means these adjustments should be made.[52] An example of a modern day movement is feminism, or more accurately, the movement to achieve a just and proper place of women within the Christian community and within society as a whole. I agree with those who hold the position than in a language like English that lends itself to sexual discrimination (fortunately, we have no such problems in many non-English languages, but we show our bias either for or against women in some other way!), inclusive language can and should be used as long as exegetical and linguistic accuracy is not compromised. Thus, while I sympathize with those who want to use inclusive language exclusively, and who would eliminate from their speech and writing all male pronouns in referring to God, I do not see this in the present time as a translational possibility. And even when we grant that such an exercise is possible, yet the language that is produced can be rather unnatural and forced so much so that so much of attractive and acceptable style is sacrificed. (I do appreciate all the efforts done in non-biblical translation in avoiding sexist language in referring to God, and in fact have been consciously doing this whenever possible in my own writing, but such activity should be distinguished from translation of the biblical text). This reservation of mine holds true also for other efforts to make the biblical text more inclusive than it really is, to the extent of sacrificing exegetical and linguistic accuracy. However,

---

[52] For example, the treatment of "Jews" in John's Gospel in the Good News Bible. See Robert G. Bratcher, "'The Jews' in the Gospel of John", in *A Translator's Handbook on the Gospel of John* (by Barclay M. Newman and Eugene A. Nida), pp. 641-649.

when such efforts can be justified both exegetically and linguistically, then these should be implemented in the translation task. Thus whenever *huioi* is used in a generic way and means "children" rather than "sons", then it should be translated as such. This would be the same case with *adelphoi* and other similar terms.

A third example may be briefly mentioned, and that is sensitivity to both biblical and receptor cultures. An awareness of the relationship of these cultures in terms of similarities and more importantly differences has led to the promulgation of translation principles which make it possible to take seriously both cultures and at the same time remain faithful to the meaning and intent of the biblical text. This is of course a very important issue which cannot be dealt with in one paragraph. It suffices to say that taking culture seriously in the translation task has made it possible for translations of the Bible to have an influence in the development of indigenization especially in Christian communities in the Third World.

To sum up, it must be stressed that every time we produce translations which are geared toward specific needs of particular audiences, then we are engaging in the normative theological task. Through meaningful and communicative translations, the biblical message becomes alive and clear not only for those within but also for those outside the believing community. A further aspect can be mentioned, and that is, that principles of dynamic equivalence break down the hard line between exegesis and translation, a position which is prevalent among Christians and in many theological schools. Translation, it is said, should stick to the text, and should never allow itself to be influenced by exegesis and interpretation. But in dynamic equivalent translations, translation and exegesis come together, and one discovers with Patrick Miller that "translation is . . . inevitably an interpretive enterprise. It must be carried out within a hermeneutical circle: both the circular relationship between part and whole and the circle that incorporates the text, the translator/interpreter, and the audience/situation".[53] Understood in this manner, the hard line between the exegesis and translation disappears, and exegesis becomes a real tool for a meaningful and faithful translation of the biblical text.

Concluding Words

In conclusion, it needs to be affirmed again that matters relating to text, canon, exegesis, in short, the whole range of scholarly endeavors applied to the biblical text are indeed relevant to the task of Bible translation, and in guaranteeing its faithfulness to the biblical text in terms of meaning, function and purpose, and its appropriateness to the intended audiences in terms of language and style.

---

[53] Miller, op cit., 541.

STEPHEN K. BATALDEN

THE POLITICS OF MODERN RUSSIAN
BIBLICAL TRANSLATION

Modern biblical translations inevitably arise out of particular political and cultural contexts. Translators are themselves products of one or another political culture. The ability to publish and disseminate the result of translation activity is also governed by local publishing conventions. Even the textual bases selected in translation and the linguistic medium employed rarely are entirely outside the influence of local political and cultural constraints. To speak of the "politics" of biblical translation, then, is not to undermine the legitimacy of the many fine modern translations of Scripture, including in this instance the Russian. Rather, attention to the politics of biblical translation can illumine broader issues in the relationship between church and society.

It is the contention of this essay that modern Russian biblical translation generated and continues to generate intense controversy precisely because fundamental questions of authority raised in the process of biblical translation have remained unresolved. Moreover, the very framing of the questions and the difficulty of their resolution reflect the highly-structured and politicized nature of modern Russian culture, while also reflecting the official position of the Orthodox Church within that culture. In the attempt to define these fundamental questions of authority, I shall try to identify the most important religio-political and cultural constraints that have attended translation of the modern Russian Bible.

In clarifying the larger cultural parameters within which Russian biblical translation has occurred, it may be helpful at the outset to identify two special features affecting the *use* of the Russian Bible. First of all, the Russian Bible has only rarely been used as a liturgical text. Rather, the biblical text used in Orthodox worship has continued to be that of an Old Slavic or Church Slavonic edition. Use of the Church Slavonic means that, in effect, the Orthodox Church has perpetuated what Professor Boris Uspenskii, among others, identifies as *diglossia* in the evolution of Russian culture.[1] Alongside a vernacular or spoken idiom, Russian culture perpetuated and enriched a stylized linguistic medium that, until the early eighteenth century and the tsarist reign of Peter the Great, remained the language of both church and state. There were efforts to introduce a modern Russian Bible into liturgical worship both during the Russian Revolution at the time of the Russian All-Church Council of 1917-1918 and in

---

[1] On the question of *diglossia*, see Uspenskii's most recent work, *Istoriia russkogo literaturnogo iazyka, XI-XVII vv.* (Munich: Otto Sagner, 1987); also his essay, "The Language Situation and Linguistic Consciousness in Muscovite Rus': The Perception of Church Slavic and Russian", in *Medieval Russian Culture*, ed. by H. Birnbaum and M.S. Flier (Berkeley, 1984).

the church renovationist movement of the 1920s and early 1930s. Still, the Slavonic Bible has remained the text of liturgical worship for Russian, as well as for Ukrainian and Belorussian, Orthodox churches. This successful attempt to preserve *diglossia* in modern Russian religious practice involves, in its own way, a political statement—albeit one that is very different from the statement of Bishop Lefebvre and contemporary Catholic Latinizers. We shall return to this issue.

A second feature bearing upon use of the Russian Bible is the relatively late development of Bible reading as an element of Orthodox piety or spirituality. Unlike Protestantism with its early sixteenth-century Luther Bible and its appeal to a Bible-reading "priesthood of believers", Russian Orthodoxy has traditionally found the clearest expression of its spirituality in the daily marking of the church calendar with its fasts, its saints' lives, its veneration of icons and, most importantly, its liturgical celebration of the eucharist. Until the nineteenth century, most Russians, including some rural parish priests and their peasant flock, were illiterate, and literacy was not required for the fulfillment of Orthodox religious observances. The artificial extension of *diglossia* in the church may well have contributed to this relative underdevelopment of Bible reading, even though there were literate Russian peasants whose literacy continued to develop in the nineteenth century out of exposure to the non-vernacular, Slavonic Bible.

Only with the growth of literacy and popular education in the later nineteenth century did Bible reading become a significant element of Russian religious life—and then only because of the development of an elaborate colportage network for dissemination of biblical literature.[2] Still, the fact that such Bible reading became most prevalent among Russian sectarians, or Protestants, confirmed for some of the more wary Orthodox prelates their suspicion that Bible reading and broad dissemination of Scripture in the common language was a distinctly Protestant, as opposed to broadly ecumenical or Orthodox, practice.

While *diglossia* and the tradition of Russian Orthodox spirituality may help to explain some of the resistance to the *use* of the modern text, it is to the history of the modern Russian Bible that one must turn to discover how it was that fundamental questions of authority arose in the process of Russian biblical translation. Although there were earlier efforts in the eighteenth century to render portions of Scripture into a modern Russian tongue,[3] the first sustained effort to

---

[2] See S. K. Batalden's unpublished article, "Colportage and the Distribution of Holy Scripture in Late Imperial Russia". This article is forthcoming in *California Slavic Studies*.

[3] The most notable examples of earlier scriptural texts in Russian are the unpublished Firsov Psalter of 1683 and Mefodii Smirnov's (Archimandrite Mefodii, 1761-1815) translation of the Epistle to the Romans first published in 1794. On the Firsov Psalter, see E. A. Tselunova, "Psaltyr' 1683 goda v perevode Avramiia Firsova", *avtoreferat* of Tselunova's *kandidat* dissertation, Moscow, 1985. For the full citation and locations of the first edition of Archimandrite Mefodii's Epistle to the Romans (1794), see the *Svodnyi katalog russkoi knigi grazhdanskoi pechati XVIII veka*, vol. II (Moscow, 1964), item #4207, p. 240.

translate and publish the Bible in modern Russian dates to the reign of Alexander I and the founding of an imperially chartered Russian Bible Society. In late 1812, British and Foreign Bible Society agent John Paterson established the Russian Bible Society in St. Petersburg. Even though the Society initially had the modest purpose of providing Scripture for non-Russian nationals of the Empire (for example, Baltic Germans and Finns), the goals of the Society quickly expanded to include publication and widescale distribution of the Slavonic Bible.

In 1816, authority was granted by Tsar Alexander I for the Russian Bible Society to translate and publish, in cooperation with the Holy Synod (the effective ruling institution of the Russian Orthodox Church), a Russian New Testament. By the time of the Russian Bible Society's closure in 1826, this landmark project to render the Bible into modern Russian had yielded a New Testament and Psalter in Russian translation, with circulation in several printings amounting to several hundred thousand copies. The translation into Russian of the Old Testament or Hebrew Bible had also been printed in sheets through the eighth book (the so-called *Octateuch*, Genesis through Ruth), although that text was never permitted distribution.[4]

Alongside the translation and publication successes of this Russian Bible Society in the first quarter of the nineteenth century, there remains the hard-nosed reality that that Bible Society was closed by imperial edict in 1826, less than fourteen years after its founding.[5] There have been many explanations offered for this closure of the Russian Bible Society. But, at the bottom of this controversy the existence of the Russian Bible Society begged what was to become the first and most fundamental of our questions of authority in the politics of modern Russian biblical translation—namely, who has the right to translate and publish Russian scripture? While we may consider that question to be rather strange in a contemporary context in which new indigenous biblical translations issue frequently and without serious challenge, the burning relevance of this question for Russian religio-political culture reflected the hierarchical nature of Russian society of the time when all publication was submitted to either secular or ecclesiastical censorial review.

What the Russian Bible Society had been able to do through the energetic executive leadership of John Paterson was to circumvent normal political and religious constraints by ingratiating itself into the confidence of the most

---

[4] There have been numerous histories of the Russian Bible Society, most notably those by Judith Cohen Zacek, "The Russian Bible Society, 1812-1826", unpublished Ph.D. dissertation, Columbia University, 1964; and A. N. Pypin, *Religioznyi dvizheniia pri Aleksandre I*, reprinted with an introduction and commentary by N. K. Piksanov (Petrograd, 1916). See also S. K. Batalden, "Printing the Bible in the Reign of Alexander I: Toward a Reinterpretation of the Imperial Russian Bible Society", forthcoming in *Church, Nation, and State in Russia and Ukraine* (London, School of Slavonic and East European Studies/Macmillan, 1990).

[5] For the official edict of Nicholas I, see the *Polnoe sobranie zakonov rossiiskoi imperii* for 1826 (St. Petersburg, 1830-1916).

powerful figures in Alexander I's Russia. The president of the Society was none other than Alexander Golitsyn, a close friend of the tsar who shared the tsar's support for religious awakening and, more importantly, held, among his other offices, the post of lay head or *ober-prokuror* of the Holy Synod. Through Golitsyn, the Russian Bible Society secured the support of the tsar, they were exempted from censorship, and they were allowed to develop their own unprecedented stereotype printing and binding establishment that ranked with the finest such institutions in England—and all this without the normal permissions and oversights assigned to such publishing activity. While the Holy Synod, under pressure from Golitsyn and the tsar, acquiesced to the Society and gave to it the formal authority to translate and publish Russian Scripture, they did so only at the expense of their former monopoly over such publication at their more primitive publishing enterprise in Moscow—a press that had held all rights to publishing scripture, much like the rights once held by Oxford and Cambridge in the case of the old authorized English edition. Such circumnavigation of the Holy Synod was ultimately to yield strong Synodal opposition to the Russian Bible Society, opposition that contributed mightily to the weakening of the Society by the 1820s, a decade after its auspicious founding.

In the matter of translation, the Bible Society took care to monitor the quality of individual book translations through its "translations subcommittee". That subcommittee was headed by an Orthodox prelate who became Metropolitan of Moscow and one of the most distinguished Russian church leaders of the nineteenth century, Filaret Drozdov. Yet, here again, the point was that the young Metropolitan Filaret was *de facto*, if not *de jure*, operating outside the parameters of direct Synodal oversight on the question of biblical translation, and his position on this issue became politically untenable after the challenge to Golitsyn's own leadership in the 1820s. The sacking of Alexander Golitsyn in 1824 marked the effective end of Bible Society independence in Russian biblical translation. By the time of the Bible Society's closure in 1826, it had already ceased to function as an organ of translation and publication.

This first fundamental question of authority—who had the right to translate and publish Holy Scripture—yielded to a temporary, though ultimately problematic, expedient in the aftermath of the Russian Bible Society era. The answer, of course, was that the Holy Synod alone had the right to translate and publish Russian scripture. Nevertheless, in an increasingly plural Russian society in which the Eastern Orthodox Church could no longer lay hegemonial claim over the religious loyalties of its multi-ethnic and variegated population, this effective response to the first fundamental question of authority left the matter for subsequent resolution in the later nineteenth and twentieth centuries. When translation efforts were at last reopened in the 1850s, a Synodally-authorized New Testament was published in 1862 and a complete and authorized Old Testament was published in 1875. Still, as in the current Gorbachev years, so also in the nineteenth century, the official church (even if they could operate as the sole arbiters of biblical translation and publication—a matter rendered more difficult in the twentieth-century due to the large Russian emigration) simply did not have within its own ranks the kind of expertise—much less at the present the printing capacity—needed to direct and control translation and publication. Thus, the issue of who has the right to translate and publish Russian Scripture remained and remains behind the scenes to this day a ticklish, unresolved problem in a religious and political culture that has in the past been conditioned to expect such questions of authority to be resolved from the top down.

Hidden behind the highly-charged early nineteenth-century debate over the Russian Bible Society was another fundamental question of authority that could not be long avoided—namely, what biblical texts were to be considered authoritative? The question of biblical texts had already arisen in the Bible Society era when the decision was taken to use the Hebrew Massoretic text rather than the Greek Septuagint as the basis for translation of the Psalter. Sensing the potential for controversy over this issue, the translations subcommittee of the Russian Bible Society prepared a preface to the Russian Psalter defending readings and numeration that differed from the established Slavonic text—a text that rested largely upon the Septuagint.[6]

The problem of textual authority returned to the politics of modern Russian biblical translation in the years immediately following closure of the Russian Bible Society. The translator of the Bible Society's Psalter and much of its undistributed *Octateuch*, Gerasim Petrovich Pavskii, continued to prepare Russian translated books of the Old Testament, using as the basis for his translations the Hebrew text. Pavskii was a white or parish clergyman of St. Petersburg, but his translations were done in his capacity as professor of Hebrew at St. Petersburg Theological Academy. Under circumstances common for the day, Pavskii's students prepared lithographic editions of his Russian translations for limited circulation as course notes. Such lithographing of course notes was acceptable, and could be done without recourse to censorial review. However, in their zeal to make available a Russian text of the Old Testament, enterprising seminarians prepared between 1838 and 1841 three lithographed editions in approximately five-hundred copies. The seminarians then proceeded to distribute these editions outside the Petersburg Theological Academy to seminarians in Moscow and Kiev, as well as to several outlying dioceses. While the history of the so-called "Pavskii Affair [*Delo Pavskogo*]" that followed in the 1840s has been reviewed in detail elsewhere, the matter became a full-blown "affair" only after the Holy Synod was alerted to this quasi-clandestine circulation and launched a series of interrogations, including the interrogation of Pavskii himself, who appears not to have cooperated with the enterprising seminarians. Before the interrogation ended, over 400 extant copies were located, seized and burned, and lengthy depositions were taken from dozens of seminarians. The

---

6 The defense of the use of the Hebrew text is included in the preface to each printing of the Russian Bible Society's Psalter, beginning with the first edition, *Kniga Khvalenii ili Psaltyr' na rossiiskom iazykie* (St. Petersburg, Printed for the Russian Bible Society at the Press of Nikolai Grech', 1822). The extended preface, of course, reflected the inability of BFBS agent John Paterson to persuade his Russian colleagues that there should be "no note or comment" added to editions of Russian scripture.

resulting archival record of over four-thousand leaves has yielded one of the most interesting documentary collections for the study of nineteenth-century Russian church history and the history of Russian censorship.[7]

What is of relevance about the Pavskii Affair is that at the center of the interrogation of Pavskii was the issue of his use of the Hebrew Bible, and particularly the rendering of certain key prophetic passages which, in the Slavonic Bible, were felt to be more appropriately direct in their messianic prophecy. Pavskii's defense of the Hebrew text and the Old Testament context met with stern rebuke from Holy Synod prelates who admonished the archpriest that the Orthodox Church received its baptism from the Greek East and need not abandon the Greek text behind the Slavonic Bible. So intense was the controversy that, at one point in the mid-1840s, the Holy Synod sought officially to canonize the Septuagint and the Slavonic readings, a decision that, in the end, was never taken.[8]

Behind the opposition to Pavskii rested a deeper level of conflict, that of a growing tension between white and black Russian Orthodox clergy. According to Orthodox tradition and practice, white clergy were to serve as parish priests, and were obligatorily to be married. Only black clergy, on the other hand, could rise to positions in the church hierarchy, but were obliged to be celibate. The conflict that brewed in the nineteenth century between the more powerful black clergy and the more impoverished, but increasingly well educated and liberal, parish clergy has been well documented in the historical literature.[9] Opposition to Pavskii on matters of textology no doubt constituted a vehicle for reaction to his well-publicized refusal to take monastic vows, and his articulate defense of white clerical liberalism against the black hierarchy. Thus, the issue of the authority of texts in this instance also served to highlight a deep-seated political conflict at the center of Russian religious culture.[10]

Despite the reaction that followed the Pavskii Affair, the rich tradition of Hebraic studies that Pavskii helped to generate and the *textus primus* of the Russian Old Testament that Pavskii himself prepared guaranteed the continuing

---

[7] On this question, see S. K. Batalden, "Gerasim Pavskii's Clandestine Old Testament: The Politics of Nineteenth-Century Russian Biblical Translation", *Church History*, vol. 57, no. 4 (December 1988), pp. 486-498.

[8] On the effort of Ober-prokuror Protasov to declare the Slavonic text inviolable, see the relevant file in the Central State Historical Archive in Leningrad (TsGIAL), *fond* 796, *opis'* 205, *delo* 195, leaves 308-310.

[9] Gregory L. Freeze, *The Parish Clergy in Nineteenth- Century Russia: Crisis, Reform, Counter-reform* (Princeton, 1983). See also Freeze's translation of I. S. Belliustin's *Description of the Clergy in Rural Russia: The Memoir of a Nineteenth-Century Parish Priest* (Ithaca, 1985).

[10] In the Belliustin memoir (p. 174), cited in note #9 above, this nineteenth-century dissenting white parish clergyman even attributed the Old Believer schism of the seventeenth century to monasticism, arguing that the separation of the Old Believers from the Moscow patriarchal church "suddenly became a reality when the monks' authority reached its apogee in the person of [Patriarch] Nikon".

use of the Hebrew text when Old Testament translation was revived a generation later in the 1860s.[11] However, as evidence of the controversy over use of the Septuagint in Russian translation, readers will note that, in the Synodal translation of the 1870s and in all subsequent Russian printings of the Synodal text down to the present, bracketed alternative Septuagint readings are provided from the very first page of Genesis onward. The controversy over the Old Testament has continued into the later nineteenth and twentieth centuries, with those committed to the use of Slavonic in Orthodox worship tending to support the Septuagint reading. The issue remains politically charged.

If anything, the politics of modern Russian New Testament textology has been thornier than that of the Old Testament. Here the problem has not been that of a conflict between rival supporters of Greek and Hebrew texts, but rather a conflict over the introduction of modern New Testament textology into Russian translation. At the base of both the Russian Bible Society New Testament and the Synodal New Testament of 1862 rested essentially the same *textus receptus*, a basic Greek text that dated with modification to the work of the Renaissance scholar Desiderius Erasmus.[12] As in western textual scholarship, so also in later nineteenth-century Russia, scholars at the theological academies followed with interest the pioneering textological work of Eberhard Nestle. The Nestle Greek texts, with their far more elaborate critical apparatus, were reviewed in Russian religious journals of the early twentieth century.[13] Indeed, this common bond of Russian textologists with their western counterparts explains in good measure the establishment in 1915 under the leadership of Petrograd Theological Academy Professor I.E. Evseev of a Russian Biblical Commission.[14] That Commission, among other things, set about the task of deciphering the textual bases of the non-extant Kirillo-Methodian text and the extant Slavonic editions of the New Testament. It was, of course, at that stage that the Russian

---

[11] In the years following the "Pavskii Affair", a rich tradition of Hebraic studies was continued at the St. Petersburg Theological Academy through the work of Professors Levison, Khvolson and Troitskii. In addition to the work of these scholars on Old Testament textology, their wider scholarship is well represented in the pages of the academy's nineteenth-century scholarly journal, *Khristianskoe chtenie*.

[12] On the *textus receptus*, see the standard work by Bruce Metzger, *The Text of the New Testament: Its Transmission, Corruption, and Restoration*, 2nd edition (Oxford, 1964).

[13] Editions of the Nestle text were routinely and favorably reviewed in each of the four major theological academy journals—*Khristianskoe chtenie* (St. Petersburg), *Bogoslovskii viestnik* (Moscow), *Pravoslavnyi sobiesednik* (Kazan'), and *Trudy kievskoi dukhovnoi akademii* (Kiev).

[14] On Evseev's Russian Biblical Commission, see the series of articles in *Bogoslovskie trudy*, vol. XIV (Moscow, 1975). In particular, V. Sorokin and K. I. Logachev, "Aktual'nye problemy russkogo perevoda sviashchennogo pisaniia", and K. Logachev, "Dokumenty bibleiskoi komissii: Organizatsiia, printsipy raboty i deiatel'nost' komissii v 1915-1921 godakh" (this latter article began in vol XIII of the *Bogoslovskie trudy* and constituted a publication of substantial portions of the earlier Commission's archival record).

Revolution and the turbulent events of the 1920s once again limited the capacity of official Russian scholarship to address serious questions of biblical textology.

The re-emergence of New Testament textology as a major issue in Russian biblical translation dates to the 1950s and the efforts of the British and Foreign Bible Society to launch a revision of the nineteenth-century Synodal Russian New Testament. With BFBS funding and the translation leadership of Bishop Cassian Bezobrazov, rector of St. Sergius Theological Institute in Paris, a new emigre Russian New Testament was completed in stages during the 1950s and 1960s, with final publication of the completed New Testament in 1970 after the death of Bishop Cassian. The strength of the text rested in its incorporation of modern textological advances represented in the Nestle-Aland critical Greek New Testament. But, this strength was more than offset by the rather unreadable nature of the Russian translation. Bishop Cassian, committed as he was to the fidelity of the finest Greek text, believed he could maintain in translation the original Greek word order in the Gospel of John. Unlike the nineteenth century when very able BFBS agents in Russia had firm command of Russian, no one from the sponsoring BFBS translations staff could sense the full dimensions of this problem until it was too late to rectify the literary unreadability of the text.[15]

Despite the limitations of the Bezobrazov/BFBS edition of 1970, that text has arguably been far more politically significant than the BFBS originators of the project could ever have imagined. For, in good measure, the Bezobrazov New Testament helped to spawn the renewal of Greek New Testament studies within the Soviet Union. Not only did the pages of the official Russian Orthodox *Zhurnal moskovskoi patriarkhii* [Journal of the Moscow Patriarchate] feel obliged in the mid-1950s to castigate the Bezobrazov emigre edition, but they went one stage further to endorse the *textus receptus* against dangerous western efforts to challenge this basic Orthodox text. So far did the reaction proceed that the patriarchate was prompted in 1956 to republish for the first time since the 1920s a complete edition of the nineteenth-century Synodal translation of the Russian Bible in a printing of fifty-thousand copies.[16]

In the reaction to the Bezobrazov text yet another feature of the politics of modern Russian culture was revealed—namely, the exaggerated sensitivity to perceptions of itself in the West. Post-World War II biblical textology in the Soviet Union has reflected a tendency similar to that of nineteenth-century Slavophilism—namely, the elevation of the West into a kind of paradigm against which Russian self-identification occurs. In this case, conservative supporters of the *textus receptus* continued and continue to the present to argue

15 On the Bezobrazov translation, see S. K. Batalden, "Revolution and Emigration: The Russian Files of the British and Foreign Bible Society", in *The Study of Russian History from British Archival Sources*, ed. by Janet M. Hartley (London, 1986), pp. 147-171.

16 On Soviet reaction to the Bezobrazov/BFBS translation, see Batalden, "The Russian Files", note 49, p. 169-170. The full title of the 1956 Moscow edition is *Bibliia, ili Knigi Sviashchennogo Pisaniia Vetkhogo i Novogo Zaveta, v russkom perevode*.

with some passion for the preservation of this important Greek, "Orthodox" text. The curiosity, of course, is the cooptation of Desiderius Erasmus of Rotterdam as the textologist of the Orthodox East as opposed to the Latin West.

Behind the anathemas directed at the Bezobrazov text rested intense curiosity over this product of modern western New Testament textology. At one stage in the process, the future Leningrad Metropolitan Nikodim even managed to secure from BFBS offices while visiting in London a microfilm copy of Bishop Cassian's notes—notes that offered a word-for-word Greek-Russian diglot of the Nestle-Aland text. Such interest has continued to the present, for there are today clear signs of openness on these textological matters. But those who enter upon these debates need to appreciate the political stakes that members of the church leadership may have in this continuing fundamental issue over the authority of texts—and, behind this, the attitude toward the West and western scholarship.

While the right to translate and the authority of texts have raised fundamental political issues for the Russian Church in modern society, a third issue is the more confounding because of the inability of the society itself to fix upon any resolution. This third fundamental question involves the basic authority of the linguistic medium. Reference has been made throughout to the politics of the *modern* Russian Bible. But, the question that has complicated the process of biblical translation—and, in fact, undermined the utility of Bishop Cassian's New Testament—is the authority of the language to be employed in Russian biblical translation. The Russian Orthodox Church in the nineteenth century developed its own official language, a variant of modern Russian that reflected its bureaucratic nature and its debt to old Slavonicisms. Thus, in some sense, the language of the Synodal New Testament constituted a regression from the more common language of the early Bible Society New Testament. Professor Evseev of the Russian Biblical Commission would later write during World War I that the authorized Synodal text utilized a "pre-Pushkin language" reflecting its failure to incorporate the richness of the common nineteenth-century literary language.[17]

Yet, the politics of the language of the modern Russian Bible has taken a curious twist in the twentieth century. Given the enormity of the changes introduced into common Russian in the Soviet period—its barren journalese and its cliche-driven formulations—it is not surprising that for many of the intelligentsia and younger generation the very "old-fashionedness" of the stilted language of the nineteenth-century Synodal Russian Bible is one of its greatest strengths. Thus, when in 1978 an experimental Russian text of the Gospel of John was prepared with United Bible Societies' support by an associate of the late Leningrad Metropolitan Nikodim, its reception—limited by its closed circulation—was less than enthusiastic among an intelligentsia that craved a

---

[17] I.E. Evseev, *Stoletniaia godovshchina russkogo perevoda Biblii,* (Petrograd, 1916). See also the same writer's *Sobor i Bibliia,* (Petrograd, 1917).

richer literary text.[18] The problem facing modern Russian biblical translation, in this respect, is that of the myriad literary voices in contemporary Russian—from the colloquial street talk of some Russian writers to the high-cultured Russian of some acmeist poets. Arguably, there is no single authoritative modern Russian literary language; there are many. And in the absence of such a norm, the Synodal text has had remarkable staying power, despite the occasional limitations of its textual base.

Finally, the problems of authority in modern Russian biblical translation have also included the profoundly divisive question of distribution. Who, the question arose, had the authority to distribute Russian scripture? Unlike its more hegemonial claims in the area of translation and publication, the Holy Synod never managed to secure in the nineteenth century monopoly rights on the distribution of Holy Scripture. Instead, there developed an unprecedented system of colportage led by the St. Petersburg agency of the British and Foreign Bible Society.[19] By the eve of World War I, BFBS agents, colporteurs and hawkers were responsible for annual sales of over seven-hundred thousand copies of Scripture in the Russian Empire. Such colportage inevitably came to arouse the concern of Synodal officials—black clerics and church bureaucrats—including the Holy Synod's head, *Ober-prokuror* Konstantin Pobedonostsev, who organized a series of "Missionary Conferences" to combat Protestant-inspired colportage in the 1890s. The ostensible concern of Synodal officials was the fear, not entirely unjustified, that colportage was becoming a front for proselytizing and recruitment into sectarian, Protestant ranks. Lurid stories were told of those who would hawk by day and proselytize by night. Although BFBS agencies successfully deflected the charges, the concern of the Holy Synod remained that biblical sales in the common language might somehow be used as a lever against the authority of the official Russian Orthodox Church.

In the Soviet period, especially since the Stalinist accords with the Orthodox Church during World War II, the authority officially to distribute Russian Scripture has been lodged squarely within the Moscow Patriarchate and its publication office. The only major exception to that has been the case of Russian scripture provided by the British and Foreign Bible Society and now the United Bible Societies to the All-Union Council of Evangelical Christians and Baptists. The assertion by the patriarchate of monopoly rights on distribution to Orthodox believers has led to understandable pressure from those who feel that the patriarchal publishing establishment has been far too conservative, empire-building and arbitrary in its distribution policies. Meanwhile, the presence of western agencies (including the United Bible Societies) providing free Scripture to Soviet churches has meant that the receiving agency, the publications' office of the Moscow Patriarchate, has become one of the

---

[18] The translation, entitled *Evangelie po Ioannu v novom russkom perevode,* was issued in Brussels by the United Bible Societies in 1978.

[19] S.K. Batalden, "Colportage," *op. cit.*

wealthiest divisions of the Russian Church, strengthening itself as it issues at profit Scriptures that are provided from the West free of charge.

Three recent and well-publicized examples of this politics of biblical distribution appear to be instructive. First, there is the case of the republication of the early twentieth-century *Tolkovaia Bibliia* [Interpreter's Bible], edited by the pre-revolutionary Russian church historian, Anatolii P. Lopukhin.[20] Much publicity attended the decision of the Scandinavian Bible Societies to mark the millennium of Christianity in Russia by providing to the Moscow Patriarchate a gift of one-hundred and fifty thousand (150,000) copies of the multi-volume sets of this coveted *Interpreter's Bible*. Yet, in the distribution of these copies the publication office of the Moscow Patriarchate began charging rates, or expecting return gifts to use the euphemism of the day, often in excess of 200 rubles for a single set of the republication. Even impoverished seminarians have been charged a routine price of fifty rubles. From such sales alone the publications office of the patriarchate could conceivably clear over fifteen million rubles, a figure that by official exchange rates amounts to nearly three million dollars. The potential for manipulation of western charity—a process dating also to the 1920s—must be considered also as a part of the politics of biblical distribution.[21]

There is, however, another different, more vulnerable side to the position of Russian Orthodox leadership in biblical distribution, a side that is currently being played out in the more open climate of Gorbachev's Soviet Union. The example, in this case, is that of one of the more noteworthy incidents at the recent June 1988 Russian Orthodox All-Church Council held in conjunction with the festivities marking the millennium of Christianity in Russia. Father Sergei Hackel, representative at the Council from the Russian Orthodox Church in England, recently has recounted the story of the Chuvash priest at the June meetings—a story that has been reconfirmed in separate accounts. According to these accounts, one of the more dramatic moments of this unprecedentedly open Church Council session was when an attending Chuvash priest asked for and received permission to address the body. In his broken Russian, the Chuvash priest rose before the assembly to tell the following story:

[20] Anatolii Pavlovich Lopukhin (1852-1904) began the editing of the Russian Interpreter's Bible, but its twelve-volume publication in St. Petersburg followed in the years after Lopukhin's death. The full title is *Tolkovaia bibliia ili kommentarii na vsie knigi sv. pisaniia Vetkhago i Novago Zavieta*, (St. Petersburg, 1904-1913). The Scandinavian reissue has combined the twelve volumes into three.

[21] On a comparable question of western charity in the 1920s involving the Russian sectarian leader Ivan S. Prokhanov, see Batalden, "Revolution and Emigration," pp. 152-156. The United Bible Societies has not been unaware of the economics of biblical distribution in the Soviet Union, and reached in 1989 an understanding with the Russian Orthodox Church that both recognizes part of this problem and looks toward future interconfessional Bible distribution arrangements in the USSR. See, in this regard, "Bible Distribution in the USSR", *UBS Background Paper*, June 1989; and "Could 'Memorandum of Understanding' Mean Organized Bible Work, Printing Press for USSR?", American Bible Society News Release, June 6, 1989.

My people are in need of the Scriptures. There are few copies of the Chuvash New Testament still available in my parish, and the last service books are in shreds. So, to forward the appeal of my people I travelled to Moscow recently to request from the publications office the republication of Chuvash New Testaments and service books. I arrived at the offices by appointment, then waited for several hours, only to be ushered in to see the secretary to the metropolitan in charge of publications. To the secretary I recounted the problem that we have no Chuvash Testaments and no service books. Then, the secretary turned to me and said, "I am sorry, but those are matters on which you will have to speak to the Metropolitan, and he is unfortunately in western Europe".

The Chuvash priest continued his account in broken Russian before the hushed All-Church Council:

Disconsolately, I took my leave and walked to the lift. At last the lift door opened, and who should appear but His Eminence, the esteemed metropolitan who was, I had just been told, in western Europe. [At this point the June Council sessions broke out into laughter—a laughter that one could not have imagined at any previous Russian Church Council of the Soviet era.] I turned to His Eminence and quickly conveyed the sense of my mission. Upon hearing my appeal, the metropolitan turned to me and said, "For those questions, you must turn to my secretary [from whence the priest had just come]".[22]

The spontaneous laughter that followed at the June Council and the ensuing reproaches directed against certain members of the church hierarchy combined to reveal a spirit of *glasnost* in this most significant of church councils since 1917. The openness, however, unveiled significant dissatisfaction with those in the hierarchy who would use their authority to limit or otherwise affect adversely the distribution of biblical literature in the Soviet Union. Such conflicts, we need hardly be reminded, were also very much at the center of the nineteenth-century Pavskii affair noted above.

The issue of the Chuvash Testament has its parallel in a third example related to the politics of biblical distribution—that is, the case of the Ukrainian Bible. Permission has recently been granted for the import of some three-hundred thousand (300,000) copies of the Ukrainian Bible. Pressed by the Vatican to

---

[22] The quotations here are drawn from the presentation of Father Sergei Hackel, priest of the Russian Orthodox Diocese of Sourozh [England] and lecturer at Sussex University, "Reflections on the Millennium Celebrations," a talk given 15 July 1988 at the conference, "Christianity in the Eastern Slav Lands (16th-20th Centuries): On the Millennium of the Baptism of Kievan Rus," a conference jointly organized by Keston College and the School of Slavonic Studies, University of London. Father Sergei Hackel was a delegate at the June 1988 All-Church Council, and his account of the Chuvash priest has been confirmed in separate recountings for this author during a visit to Moscow in late July 1988.

provide recognition for the Ukrainian Uniate or Greek Catholic Church and recent Gorbachev talks at the Vatican confirming the recognition of Greek Catholics in the Ukraine, the Moscow Patriarchate has taken the cautious step of distributing some Ukrainian Bibles.[23] Such a cautious step is a part of wider efforts designed to coopt those Ukrainian Catholics who would see their national and linguistic identity linked with their ecclesiastical, in this case Catholic, loyalties. Still, it is doubtful that the Moscow Patriarchate is prepared to countenance the use of a Ukranian text in liturgical worship.

The point, of course, is that in using biblical distribution in the common language as a tool for cooptation, the Orthodox Church may well be raising fundamental new questions about the use of the Church Slavonic text—the liturgical text so reflective of *diglossia*. If the preservation of the Church Slavonic for liturgical worship has indirectly served the interests of Russian imperial, political domination of the Orthodox Church—especially against the threats of late nineteenth-century clerical liberalism and twentieth-century interwar renovationism (*obnovlenchestvo*)—then any challenge to that domination may have significant consequences for the church in Soviet society, for its seminaries, its clergy, and, most significantly, for its millions of lay believers.

Modern Russian biblical translation has been inevitably drawn into politically controversial questions of authority in a highly structured Russian and Soviet politicized environment. The authority of translations and publishing, the authority of texts, the authority of the language itself, and the authority to distribute Scripture are all a part of this political context. Just as the political culture has affected earlier biblical translation and publication, so also in the Gorbachev years changes now affecting the political culture may fundamentally alter the politics of biblical translation and distribution in the Soviet Union.

However, alongside the restructuring of Soviet political culture and its potential ramifications for the politics of biblical translation, there remains the powerful and, one may even say, creative disposition to preserve tradition in the Orthodox East—a propensity seen clearly in earlier centuries when the Old Believers or schismatics refused to conform to modernizing innovations introduced into their Old Slavonic service books.[24]

---

[23] The Ukrainian Bible, like the Russian Synodal translation, has its origin in the nineteenth century. However, the text now being distributed is that prepared by Metropolitan Ilarion (Ogienko). The Ilarion translation was begun during the interwar period with funding from the British and Foreign Bible Society.

[24] The reference here to the Old Believers of the seventeenth century is because of their opposition to Patriarch Nikon's "modernizing" changes introduced into the liturgical service books. See, in this connection, the most recent critical English edition of seventeenth-century Old Believer Archpriest Avvakum's autobiography, *Archpriest Avvakum: The Life Written by Himself*, translated with annotations, commentary and an historical introduction by Kenneth N. Brostrom, Michigan Slavic Translations Series #4 (Ann Arbor, 1979).

SAMUEL ESCOBAR

THE ROLE OF TRANSLATION IN DEVELOPING
INDIGENOUS THEOLOGIES—A LATIN AMERICAN VIEW[1]

One of the characteristics of our time is the rise of a lively and thriving
Christianity in the so called Third World. Missiologists and historians who
watch this development are usually impressed by the contrast between the
spiritual and missionary vitality of these churches among the masses of poor
people in Asia, Africa and Latin America, and the decline of commitment and
vitality in the churches of what was Christendom in the past. For Scottish
missiologist Andrew Walls this is a fact that corresponds to a pattern of retreat
and advance in the history of Christian mission and the spread of the Christian
faith,

> The recession of Christianity among the European peoples appears to be
> continuing. And yet we seem to stand at the threshold of a new age of
> Christianity, one in which its main base will be in the Southern
> continents, and where its dominant expression will be filtered through
> the culture of those continents. Once again Christianity has been saved
> for the world by its diffusion across cultural lines.[2]

1. The Coming of the Third Church

The significance of the above mentioned facts, and the need to pay attention to
them as we look to the future of the Christian mission, have also been stressed
by Swiss missiologist Walbert Buhlman, who has coined the expression "The
coming of the Third Church". Outlining a historical panorama with great bold
strokes, Buhlman explains the meaning of this expression,

> Roughly speaking we can say that the first Christian millenium, with the
> first eight councils all held in the East, stood mainly under the leadership
> of the First Church, the Eastern Church; the second millenium stood
> under the leadership of the Second Church, the Western Church, which
> shaped the Middle Ages and, from the time of the "discovery" of the New
> World, undertook all missionary initiatives. Now the coming third
> millenium will evidently stand under the leadership of the Third Church,

1 I am thankful to Dordt College, Sioux Center, Iowa for permission to use there some
portions of my monograph *Liberation Themes in Reformational Perspective*, that has been
published in the "Dordt College Lecture Series".

2 Andrew Walls, "Culture and Coherence in Christian History", *Evangelical Review of
Theology* 9,3(1985):221.

the Southern Church. I am convinced that the most important drives and
inspirations for the whole church in the future will come from the Third
Church.[3]

Theology cannot be separated from the life of the church, and it is only natural
that new churches when they are free to live their life and testimony for Christ
within their own context, will enter sooner or later in the task of developing
their own theology. Evangelism, the communication of the faith to the new
generations, the prophetic stance demanded by history and society, the demand of
pastoral answers for ethical problems, are all aspects of mission that press for
the development of a lively theology, and benefit from it. In some cases
theology has accompanied the effort of these churches to find their own identity,
away from colonialist traps linked to their origin. Indigenous theology is much
more than an adolescent rebellion or a curiosity for academics interested in exotic
things. It has to do with the life of the Church and her faithfulness to the Lord.

Theologians from the Third Church are now walking in the promising and
risky path of forging indigenous expressions of what could be described as the
Third Church theology. Because of the kind of world in which we live and the
characteristics of our moment of Christian history, this task can only be
accomplished in dialogue with Christians from the Eastern and the Western
Churches. There are very promising signs that when true dialogue takes place
there can be a communal perception of the road for the future. From such kind of
dialogue came for instance this eloquent statement of the "Willowbank Report":

> We should seek with equal care to avoid theological imperialism or
> theological provincialism. A church's theology should be developed by
> the community of faith out of the Scripture in interaction with other
> theologies of the past and present, and with the local culture and its
> needs".[4]

The impact of liberation theologies and Black theology in many parts of the
world is a testimony to the significance of efforts on the part of Third World
churches to forge their own way of thinking and articulating their faith. As
several of their representative voices have expressed, these theologies have in
common their origin in the lively struggle of young or renewed churches among
the masses of the underprivileged and poor. Their indigeneity is in some cases
the result of a revolt against decades or even centuries of imposition of a foreign
theological pattern that was passively accepted within a colonial situation. It is
an indigeneity that comes from the new active role taken by those that were
before reduced to silence, whose presence was not recognized or given
expression. Gustavo Gutierrez refers to it in this way,

---

[3] Walbert Buhlman, *The Church of the Future*, (Maryknoll, NY: Orbis Books, 1986), 6.

[4] John R.W. Stott and Robert Coote, eds. *Down to Earth, Studies in Christianity and
Culture* (Grand Rapids: Eerdmans, 1980), 334.

The theological schools that are growing up in the so-called Third World countries, or among the racially and culturally oppressed minorities of the wealthy nations, or in the context of women's liberation, are expressions of the new presence of those who have previously been "absent" from history. Their efforts spring from areas of humanity that have previously been arid theologically speaking but in which Christian faith has old and deep roots. Hence their present fruitfulness.[5]

In reference to Black theology, Deotis Roberts has pointed out the "affinity between the mood of black theologians and the liberation theologians of Latin America . . . because both are tuned in on an oppressed human situation".[6] At the same time he has described the uniqueness of Black theology in these terms:

It is seeking to be indigenous by rooting itself in the African/Afro-American religious heritage. Ours has been an experience of suffering without bitterness. But out of this crucible has emerged a robust faith that now deserves theological interpretation. We have discovered deep in our African roots the basis for sharing and caring in the notion of "familyhood" in African society. We note a sense of servanthood, togetherness, and stewardship in primitive Christianity and our religious heritage.[7]

The rise of indigenous theologies is a principle at work all through the history of Christianity. Such theologies could be considered as the plants native to their own cultural soil, that have sprung forth from the eternal seed of the Gospel which is incorporated in the Holy Scripture. There is a way in which the Protestant Reformation of the 16th century could be considered as the rise of a form of Christianity more contextualized in the Northern European countries, breaking away from the Latin center and the Latin theology that up to that point had dominated the life of the Church. A.M. Chirgwin has said,

The Reformation was not just the throwing off of the Roman yoke. It was a deeper movement with more sides to it than that. In part it was a protest against the abuses and corruptions of the medieval Church; in part it was an assertion of the new sense of nationhood against the dominance of Rome; in part it was a rediscovery of the Bible.[8]

---

[5] Gustavo Gutiérrez, *We Drink From Our Own Wells: The Spiritual Journey of a People,* (Maryknoll, NY: Orbis Books, 1984), p. 27.

[6] J. Deotis Roberts, *A Black Political Theology,* (Philadelphia: Westminster Press, 1974), p. 206.

[7] Ibid., p. 208.

[8] A.M. Chirgwin, *The Bible in World Evangelism,* (New York: Friendship Press, 1954), p. 29.

During the same period there is another theological stream that has its own contextual dimension—the theology of the Spanish mystics like San Juan de la Cruz and Santa Teresa de Jesus. Only in recent years, thanks to the work of scholars like Americo Castro and Marcel Bataillon, we have come to realize how much that powerful spiritual reformation and its vigorous missionary thrust was partly influenced by the use of insights from Erasmus, but also by elements from the Islamic and Jewish spirituality that had been present in Spain during eight centuries.

In these two great movements it is possible to say that we are confronted with the rise of indigenous theologies. The measure of continuity and discontinuity that they represent in the general history of theological inquiry is an area yet to be explored critically. We are dealing here with something which is essential to the very center of the Christian faith, what Andrew Walls has called its "translatability". Referring to the contrast with other faiths like Islam, which have key elements that cannot be translated, Walls says that,

> the great act on which Christian faith rests, the Word becoming flesh and pitching tent among us, is itself an act of translation. And this principle brings Christ to the heart of each culture where he finds acceptance; to the burning questions within that culture, to the points of reference within it by which men know themselves. That is why each phase of Christian history has produced new themes: themes which the points of reference of that culture have made inescapable for those who share that framework. The same themes may lie beyond the conception of Christians of an earlier or another frame of thought. They will have their own commanding heights to be conquered by Christ.[9]

Walls finds that in the history of Christianity there is a constant tension between, on the one hand, this "indigenizing" principle and, on the other hand, a universalizing factor that he calls the "pilgrim" principle. Both are present in the Gospel, because God in Christ takes people "as they are" (including their inmersion in their culture), but takes them in order to transform them, making them aware that here they have no abiding city.[10] It is within the frame of reference of the tension of these principles that we are to understand the validity and relevance of indigenous theologies. On the one hand the urgency to be open to the way in which the Third Church is exploring new theological territory, but also to be open to the dialogue that will bring mutual enrichment as the church universal looks backward in thanksgiving and forward in faith.

---

9 Walls, 1985. p. 222.

10 Andrew Walls, "The Gospel as the Prisoner and Liberator of Culture", in *Evangelical Review of Theology*, 7,2(1983):223-225.

2. The Bible and Theological Method

The experience of churches after the Reformation demonstrates the close relationship between theological developments and the wide diffusion and use of Scripture. Probably one of the most dynamic aspects of the Reformation was the return to Scripture and the development of a theological method that had the study of Scripture at its center. We must not forget that Bible translation engaged the attention of the Reformers as a decisive part of their theological and pastoral work.

> In 1516 Erasmus published his Greek New Testament and the very next year Luther nailed his thesis to the church door in Wittemberg. In 1522 Luther translated the New Testament into German and a few years later German princes and cities began to call themselves "Protestant". Again in 1525, Tyndale translated the Bible into English and in two years' time Reformation doctrines were being openly advocated in Oxford and Cambridge. Once more in 1535 Olivetan translated the Bible into French and a year later Calvin published his *Institutes* and Geneva went Protestant. Every new step in biblical discovery or translation seemed to be the occasion if not the cause of another development in Protestantism. The biblical renewal and the Reformation moved forward together, with the biblical renewal generally taking the lead.[11]

If we look at these facts of history from the specific perspective of theological development, of the rise of a theology that would be indigenous to the lands where the church was being revived and reformed, we have to refer also to the development of a new theological method for which the reading and interpretation of Scripture was central. There was in the Reformation a return to Scriptures and an effort to formulate and explain the Christian faith anew, basically as a commentary to Scripture. A strong impulse in this direction came from Luther, but the systematic working of it was elaborated by Calvin:

> a law . . . governed the pattern of Calvin's thought. The Reformer sought not merely to take the materials of his theology out of the Bible but also to make his theology a complete and consistent representation of the Bible.[12]

As both Luther and Calvin were not only theologians but mainly preachers and pastors, their theology was a process of contextualization within the new social conditions of nationalist upsurges and the initial steps of Western society into modernity. Rather than a commentary upon the accumulated traditions of the Latin church centered in Rome, theology became a commentary on Scripture,

---

[11] Chirgwin, 1954, p. 30.

[12] Frank H. Littell, *Reformation Studies*, (Richmond, VA: John Knox Press, 1962), p. 107.

written in the vernacular language of the masses to which Scripture had already been translated. We are not only referring to systematic theological treatises but to the hymns, to the books on spirituality, to the creedal formulations which expressed the intense process of doing theology that was taking place. When it came to the systematic task, as theologian Bernard Ramm says,

> The historic Protestant position is to ground theology in biblical exegesis. A theological system is to be built up exegetically brick by brick. Hence the theology is no better than the exegesis that underlies it. The task of the *systematic* theologian is to commence with this bricks ascertained through exegesis and build the temple of his theological system. But only when he is sure of his individual bricks is he able to make the necessary generalizations, and to carry on the synthetic and creative activity that is necessary for the construction of a theological system.[13]

Before Protestantism became a missionary force, the role of the Pietist movement and the Evangelical Revival was to foster a return to the Scriptures rediscovered in the Reformation, but this time with an intense emphasis on the application of its message. Chirgwin has pointed out that "In the years immediately before the Revival the Bible had not been suppressed; it had merely been neglected".[14] The pattern is well illustrated by the case of John Wesley and his well known experience of spiritual revival at a famous meeting on Aldersgate Street, where the commentary of Luther on Romans was being read. That meeting turned Wesley into a great evangelist and missionary to the masses of England. Chirgwin calls our attention to the centrality of Scripture as a connecting factor in a succession of decisive movements—Hus and Wycliffe, the Reformation, the Moravian Pietists, and Wesley—"It was a remarkable chain and every link in it was concerned with the Bible".[15] As it has been pointed out recently by historian Donald Dayton, Wesley's way of doing theology differed from the method of the Reformers. In his famous "quadrilateral" of Scripture, reason, tradition and experience, there was "a subtle interplay of theological norms and sources that Wesley understood to be guided and directed by the Scriptures". Besides that we are reminded that "Wesley plumbed the whole of the Christian tradition and the Scriptures but bent this work to practical rather than speculative purposes".[16]

---

[13] Bernard Ramm, *Protestant Biblical Interpretation*, (Grand Rapids, MI: Baker Book House, 1970), p. 179.

[14] Chirgwin, 1954, p. 43.

[15] Ibid., p. 44.

[16] Donald W. Dayton, "The Use of Scripture in the Wesleyan Tradition", in Robert K. Johnston, ed., *The Use of the Bible in Theology: Evangelical Options*, (Atlanta: John Knox Press, 1983), pp. 136, 128.

When Protestantism became a missionary force during the second half of the 18th century, a distinctive mark of its methodology was the translation of Scripture to the language of the people that were to receive the Gospel. A historian of unequivocal ecumenical vocation like Stephen Neill says that,

> The first principle of Protestant missions has been that Christians should have the Bible in their hands in their own language at the earliest possible date. The Roman Catholic method has been different. It is not true to say that nothing has been done; we have heard of some translation of Scripture. But for the most part such literature as had been produced was made up of catechisms and books of devotion. It is a fact that though the Roman Catholics had been on the Fisher Coast in South India since 1534, the first translation of the New Testament into Tamil was that completed by the Protestant Ziegenbalg in 1714. The first Roman Catholic missionaries arrived in the Philippines in 1565. In three centuries almost the whole population had become Christian, yet it appears that the first translation of any part of the Scripture into any language of the Philippines, the Gospel of Luke in the Pangasinan language, was made only in 1873.[17]

This has accounted for the rise of truly indigenous theologies, sometimes taking missionaries by surprise. In the recent case of Africa the explosion of spiritual vitality is linked to the existence of Scripture in the languages of the people. The case of Africa is probably one of the most representative in our century. David Barrett has studied in depth the vitality of new religious movements in that continent, the explosion of independent churches and the theological revolution that has accompanied it. For Barrett the key in the process is the availability of the Bible in the vernacular. It has not been a fact that has influenced only life within the Christian community but has generated projections to society at large, thus creating a dialectical movement of mutual influences.

> It is impossible to overestimate the importance of the Bible in African society. The portions of it that are first translated are in most cases the first printed literature in the vernacular language. Vast literacy campaigns are based on it. Ability to read a Gospel is a requirement for baptism in many Protestant churches.[18]

Barrett points out the importance of these translations of the Bible in the development of the self-image of many tribes, and consequently in the

---

[17] Stephen Neill, *A History of Christian Missions,* 2nd edition, (New York: Penguin, 1986), p. 177.

[18] David B. Barrett, *Schism and Renewal in Africa,* (New York: Oxford University Press, 1968), p. 127.

movement towards independence, but he also shows the effect this had in the rise of independent churches and of an independent theology.

> Up to this point the missions had had the same absolute control over the Scriptures as they had exercised over the church. They alone had access to the Hebrew and Greek sources; their interpretation was final. But with the publication of African translations, a momentous change took place: it now became possible to differentiate between missions and scriptures. Through these scriptures God, Africans perceived, was addressing them in the vernacular in which was enshrined the soul of their people . . . the vernacular therefore provided an independent standard of reference that African Christians were quick to seize on.[19]

Going beyond some of the debates of the past, both Catholic and Protestant historiography acknowledge nowadays the vitality of spirituality and theology centered in Scripture. It can certainly be said today that the return to that source of vitality has been one of the hallmarks of post-Vatican II Catholicism. Writing on the wake of that Council, Jesuit scholar Walter M. Abbott said,

> According to Vatican II, "all the preaching of the Church must be nourished and ruled by Sacred Scripture"; the Bible is the chief source of theology and the training of priests should be built around a Bible-centered theology rather than polemically oriented theology; not only preaching but catechetics and "all other Christian instruction" should be nourished by the "primary and perpetual" source of the Bible.[20]

Without the official sanction from the Vatican to a new way of doing theology, in which the reading of Scripture is central, we could not have seen the flourishing of indigenous theologies in Latin American Catholicism.

3. The Rise of Indigenous Theologies in Latin America

Like the existence of living forms of Christianity, the promise of a new indigenous theology is closely linked to the availability of Scripture in the language of the people. It has proved its value in terms of mission and the planting of the Church. It will show its possibilities in terms of an intelligence of the faith that will accompany the life of the church. The question of the delay of a contextual and indigenous theology is linked to the question of the persistence of colonialist patterns of mission and church life. These have been made impossible by the new post-colonial situations that are lived in the world, by the vigour of new churches or revived churches that have come to the scene,

---

19 Ibid., p. 127.

20 Walter M. Abbott, "Bible Needs of Roman Catholics", in *United Bible Societies Bulletin*, Third Quarter, 1967, p. 103.

and by the existence of international platforms of dialogue that have come to existence in recent decades.

Probably the rise of liberation theologies is the best illustration of this kind of development. It represents a break away from the past, a movement of return to the biblical sources of the Christian life, and a new reading of history. The emphasis on a praxeological source for the reflection is a hermeneutical emphasis, because a mark of these theologies is the search for a new reading of the biblical material. That effort to ground theology in praxis, but to do it "in the light of Scripture", has been probably the best common ground that exists for dialogue with other theologies across cultures and continents.[21]

Liberation theologies have rediscovered the centrality of new themes for theological discourse[22] which are closely related to the central themes of classical theology—God as liberator, social oppression as sin, a Christology that may be "operative" for political and social action, salvation as a holistic experience, poverty and justice, the God of the poor, the preferential option for the poor. In some cases these are themes that had been more or less "hidden" in the predominant theology of the countries that missionized in Latin America. What is worse, in other cases theological themes were used to construct an ideology supportive of the foreign conquest and the *status quo*. As long as Latin American theological efforts were nothing more than a carbon copy of what was done in Europe and North America those themes also remained hidden or manipulated. It has taken the crisis of the post-colonial situation and of the revolt against neo-colonialism, for the indigenous churches to question the traditional schemes.

The indigeneity of the theologies of liberation has been questioned because of their use of Marxism, a European philosophical product.[23] Some liberation theologians, especially Gustavo Gutierrez in recent times, have clarified the limits of their use of the Latin American social sciences, in which some ideas of Marxism are present as a component. They are used for the analysis of the social situation in Latin America, in order to define the kind of contribution that Christians will make in it. However, Gutierrez argues that, in his own case, Marxism as a complete philosophical system, including its atheistic presuppositions, has not been used for the theological task.[24] On the other hand, Gutierrez and others have insisted that the indigeneity of their theology comes from the fact that they are trying to develop a creative and "new" reading of Scripture "from the perspective of the poor". The ground of indigeneity would be the place where the theologian has chosen to stand—among the poor. And the fact is that in many cases this puts the interpreter in a situation that

---

[21] Andrew Kirk, *Liberation Theology: An Evangelical View From the Third World,* (Atlanta: John Knox Press, 1979).

[22] Elsa Tamez, *Bible of the Oppressed,* (Maryknoll, NY: Orbis Books, 1982).

J. Severino Croatto, *Hermeneutica Biblica,* (Buenos Aires: La Aurora, 1984).

[23] Jurgen Moltmann, "An Open Letter to Jose Miguez Bonino", *Christianity and Crisis,* 36,5 (March 29, 1976).

[24] Gustavo Gutiérrez, *La Verdad: Los Hara Libres,* (Lima: CEP, 1986), pp. 90-94.

sociologically is very similar to that of the human author of the biblical material—the jail, exile, sociological poverty.

Liberation theologians have become known in Europe and North America because of a type of discourse that has been able to penetrate the academic world where theology is traditionally developed. But indigeneity as a new way of reading Scripture is also taking place at pastoral and popular levels, within the actual living conditions of the poor, as they try to live and express their faith in the midst of misery, social unrest and repression. Such is the case with the Basic Christian Communities, and the result could be summarized in the words of Frei Betto, one of the theologians close to those communities in Brazil:

> The difference between the reading that we traditional priests make of the Bible and that which the communities make is that we look at the Bible as though we are looking through a window, curious to see what is happening outside, while the people of the communities look at the Bible as one looks at a mirror, to see a reflection of their own reality.[25]

Frei Betto goes on to say that the traditional way of reading Scripture is to look back at what God did in the past in a bygone era in which he was present, but that the poor in the Base Ecclesial Communities "feel as they are seeing their own lives revealed in the accounts of the Bible". Consequently the primary task of the theologian should be "returning the keys of the Bible back to the people".[26]

The centrality of the use of Scripture in some of the Base Ecclesial Communities within the Roman Catholic Church is partly due to the motivation and stimulus that came from the experience of early Protestantism in Latin America.[27] One very known fact in the history of United Bible Societies in that part of the world is the decisive role played by Scriptures in the rise of a vigorous Evangelical minority during the first decades of this century. Methodist theologian Jose Miguez Bonino says,

> In Latin America the Bible was not simply a book of doctrine or a devotional guide. It was the basic tool for evangelism, the seed of the Church. Again and again a missionary traveled from place to place leaving Bibles, New Testaments and single books, and evangelical congregations sprang up in his trail and gathered around the Word of God. Lay preachers, many times without theological or even secular

---

[25] Guillermo Cook, *The Expectation of the Poor,* (Maryknoll, NY: Orbis Books, 1985), p. 110.

[26] Ibid., p. 111.

[27] Samuel Escobar, "Christian Base Communities: A Historical Perspective", *Transformation*, 3,3 (1986).

education became powerful evangelists resting their authority solely on the Bible.[28]

The theology of these nascent communities was centered around Scripture, and in their initial decades it was very much the Evangelical theology brought by the missionary movement. Some aspects of the Protestant heritage were accentuated partly because of the polemical attitude of some of the missionaries, and also partly because of the critical role these Evangelical minorities came to play in a society where the Roman Catholic Church had enjoyed a religious monopoly. Ivan Vallier has studied the issue from a sociological perspective,[29] and I have explored it from the theological angle.[30] The search for theological indigeneity started already with the first generation of Latin American Evangelical thinkers that entered in a global dialogue within the ecumenical movement, men like Gonzalo Baez Camargo and Alberto Rembao. Some of the thinkers of a second generation looked for theological renewal following especially European theologies. Men like Rubem Alves, Julio de Santa Ana, Jose Miguez Bonino and Emilio Castro became the pioneers of an effort to reformulate a reading of Scripture around themes like God's action in history, hope and human utopias, the sociological dimension of the Christian community and the relationships between empire and Christian mission. Later on, some of their perceptions were taken by Roman Catholic theologians of liberation.[31]

More recently, an Evangelical theology of mission in Latin America has also been calling insistently for a more indigenous form of theological reflection. Within the Protestant tradition of theological method that was outlined above, we have had a creative reading of Scripture around themes like Christology,[32] Church and World[33] and Providence and History.[34] Ecuadorian theologian Rene Padilla is representative of a generation that has been working through the years in the critical task of reading the Evangelical theological heritage through Latin American eyes. He stresses the fact that "an *evangelical*

[28] Jose Míguez Bonino, "Main Currents of Protestantism", in Samuel Shapiro, ed., *Integration of Man and Society in Latin America*, (Notre Dame, IN: University of Notre Dame Press, 1967), p. 193.

[29] Ivan Vallier, *Catholicism, Social Control and Moderization in Latin America*, (Englewood Cliffs, NJ: Prentice Hall, 1970).

[30] Samuel Escobar, "The Kingdom of God, Eschatology and Social and Political Ethics in Latin America", in *Theological Fraternity Bulletin*, No. 1, 1975.

[31] Alan Preston Neely, "Protestant Antecedents of the Latin American Theology of Liberation", Ph.D Thesis, The American University, Washington, D.C., 1977.

Emilio A. Nuñez, *Liberation Theology*, Translated from Spanish by Paul E. Sywulka, (Chicago: Moody Press, 1985).

[32] Justo L. Gonzalez, *Revolución y Encarnación*, (Rio Piedras: La Reforma, 1967).

[33] C. René Padilla, *Mission Between the Times*, (Grand Rapids, MI: Eerdmans, 1985).

[34] Pedro Arana, *Providencia y Revolución*, (Lima: Estandarte de la Verdad, 1970).

theology can never be less than a *biblical* theology", stating the normativity of Scripture as our point of departure. Theology includes then,

> a process of transposing the Word of God from its original Hebrew or Greco-Roman *milieu* into a contemporary situation for the purpose of producing in the modern readers or hearers the same kind of impact that the original message was meant to produce in its original historical context.[35]

The pastoral and missionary ground of the theological task proposed is evident here. It is a hermeneutical task at the service of the life and mission of the church. Such hermeneutics, Padilla suggests, is to be characterized through a fourfold description: *communal*, because it is done by all the people of God; *pneumatic* because it confesses dependance on the assistance of the Holy Spirit; *contextual*, because it takes seriously the social and historical context; and *missiological*, because it is geared to the fulfillment of the mission of the church. The contextual dimension of this task is the one that takes us to the heart of the indigeneity:

> The contextualization of the Gospel will not consist of an adaptation of an existing theology of universal validity to a particular situation. It will not be merely the result of an intellectual process. It will not be aided by benevolent missionary paternalism intended to help the native theologians to select "positive elements" from their own historical situation which then may be used in the communication of a foreign version of the Gospel. It can only be the result of a new open-ended reading of Scripture with a hermeneutic in which the biblical text and the historical situation become mutually engaged in a dialogue whose purpose is to place the Church under the Lordship of Jesus Christ in its particular context.[36]

4. New Indigenous Theologies

When talking about Liberation theologies and the contemporary Evangelical theology of mission in Latin America, we are still referring to the Spanish and Portuguese-speaking segments which are the majority of the population of Latin America. Either in the Iberian form of Catholic Christianity or in the more Anglosaxonized forms of Protestantism that have spread in Latin America, we are talking of a westernized cultural environment. It is yet to be seen in these lands what is going to be the effect of Bible translation on the large native communities that have kept a singular cultural identity in spite of centuries of Iberian and Westernized domination.

---

[35] C. René Padilla, "Biblical Foundations: A Latin American Study", *Evangelical Review of Theology*, 7,1, April 1983, p. 79.

[36] Ibid., p. 86.

A relentless process of urbanization has brought the native cultures to the great cities where instead of being absorbed by the urban culture, they have in some cases managed to change the face of the city. The missionary efforts that have tried to continue their work giving due regard to the cultural indigeneity have seen a reward in terms of fruitfulness of their efforts. Keith Hamilton, several years ago, and more recently Ruben Tito Paredes, have documented the amazing growth of indigenous Evangelical churches among the Andean communities of Quechua and Aymara-speaking peoples.[37] The vitality of these growing churches is surpassing that of their Spanish-speaking counterparts in countries like Bolivia, Peru and Ecuador.

A new era opened for these communities some decades ago, when for the first time the New Testament became available in their own language. The long process of translation started already by the pioneering efforts of James Thomson in the 1820's, is a testimony to the sacrificial and patient style of the Bible Societies and the missionary groups that have worked with them. A new crucial time has come now with the availability of the Old Testament in those native languages. Precisely this year of 1988 will see the publication of five complete Bibles in the languages of people that have been in some kind of contact with Christianity since the middle of the 16th century but only now have access to the totality of Scripture in their own mother tongue.

William Mitchell, a United Bible Societies Translation Advisor that knows the Andean reality from experience of years as an insider in the area, says that "Recent studies suggest that it is in no way pretentious to imagine that the Old Testament in Quechua and Aymara could have an impact on the Andean peoples".[38] Mitchell analizes the historical moment we live today, the development of native churches, the varying experiences of Catholics and Evangelicals in the area, and the rise of some indigenous religious movements. From such observation and from his own missionary experience, he comes to the conclusion that the introduction of the Old Testament at this point in time is in no way a neutral stance, and that the Andean people will appropriate it in a unique way.

The Andean indigenous theology will sooner or later deal with two areas that are decisive for the life of the churches in the Andean zone. In both the fermenting factor of the Old Testament teaching will be decisive. One is the perception of history as a linear rather than a cyclical phenomenon. Here Mitchell quotes Brazilian theologian Carlos Mesters who believes that for the Andean peoples this will mean a new reading of their own history, and will have tremendous consequences for their participation in the processes of

---

[37] Keith E. Hamilton, *Church Growth in the High Andes*, (Lucknow, 1962).

Ruben E. Paredes-Alfaro, "A Protestant Movement in Ecuador and Peru: A Comparative Socio-Anthropological Study of the Establishment and Diffusion of Protestantism in Two Central Highland Regions", Ph.D Thesis, (University of California, Los Angeles, 1980).

[38] William Mitchell, "The Old Testament and the Andean Peoples", *United Bible Societies Bulletin*, No. 148-149, Third/Fourth Quarters, 1987, p. 129.

transformation. The second area that seems important in my opinion is the view of the human, and especially of the humanity of the Andean people. This was the great debate of the theologians and missiologists of the 16th century in the University of Salamanca.[39] But in that memorable occasion it was a debate *of Europeans about the Indians* of the New World. Only in our times, and with the complete text of Scripture in their hands, the Andean people themselves will reflect theologically on the key anthropological questions about their identity, their future and their liberation.

I think there are reasons to believe that the rise of indigenous churches and indigenous theologies, facilitated by the existence of Scripture in the Andean languages, will have a deep and lasting social impact. Peruvian anthropologist Jose Matos Mar, quoted by Mitchell, has described the condition of Peru today using the 16th century as a point of reference:

> As at the time of the Reformation, the growth of literacy and the Bible put into the hands of the masses of the people ignite a new religiosity, intransigent in its evangelisation of the poor and meeting the formal structures of the church head-on, identified as these structures are with the apparatus of the State.[40]

Writing also about the 16th century, the well-known Reformed theologian and economist, Andre Bieler, who is a specialist in the social and economic dimensions of the Reformation has stated that,

> The Reformation gave the leaven of the Gospel back to the people. But this leaven no longer acted upon these tormented masses as a pious consolation justifying the injustices of the great and the oppression by the mighty, but rather as an energetic stimulant which gave to believers the courage to think and to speak the truth.[41]

The Bible in the language of the people has played a decisive role in the rise of thousands of Evangelical communities among the poor and the native peoples across Latin America. In our times, the promise of indigenous theologies is again the promise of what can happen when such theologies are a way of giving back to the people the leaven of the Gospel, when the way in which these people think their faith and their life is shaped by the Word of Jesus Christ who said: "truth will set you free".

---

[39] Lewis Hanke, *All Mankind is One,* (De Kalb, IL: Northern Illinois University Press, 1974).

[40] Mitchell, 1987, p. 129.

[41] André Biéler, *The Social Humanism of Calvin,* (Richmond, VA: John Knox Press, 1964), p. 29.

KOSUKE KOYAMA

THE ROLE OF TRANSLATION IN DEVELOPING INDIGENOUS THEOLOGIES—AN ASIAN VIEW

Thesis

One hundred sheep in the fold (completeness) does not signify universality. The image of a shepherd who seeks the one lost sheep (moving towards completeness) does. Because of this the symbol of universality has salvific meaning. How is it related to Christian theology and the translation of the Bible?

(1) Tension Between Jeremiah and Nebuchadnezzar

(A) Two languages Responding to the Hierophany:

Translators of great religious documents such as the Bible are likely to have the experience of hierophany, the manifestation of the sacred. Bible translation can be, in its depth, a mystical experience. The human spirit has responded to hierophany in two ways: with a spirituality of discontinuity (revelation) and with a spirituality of continuity (enlightenment). Revelation uses a language of surprise, enlightenment one of confirmation. The spirituality of discontinuity between "God" and humanity is expressed in the burning bush story of Moses;

> "Do not come near; put off your shoes, from your feet, for the place on which you are standing is holy ground". . . And Moses hid his face, for he was afraid to look at God. (Ex. 3:5.6)

The sacred appeared to Moses unexpectedly. So, too, Jeremiah, at the call of God, says "I do not know how to speak" (Jer. 1:6). On the cross, Jesus "cried with a loud voice, *Eloi, Eloi, lama sabachthani*? (Mk. 15:34). Muhammad was shocked and terrified when the words came to him in the cave on Mount Hira. Martin Luther speaks of *Anfechtung*. Hierophany attacks human confidence. The Semitic spiritual tradition tends to negate the continuity between hierophany and human preparedness or achievement. "The Lord sees not as man sees" (I Sam. 16:7. See also I Cor. 1:25).

With the second kind of spirituality, enlightenment spirituality, the Asian, Buddha, searched for the ultimate *dharma* (truth, reason, law, or word) that could free humanity from suffering (*dukkha*). The contents of his Enlightenment may have been the thought of Conditioned Arising (*paticcasamuppada*). Very briefly it means that from ignorance (*avijja*) comes greed (*tanha*), and from greed comes suffering (*dukkha*). This was the dharma that he finally arrived at in his meditation-concentration (*samadhi*), but at the same time, according to the ancient layer of the Buddhist text, the *dharma* revealed itself (*patubhavati*) to him. It was hierophany. Between his own good thinking and the hierophany there was a remarkable continuity (simultaneity). Experiencing this simultaneity he became confident of his Enlightenment.

I find this continuity in the center of the Buddhist tradition significant. I have noticed the same depth of continuity in the teachings of the ancient sages of China. For them the ideal life is built upon the mysterious simultaneity between necessity and freedom. In the philosophical and religious tradition of the East, the "hierophany" and the best working of human reason coincide. "The Lord sees as man sees".

Thus, human response to hierophany intimates two types of religious languages; the language of discontinuity (profound surprise, Mark, 2:17: "I came not to call the righteous, but sinners") and that of continuity (good reasoning, diagnosis and therapy, best represented by the Buddha's Four Noble Truths). In discontinuity the sacred disturbs us while in enlightenment the sacred confirms us. In Bible translation we may, on occasion, find ourselves challenged to express the message of revelation, of discontinuity, using words from the language of continuity, of enlightenment.

(B) In the Dialogue Between These Two Languages Universality is Intimated

The basic orientation of Christian theology is expressed in the primacy of discontinuity (divine grace) over continuity (human achievement). Both the Israelites and the Egyptians were stubborn. So, too, the Assyrians, the Babylonians, the Romans, . . and by implication, the Chinese and Indians, . . are stubborn people. "I have seen this people; and behold, it is a stiff-necked people" (Ex.32:9, Dt. 31:27, Mk. 3:5). "There is none that does good" (Ps. 14:1). It was by the unexpected command of God that Aaron's rod became a serpent and swallowed the serpents produced by the magicians of Egypt (Ex. 7:10-13). The outcome must have surprised both the Israelites and the Egyptians. The primacy of the discontinuity-dissimultaneity over continuity-simultaneity suggests the primacy of Will over Wisdom.

For three milleniums, through the peoples of the Bible and the Qur'an, the message of Samuel, that "the Lord sees not as man sees", has spoken to the human mind and challenged civilizations. How do we understand this discontinuity-oriented eschatological saying of the ancient seer? My understanding is that "the Lord sees not as man sees" will become meaningful to humanity when it is placed in dialogue (or in controversy) with the view which says "the Lord sees as man sees" or even "man sees as the Lord sees". When our souls ponder on personal and public morality—on political powers, economic justice, ecological restoration, distribution of wealth, world hunger, militarism, racism, sexism, and all that, we are inevitably making our own existential stance against the words of Samuel. The work of Bible translation is situated in the midst of the linguistic context of this dialogue or controversy. Samuel is always sitting on your Bible translation committee. Translation is an act of participation in this kind of universality.

The Biblical prophets had remarkably picturesque ways to present the symbol of universality as an eschatological move towards completeness. For example; Jeremiah 10:5:

> Their idols are like scarecrows in a cucumber field, and they cannot speak; they have to be carried, for they cannot walk. Be not afraid of them, for they cannot do evil, neither is it in them to do good (Jer. 10:5).

The twentieth century theologian Paul Tillich recasts Jeremiah's passage as follows:

> Idolatry is the elevation of a preliminary concern to ultimacy. Something essentially conditioned is taken as unconditional, something essentially partial is boosted into universality, and something essentially finite is given infinite significance.[1]

The focus is on idolatry. We are warned to move away from idolatry to the condition of complete spiritual and social healing. More than anything else idolatry produces "dialogue". "What we see" and "what the Lord sees" are in controversy. I am tempted to say that all human controversies originate from this particular controversy on the idols. The scale of such dialogue ranges from pious personal words to the overwhelming collective arrogance demonstrated in the massive nuclear build-up and in the realities of the global ecological crisis. No culture and language is free from idolatry. What Jeremiah says is simple, clear, and unforgettable. What "the Lord sees" and what "we see" are in a passionate dialogue-controversy focused for which Jeremiah's critical words, "they have to be carried" (See also Acts. 19:26) provide an apt metaphor. I present this observation of Jeremiah, so simple, profound and passionate—as a guide for a universal theology. For Abraham Heschel this universality is rooted in the "pathos of God".[2] Prophetic universality persuasively invites all people to discussion. The symbol of universality invites all to the dispute God initiates (See. Hos 4:1-3). We have the image of a shepherd who is on the move because one from the fold is lost.

Let me expand a bit on Jeremiah's scarecrow verse. The sight of scarecrows (we call them *kakashi*) in the rice paddy field is a familiar one for every Japanese, though traditionally we have thought of it more as being a scaresparrow than a scarecrow. The word *kakashi* might have derived from *kagu*, "to smell". Birds, people learned, are discouraged by the bad smell produced by burning animal

---

1 Paul Tillich, *Systematic Theology*, Vol. I. (London: Nisbet & Co., 1953), p. 16.

2 Abraham Joshua Heschel, *The Prophets*, (New York: Harper & Row, 1962), p. 224.

flesh in the field by the scarecrows. The *kakashi*, attired like a farmer, capped with a straw hat, stands in the midst of the rice field. It is one-legged. Nose and mouth are painted on its straw face.

The Hebrew word for scarecrow, *tomer*, means palm tree, or post. It comes from the verb that conveys the image of something erect and stiff. It does not quite give the image of the scarecrow I have in my mind. Did Jeremiah see a human shaped scarecrow? Did he smell a bad smell? How about the people who live in the Arctic Circle? Do they have scarecrows? Yet, I believe that the message of the critique of idols comes through with an astounding clarity bridging a time span of 25 centuries and cultural-linguistic barriers. The universality is not in the physical universality of scarecrows from the Arctic Circle to the Tropics, but in the ability of the truth so presented to create a fascinating way of communicating itself. If there is no airstrip for the universal truth to land on, it will make one while it is flying and land on it.

Jeremiah's universal theology goes even further to the critical core of human history and civilization. It's social ethical implication is both extensive and profound. What if someone were to insist, against Jeremiah and all good human judgment, that scarecrows "can walk" and that they "can do evil and do good?" In all human civilizations this happens repeatedly, persistently and incorrigibly in both larger and smaller scales.

> You are commanded, O peoples, nations, and languages, that when you·
> hear the sound of the horn, pipe, lyre, trigon, harp, bagpipe, and every
> kind of music, you are to fall down and worship the golden image that
> King Nebuchadnezzar has set up (Dan. 3:4.5).

Thus Jeremiah confronts Nebuchadnezzar. This is, in fact, a main theme of the the entire Bible. "We must obey God rather than men" (Acts. 5:29).

A mere human being was "boosted", with "every kind of music", to divinity in the imperial cult of Japan during the war years. In 1945 Japan was utterly destroyed for believing, as I see it, in a scarecrow. Thus the words of Jeremiah became a devastating historical reality. For me it was a historical, theological and mystical experience. It was the power of the symbol of universality that I experienced.

****

The Bible is the literature in which the two languages: that of discontinuity, "The Lord sees not as man sees" and that of continuity, "Man sees as the Lord sees", are in extensive and profound dialogue (controversy). The purpose of this dialogue is to inspire humanity to become free from the power of idolatry. This is a vision for a universal theology which derives from the nature of God presented in the Bible. There is a shepherd who goes after the one lost in idolatry. While history as we know it continues, there will be idolatry. There the shepherd will be also. This is the basic "heat"—*tapas* in Sanskrit—of human history as Christian theology understands it.

2) Theological Construction

A) The 1837 Gützlaff Translation

Let me relate my appreciation of Gützlaff's 1837 translation into Japanese of the Gospel of John to the discussion on the symbol of universality so far presented. Karl Gützlaff was a missionary-scholar of the Netherlands Mission Society. The Gospel was published in Singapore by The American Board of Commissioners for Foreign Missions. Gützlaff was aided in his work of translation by three Japanese sailors.

> In November 1831, a coasting junk of 200 tons, bound for Yeddo with tribute for the Emperor and a cargo of rice, left the port of Toba, in the principality of Sima, about a couple of hundred miles to the south-west of the capital. It was caught in a gale, dismasted, blown into the trackless expanses of the Pacific. . . . For fourteen months it drifted at the caprice of wind and current. . . . the junk was cast upon the Oregon coast, near the Columbia River. The wreck was plundered by the Indians, who kept the three as prisoners until the factor of the Hudson's Bay Company obtained their release, and took measures for their being returned to their homes. They reached England by way of the Sandwich Islands and Cape Horn; were shipped out to the care of the Superintendent of British trade in China; and in December 1835 landed at Macao, where Mr. Gützlaff took charge of them, and set himself to the task of acquiring their language and preparing a version of the New Testament.[3]

Gützlaff learned the Japanese language from them. The famous opening words in the Prologue of John's Gospel (1:1) were set down in the Japanese katakana script. The translation is fascinating for its richness of imagination and association.

> Hajimari ni kashikoimono gozaru. Kono kashikoimono gokuraku tomoni gozaru. Kono kashikoimono wa gokuraku.

There is a profound spiritual and theological connection of these opening words of John's Gospel with the word of Jeremiah warning of idolatry. A look at some of the Japanese words used in this translation will bring out their original meanings from which the modern usages have come and help us to see this connection.

---

[3] William Canton, *A History of the British and Foreign Bible Society*, Vol. II, (London: John Murray, Albemarle Street, W., 1904), p. 393f.

The word *hajimari* [*hajime*], beginning, tends to mean one *hajime* among many *hajime*[s]. "Everything has *hajime* and *owari* [end]" says a well-known Japanese proverb. Even when the concept of "the" *hajime* is carefully presented, it may not suggest a sense of critical urgency to the Japanese people. In the colloquial translation published in 1955, we read *hajimeni*. The translation used before 1955 also reads *hajimeni*, specifically indicating that the meaning is "in the great beginning" by the use of a certain Chinese character. But "the great beginning" is not necessarily able to introduce the quality of eschatological surprise into the Japanese language, since Chinese cosmological speculation from ancient times makes "the great beginning" the primary principle as in I–Ching, the Book of Changes. How, we must ask, can cosmological words (continuity) be made to speak an eschatological message (discontinuity)?

The Japanese word, *kashikoimono*, is used by Gützlaff for *logos*, "The Word". *Mono* means all that which is tangible to us as things are [tea cups, umbrellas]. When one wants to speak something in general, prefering not to make it clear, that something is called *mono*. "I have eaten some *mono*". *Mono* does not suggest the changes that take place in the course of time because *mono* does not contain a sense of time. Thus, it has come to refer to that which is unchangeable and inevitable, hence, fearful. Fearful objects may be demons, unpacified departed spirits, and all kinds of evil beings. When an unpacified departed spirit possesses a person, that person is said to be *mono noke*, [*noke* meaning "under the influence of"]. Such possession can be fatal. A view which is culturally and theologically important is suggested here, namely, that that which is inevitable is fearful.

Kashikoimono means one who is wise and should be approached with a sense of awe and veneration [*kashikoshi*]. The original meaning of *kashikoshi* was the fear that the ancient Japanese felt for the overwhelming and uncanny powers of the spirits dwelling in the sea, mountains, mountain paths, rocks, wind, and thunder. From this animistic fear of natural forces, *kashikoshi* began also to include persons who have similar power. So, in applying the concept to *logos* it is "something that is wise which arouses the sense of awe in the human mind".

This *kashikoimono* was with *gokuraku*. For the Japanese, *gokuraku* means paradise. (Literally, in the Chinese characters, "extremely [*goku*] pleasurable [*raku*]". It signifies the *jodo*, "pure land" [*sukhavati*] of Japanese Jodo Buddhism of the thirteenth century represented by the monks Honen and Shinran). "God" is translated as "Paradise". This *logos* [*kashikoimono*] is with paradise [*gokuraku*].

Japanese word for god or gods is *kami*. The Japanese classic scholar Motoori Nobunaga (1730-1801) writes about *kami*:

> It is hardly necessary to say that it includes human beings. It also includes such objects as birds, beasts, trees, plants, seas, mountains and so forth. In ancient usage, anything whatsoever which was outside the ordinary, which possessed superior power or which was awe-inspiring was called *kami*. Eminence here does not refer merely to the superiority

of nobility, goodness or meritous deed. Evil and mysterious things, if they are extraordinary and dreadful, are called *kami*.[4]

The three Japanese helpers must have known the word *kami*, yet the word *gokuraku* was chosen. With this choice of word, the translation adopted the word which is full of the emotional and intellectual contents of Mahayana Pure Land Buddhism.

Kashikoimono, on the other hand, carries animistic overtones. It is on the side of the Way of Kami, Shinto. Thus the translation presents the *logos* with animistic, and the *theos* with Buddhistic connotations. The 1837 Gützlaff translation of the beginning of John's Gospel brings together the two streams of religious thought and emotion of the Japanese people. The gospel brings the animistic outlook of human life and the Mahayana doctrine of the *summum bonum* together in order to present itself to its audience. The situation is as complicated as it is dynamic. In my view, however, it is not exceptional. Bible translation always encounters linguistic and cultural situations in which "other" traditions are called in. These situations point us to the importance and the creative possibility in the symbol of universality.

Questions

a) Cosmological and eschatological languages

The human mind is blessed with the ability to create a syntax with which eschatological meaning can be suggested through the use of everyday words. This can happen because we have the spiritual and mental capacities of imagination and association. Cosmological language can intimate an eschatological message.

> Who makes the sun rise on the evil and on the good, and sends rain on the just and on the unjust (Mt. 5:45).

> Why do you see the speck that is in your brother's eye, but do not notice the log that is in your own eye? (Mt. 7:3).

An unforgettable verse from the Qur'an reads:

> We indeed created man; and We know what his soul whispers within him, and We are nearer to him than the jugular vein (Qaf. 15).

---

4 H. Byron Earhart, comp., *Religion in the Japanese Experience: Sources and Interpretations*, (Encino, CA: Dickenson Publishing Co., 1974), p. 10.

It is important to notice that these sayings contain a sharp edge of judgment upon human life. They are not easy words to hear (Jn. 6:60). They are against idolatry. True eschatology criticizes idolatry.

It is in the world of human language that idolatry first originates. The false god (*molok*) skillfully propagates its own eschatology of self-aggrandizement creating pseudo syntaxes. It is not just by accident that the proclamation of Nebuchadnezzar begins with the call; "O, peoples, nations and languages, . . "

b) The logos as "the wisdom which evokes awe"

This combination of wisdom and awe reminds us of the rich religious and philosophical traditions associated with such inspiring Asian names as the Buddha, Confucius and Prince Shotoku. Such wisdom contains uncommon depth. Can this wisdom-depth become "eschatological" (dis-simultaneous, discontinuous)? What is the theological value in the religious world of simultaneity and continuity?

Confronted by such a question, the meaning of the Greek word *logos* placed in the context of John 1:1 will expand. When the Vatican Council II (1962-65) affirmed the presence of the goodness of God in other religions[5] the Catholic Church effectively initiated a discussion of the meaning of *logos* in the context of humanity's religious life in the twentieth century.Vatican II was more positive about "other religions" even than the famous words of the Indian Christian mystic Sundar Singh (1889-1929) who said, "Christianity is the fulfilment of Hinduism. Hinduism has been digging channels. Christ is the water to flow through these channels".[6]

To reject "Asia's Wisdom" would be an act of self-idolatry on the part of the Church. If the Semitic transcendence is vertical transcendence, Asia's could be called horizontal transcendence. Both have the dimension of transcendence. When the vertical transcendence engages in dialogue with the horizontal transcendence, we may come to a new appreciation of the symbol of universality.

c) The presence of the awe

In the 1955 Japanese translation of John 1:1 the *logos* is *kotoba*, the word. *Kotaba* comes from *koto* which meant simultaneously both word (what is spoken) and event (what happened). Gradually, however, a separation took place between word and event. *Koto* remained to signify event, while *kotoba* appeared to mean speech. Sometimes *kotoba* meant "words only" apart form the question of a person's sincerity. Here *kotoba* is placed in opposition to *kokoro* or sincere

---

5 *Declaration on the Relation of the Church to Non-Christians*, #2, October 1965.

6 Robin H. Boyd, *An Introduction to Indian Christian Theology*, (Madras: Christian Literature Society, 1975), p. 107.

heart. *Kotoba* does not convey the feeling of awesomeness. It no longer suggests the unity of word and event. William Temple says that the original intention of the Evangelist in the Prologue was to communicate the idea that "in the beginning was the Messiah . . .". If so, *kashikoimono* comes relatively closer to the mind of John than *kotoba*. Yet, *kashikoimono*, cannot be used today. It is not in popular use today. I have noticed that, in a subtle change, the Catholic-Protestant joint translation (1980) replaces *kotoba* with *mikotoba*. *Mi*, like the Thai *pra*, is a prefix meaning excellent and sacred. Thus the Japanese *mikotoba* or "sacred word" would correspond to the Thai *pra-tham* [*dharma*] or sacred law used in the 1977 Thai colloquial translation of John's prologue. Does this succeed in avoiding or controlling the suggestion of insincerity attached to the word *kotaba* (*logos*)?

Whatever word is used, it must not convey insincerity. Originally, *Koto* meant simultaneously word and event, sincerity demonstrated in action. Does the English word "Word" have clear social ethical connotation for us today? What is the relationship between social responsibility and the presence of someone who is wise and to be awed? Liberation theology is concerned about the social ethical meaning of the *kotaba* which was in the beginning. The *kotaba* of redemption in isolation from the word of social justice can produce idolatry (Mt. 7:21).

d) Paradise for God

Why was the Greek New Testament word *theos* translated by Gützlaff as "paradise"? The intellectually alert and culturally sensitive sixteenth century Jesuit mission in Japan decided, after making many attempts, including the disastrous one of *Dainichi* [Mayahana Buddhism's metaphysical solar Buddha], that the Latin word *deus* was safest to designate Christianity's God in the religious and cultural world of Japan.

Gützlaff's use of the word "paradise" for God must have placed the Christian gospel in the very proximity of the spiritual life of the Japanese people at that time. Gokuraku was the central religious word that could nearly summarize the totality of religious thought and emotion. With the word Gokuraku in 1837 Gützlaff began a Christian-Buddhist dialogue! Will this Mahayananize the Christian gospel or Christianize the Mahayana message?

The Burmese theologian Khin Maung Din writes,

> Presentation of biblical stories in the cultural style of Burmese drama, dressing up of the Nativity Scene in Burmese costumes, use of indigenous musical instruments and melodies for religious hymns and songs, etc., were merely attempts to put the gospel wine into Burmese cultural bottles. . . But to me, the basic theological problem for Burmese Christian theology is not that which is concerned with "the bottle", but that which concerns the "wine" itself. The gospel must not only be understood in a Burmese way, but the Burmese and Buddhist understanding

of Man, Nature, and Ultimate Reality must also become inclusive as a
vital component in the overall content of the gospel.[7]

Is the Bible translation a matter of "bottle" only, or does it touch on the "wine"
itself? In the Chinese translation of the Bible, Chinese language which carries
the Chinese meaning of "Man, Nature and Ultimate Reality" is used. In that
sense the translation inevitably touches upon the wine. This translation situation
is different from making the Chinese understanding of "Man, Nature and
Ultimate Reality a vital component in the overall content of the gospel". In
theology, not in Bible translation, we can do what Din proposes. But this
general statement must be examined very carefully. Stanley Samartha writes,

> Just because it was a "scandal" to the Jews and a "stumbling block" to
> the Greeks in Paul's time, it is foolish to insist that it ought to be a
> skandalon to all Hindus and Buddhists.[8]

This comment is directed, not to the bottle, but to the wine of the gospel. Bible
translation sits in the front row of the bottle-wine discussion because it provides
the fundamental tool for such theological reflection.

e) Gokuraku is not a native concept to Japan

Kono kashikoimono was *gokuraku*. Is this indigenous theology? The concept of
gokuraku was not native to Japan. They came from the advanced civilizations of
India and China. In that sense we cannot say this translation, though refreshing,
contributed to the building up of indigenous theology. What does indigenous
theology mean?

B) Indigenous Theology

In terms of culture and language only the Palestine of Jesus' time may have had
the possibility of creating an indigenous Christian theology. But even the gospel
narratives as they have come down to us in the Bible are more of an international
and intercultural creation already in their earliest possible stage of development
than we may unwarrantedly think. The New Testament uses such current
religious words as *logos, soter, mysteria, metamorphosis*.[9] The apostle Paul

---

[7] Douglas J. Elwood, ed., *What Asian Christians are Thinking: A Theological Source
Book,* (Quezon City: New Day Publishers, 1976), p. 88ff.

[8] Gerald H. Anderson and Thomas F. Stransky, eds., *Christ's Lordship and Religious
Pluralism,* (Maryknoll, NY: Orbis Books, 1981), p. 25.

[9] Visser't Hooft, "Accommodation True or False" *The South East Asia Journal of
Theology,* Jan. 1967.

spoke both Greek and Hebrew (Act. 21:37-40). Any simplistic idea that once there was an intact ("chemically pure"—as H.R. Schlette calls it) indigenous theology functioning in a neatly packaged culture and that all troubles began after the gospel left its homeland is not acceptable. In the minds of Jesus and Paul, and their audiences "Bible translation" was already going on. The process of accommodation or contextualization is as old as the apostolic preaching itself.

What the expression "indigenous theology" means may be better suggested by such adjectives as "accommodated" or "contextualized". The gospel must be accommodated to a given language in order to speak sensibly to the people who live in that culture. In our reflection on "Christ and Culture" the images of accommodation and contextualization seem to be more promising than that of indigenity. In fact, the name "indigenous theology" given by the Western theologians to Asian and African theologies has a smack of Eurocentered parochialism.

Ultimately the gospel is indigenous only to Jesus of Nazareth or, doctrinally put, to the Holy Trinity. This is the primary theological sense of indigenity. But this indigenity is shared with us. "The Word became flesh and dwelt among us" (Jn. 1:14). This is the gospel of God's self-giving. This sharing is pointed to in the symbol of universality. So the indigenity is shared in the most intimate and universal way.

> Glory to God in the highest, and on earth peace among men with whom he is pleased (Lk. 2:14).

Geoffrey Wainwright writes:

> Wherever self-giving love is shown by a human being in any degree at all, God must be said to be present in the transformation of human character into God's own moral and spiritual likeness. There redemption is happening, as people are being set free from self-regard and self-interest.[10]

I understand the word "indigenous" of indigenous theology this way. If a well accommodated or contextualized theology did not inspire us to demonstrate self-giving love, what use is it?

What if the gospel began to speak competently in the local cultural language, to the extent of distinguishing "cucumber field" from "melon patch", if not love (I Cor. 13:1-3)? We are called to accommodate and contextualize the gospel. The reason for this is the sharing of the Self-hood of God, the ultimate indigenity.

---

[10] Geoffrey Wainwright, *Doxology: The Praise of God in Worship, Doctrine, and Life: A Systematic Theology,* (New York: Oxford University Press, 1980), p. 68ff.

C) *Casting Out the Dumb Spirit*

On the basis of this understanding of the theological meaning of indigenity, I would like to think about the theme of "casting out the dumb spirit" (Mk. 9:14-29). Can we see the purpose and meaning of the Christian gospel as "casting out the dumb spirit?" This would be a dramatic expression of universality, "the move toward completeness". Is this the "indigenous" concern of God of the Bible? The word of God is against the dumb spirit that makes us to trust in lifeless scarecrows, forces us to fall down before the image that Nebuchadnezzar sets up, and instigates in us a spirit that would boost the relative to the absolute.

Mark places the story of the healing of an epileptic boy almost immediately after the transfiguration of Jesus at which Moses and Elijah appear. The indigenous glory of Jesus Christ manifested at the moment of transfiguration was reenacted in this world of humanity exemplified by the agonizing sickness that inflicted a boy. What a despairing distance from the *gokuraku*!

The saviour figure coming down from the mountain to the world below which is full of human miseries has been an inspiring Mahayana Buddhism theme. Great painters were inspired by this theme, which is called in Japanese *Shutsusan Shaka*. Gotama Siddhattha comes out of the mountain after realizing the futility of the way of self-mortification to achieve enlightenment. The emotional impact of the painting is that of the saviour figure coming down from the mountain to save suffering humanity. His hands are half hidden by the wornout robe he wears. The half hidden [hence, half revealed] hand is a symbol for the simultaneity of continuity-simultaneity that should engage in dialogue with the Semitic universality of discontinuity-dissimultaneity.

> "Master, it is well that we are here; let us make three booths, one for you and one for Moses and one for Elijah". For he did not know what to say, for they were exceedingly afraid (Mk. 9:5,6).

The glory seized Peter. He "did not know what to say". The dumb spirit seized the boy. The boy could not speak. The two could not speak for different reasons. Theology must be aware of these similarity and dissimilarity.

> Whenever it/the dumb spirit/seizes him, it dashes him down; and he foams and grinds his teeth and becomes rigid.

It is *mungo* [dumb] *atma* [spirit] that does this violent seizure (in Gujarati). *Chiwanda*, harmful spirit, does it (in Chichewa, the national language of Malawi). Chiwanda is *pneuma akatharton* because it separates persons from God and the community. Spirit is invisible and it is extremely mobile, like wind. Evil spirit (*ashuddha atma*, unclean spirit [Gujarati]; *muzimu oipa*, bad spirit [Chichewa]; *aku rei*, evil spirit; *kegareta rei*, unclean spirit [Japanese]) possesses people. The New Testament does not present situations in which good spirit possesses people as the evil spirit does. Instead there is the command of Jesus;

"You dumb and dead spirit, I command you, come out of him, and never enter him again". Then, from the father of the boy comes one of the most memorable words in the New Testament, "I believe; help my unbelief!" ("I do believe. If my faith is not enough, help me" *The Translator's New Testament.*)

The response of the father is fitting for the crisis we experience in the depths of our own soul, and in the depth of the language we speak. Even when we say "we believe" we are very much aware of our unbelief. This is paradoxical and scandalous (I Cor. 1:20-25). The paradox belongs to the image of universality I am presenting.

****

Bible translation is a participation in God's act of sharing God's indigenous glory with humanity. Theology that speaks about this ongoing sharing is a universal theology. This theology keeps humanity aware of idolatry.

LOUIS J. LUZBETAK

CONTEXTUAL TRANSLATION:
THE ROLE OF CULTURAL ANTHROPOLOGY

At this conference we are discussing the spread of the Church through the instrumentality of translation, especially during the last 200 years. I would like to limit my observations to *the role of culture* in translation and to show how *cultural anthropology* might help the translator in this important dimension of his or her work.

Contextual Translation: What It Is

What do we mean by contextual translation? Let us for a moment say that we are somewhere in the North of Ghana, among the Dangombas, and that we would like to thank someone. The Dangombas, we are told, do not have a word for "Thank you". So, what do we do? Most likely we would just go ahead and coin a word ourselves, one that would be more or less what we are trying to say, something more or less the equivalent of what we Western native speakers of English understand by "Thank you", perhaps something like "I wish to acknowledge your goodness" or "I greatly value your kindness". The only trouble with this solution is that it is not a solution at all; we are overlooking an extremely important presupposition of the Dangomban traditional world-view. These Africans, as a rule, do not think in terms of generosity, kindness, or goodness; rather, they express their appreciation in terms of duty. But this is precisely the difficulty: whatever is done out of a sense of duty—that is to say, whatever is *expected*—does not call for a thank you. (There seems to be some logic in this manner of thinking. Sometimes we think in these terms ourselves. At least I can't remember a traffic policeman ever thanking me for not driving through a red light.) The Dangombas might, in fact, be offended if we expressed our appreciation to them for what is expected of any and every decent individual, as if we were implying that the people we happen to be thanking were not respectable individuals. The harmonious family cooperation, so thoroughly human, is viewed by these people as being basically a fulfillment of a duty or of an implied contract with one's social group, and therefore an expression of gratitude would be out of place here. In fact, according to this deeply duty-conscious culture, God's gratuitous love would be difficult to grasp, for gratuitous love, especially such as was Christ's death on the cross, might even suggest gullibility and weakness on the part of God instead of what the cross really was, the absolute proof of God's infinite love, wisdom, power, and supreme victory—anything but gullibility and weakness. This duty-conscious mentality—this particular cultural context—whether we agree with it or not, must not be overlooked when we try to translate verbally or nonverbally the simple English "Thank you!" (or anything else for that matter) into the language, and especially the *world*, of the Dangombas.[1] This, I think, would be a good example of *inculturating* or *contextualizing* a translation.

The sacred writers always had very definite audiences in mind. What is important is that these audiences had specific *social and cultural* identities—social and cultural identities through which the sacred writers' message would be filtered, interpreted, and understood. Sacred writers wrote also with specific goals in mind: that is, they wanted to provide specific information; they wanted to arouse certain emotions; and they wanted to stimulate their audiences to a particular form of action. In a word, the sacred writers were deeply concerned about their message having a specific, largely *culturally conditioned* cognitive, emotive, and motivational impact. This nonlinguistic largely culturally conditioned impact on today's translators, despite the cultural filtering that this meaning first goes through in the *translator's* mind, must now as much as possible be expressed in terms of possibly a third culture, one perhaps different from that of the translator, namely, the culture of the society into whose language the translation is being made. (Where this cannot be satisfactorily accomplished, an occasional marginal comment may, and at times must, be added). In other words, a Bible translation must very often take at least three different cultural contexts into account. In a word, what I am saying is that good translations are always highly contextual translations.

Consequently, translators must be veritable circus jugglers. Having tossed not one but several cultures into the air, they must now concentrate simultaneously on whatever they tossed up—the particular biblical culture, the culture of the readers of the translation, and the translators' own culture. Translations, like all communication, are deeply imbedded in cultural presuppositions.

Much of what I am saying about Bible translation holds, of course, also for other types of translation, which have made the Church what it is today. As we all know, Christian churches today are greatly dependent on translation. Besides Bible translation, the Church needs a considerable amount of translation as a worshipping People of God in its liturgies and rituals. The Church needs translation to carry out its role as religious and moral leader. The local churches need translation to be able to share their experiences and growth with one another and to transmit their religious and moral message across generations and other subcultural boundaries. The Church with its thousands and thousands of schools under its direction at every level from kindergarten to universities, needs translation to carry out its role as teacher of humanity and as promoter of cultural growth and development. The Church needs translation in connection with its countless socioeconomic programs. The best medicine and food comes

---

[1] The problem of expressing gratitude among the Dangombas was discussed in the newsletter of the Tamale Institute of Cross-Cultural Studies (Tamale, Ghana), September 1988, pp. 4-5.

packaged in the form of education, and education is basically culture learning, largely across cultures.

At one time, the quality of a Bible translation was judged in no small measure by its faithfulness to the *form* of the message being translated—that is, by its faithfulness to such things as its literalness, its closeness to the original grammatical structure, its adherence to the original style and idiom, and the like. Today, the main emphasis in all translation work, biblical and otherwise, is clearly and rightly placed on *content* (on *meaning*); and of concern is not only linguistic meaning but also the important meaning hidden in the nonlinguistic background—particularly in the implied *cultural* context, in the countless cultural presuppositions hidden in words. The translators today must be keenly aware of and constantly attuned to these various cultural contexts in order that they themselves do not misunderstand the original message and impact and that they tailor their translated message as much as possible to the cultural context of *their* particular audience. A good Bible translator is, therefore, not so much a walking biblical encyclopedia as an individual who has somehow acquired a sixth sense, an individual who has been *sensitized* to culture as such—and I want to stress the word *sensitized*. This is precisely where cultural anthropology comes into the picture—it enters into the process of cultural sensitization. We come, therefore to our second question: What is the role of cultural anthropology in translation?

The Role of Cultural Anthropology in Translation

By no means do I wish to suggest that culture is the sole source of translation problems, or that translation calls for anthropologists rather than linguists. Languages, as we all know, are themselves complex networks of enigmas, even if language is that particular aspect of culture that has been most thoroughly studied, and even if, as in the case of Bible translation, the translator can actually be overwhelmed with translation aids. Superb Hebrew, Greek, and other dictionaries are now available. Today, there are whole libraries of commentaries, concordances, archaeological handbooks, biblical encyclopedias, and translation guides at our disposal. Nor by stressing culture am I overlooking the psychological and noncultural situational factors that come into play.[2] In fact, as I speak to you, I am very much aware of my own possible cultural anthropological bias, since cultural anthropology happens to be my field.

This reminds me of an old comic strip I used to enjoy very much in my younger days. I know this is going to date me, but in this connection I cannot help being reminded of how one dark night Mutt found his good friend Jeff crawling on his hands and knees under the corner streetlight furiously looking for

---

2 For an excellent treatment of such factors, see especially Eugene A. Nida and William D. Reyburn, *Meaning Across Cultures* (Maryknoll, NY: Orbis Books, 1981) and Charles H. Kraft, *Communication Theory for Christian Witness* (Nashville, TN: Abingdon Press, 1983).

a quarter he had lost about halfway down the block. (At that time a quarter evidently was worth a quarter.) Mutt, unable to contain his curiosity, asks Jeff, "Why in the world are you looking for your quarter *here* if you know you dropped it somewhere in the *middle* of the block?" In his inimitable way Jeff looks up and says, "Can't you see, dummy? This is where the darn city put up the streetlight".

Anthropology is where *my* light happens to be located, but that is not why I am suggesting you look there. Culture *is* indeed where many, if not most, translation problems (especially biblical problems) lie and where many, if not most, of our solutions *should* be sought. Speaking of cross-cultural problems that missionaries have had to face from time immemorial, David Hesselgrave[3] was right on the mark when he observed that it has not been the long arduous distances between homeland and mission that have been the most difficult for missionaries—no, not the first 10,000 miles of their missionary journey but the last eighteen inches. Like missionary work, translation is *cross-cultural* communication, and culture becomes a problem the moment we come within an arm's length of our task as translators. A good missionary is a culturally sensitive missionary, and the same holds for a good translator. *The best translators, like the best evangelizers, are not necessarily the best preachers and orators who know their language and their Bible, but such who are at the same time the best listeners*. Translators must know how to listen to the cultures that they as translators are juggling in their particular act, not least important of which is their own culture and that of the society into whose language the translation is being made. I like the observation of the Greek philosopher Epictetus, who wisely observed that God gave us two ears and only one mouth so that we would listen twice as much as we would speak. Wise ol' chap, that Epictetus! And excellent advice indeed he has for translators! The answer to the question we posed a moment ago regarding the role of cultural anthropology in translation is this: *Cultural anthropology teaches the translator how to listen to cultures*. It does not so much fill the translator's head with a lot of specific ethnographic details about specific cultures (although that too can be helpful) but rather cultural anthropology *sensitizes* the translator's eyes, mind, and heart to cultural presuppositions.

In cold terms, to be able to listen to cultures, in a word, to be sensitized to cultures, one must understand (1) what culture is; (2) how culture is organized; and (3) how culture operates. To be culturally sensitized, the translator must know at least the basics of the nature, structure, and dynamics of culture.

---

[3] David J. Hesselgrave, *Communicating Christ Cross-Culturally: An Introduction to Missionary Communication* (Grand Rapids, MI: Zondervan, 1978), p. 69.

1) The Nature of Culture

It is quite true that there is much that anthropology cannot tell us about culture, but as Alfred L. Kroeber, one of the leading anthropologists of his time, pointed out almost forty years ago: "The most significant accomplishment of anthropology in the first half of the twentieth century was the extension and clarification of the concept of culture".[4] Since Kroeber's time, you can be certain, anthropology has not just stood still; the extension and clarification of the concept of culture from various perspectives has been going on and is still going on. During Kroeber's time, anthropologists were greatly interested in finding a suitable definition for their extremely complex concept, and Kroeber and Kluckhohn in their search for such an ideal definition merely found out that at the time there were no less than several hundred definitions in use in anthropological literature.[5]

Today in many fields, including anthropology and theology, emphasis is being placed not so much on essential definitions as on models. Instead of trying to define in one concise sentence the essence of complicated realities, today we are using models more and more such as the concept of *Church* and the concept of *culture*.[6] Reality is being looked at from a very definite perspective and is being described by means of a simplified analogy or rough draft, rough but effectively capable of calling up useful, fitting and stimulating images. A model, we are saying, is something between an abstraction and a reality. For instance, a map could be called a model; so could a diagram, a drawing, a picture, a three-dimensional miniature, a mathematical symbol, a chemical formula or molecular model, or even a word or statement. A model is basically an analogy around which inquiry can be usefully and effectively organized and described. A model is something to be taken seriously but not literally. Nor is a model presented as the final word but rather as a statement inviting challenge, inviting supplementary detail, and perhaps even correction—in a word, as something open to ever further refinement. A model, we are saying, has the advantage of proceeding pedagogically from the known to the unknown. In fact, a good model often dramatizes the implications of the analogy in question. Paul, for instance, used the most familiar bit of reality known of human beings, their own bodies, to describe the extremely complex notion of the Church (Eph 4:1-13; 1 Cor 12). To this day, Paul's analogy continues to stimulate theological thought and to

---

4 Alfred L. Kroeber, "Anthropology," *Scientific American* Vol. 183 (1950), p. 87.

5 Alfred L. Kroeber and Clyde Kluckhohn. 1952. "A Critical Review of Concepts and Definitions", in *Papers of the Peabody Museum of American Archaeology and Ethnology* , p. 149.

6 The major topics discussed in the present paper are treated fully in the author's new *Church and Cultures: New Perspectives in Missiological Anthropology* (Maryknoll, NY: Orbis Books, 1988). For the meaning and usefulness of models, see pp. 135-137.

A recent work on the cultural factors in translation is R. Daniel Shaw's *Transculturation: The Culture Factor in Translation and Other Communication Tasks* (Pasadena, CA: William Carey Library, 1988).

open new vistas to further theological investigation into the organic nature of the Church, the close interdependence of its members, their relation to the Father through their relationship as limbs to Christ their Head and to the Holy Spirit, the common Life of the entire Body.

Not all models or perspectives of culture are equally suitable, or perhaps even usable, as far as translators are concerned. The model of culture that will sensitize the translator to culture will, first of all, have to be *holistic*, that is, it must be able to deal with our total humanness, able to deal with our physical, social, and spiritual wholeness. The model I am speaking about—the kind that sensitizes—will also be *emic*—a term taken from the linguistic term *phonemic* in contradistinction to *phonetic*, a term invented by Dr. Kenneth Pike, known, I am sure, to most of us. By *emic* we mean that our model will enable the translator to *feel* the organization of culture as much as possible from the *inside*, the way the community whose culture is being translated and the community into whose language the translation is being made do. The model I am speaking about should be able, above all, to reveal the systematic structure of culture and especially a people's "soul", the deepest cognitive, emotive, and motivational aspects of culture.[7] The model I am speaking about will have to be able to deal with social change since culture is never still, unless, of course, it is dead—but the translator's target society as well as his or her own culture, the translator's main source of bias, are anything but dead: the cultural model that can sensitize the translator to culture will necessarily be a highly dynamic model, as dynamic as culture really is.[8]

I don't intend to bore you with a description of the various models as found in current anthropology. (I wouldn't have enough time to do that even if I were malicious, and foolish, enough to try.) Let me merely suggest that no single model of culture is able by itself to do the job, whether it be the old or the updated version of functionalism, a perspective that uses a living organism as a model of culture, much like Paul's model of the Church; or whether our model is that of cognitive anthropology (also called ethnoscience and new ethnography), which uses language as analogue, making culture itself into a society's body of knowledge; or whether the model is that of symbolic or semiotic anthropology, which views culture as a very complex and busy communication network that sends messages along vast and elaborate interconnected routes following complex but definite rules of the road, making culture itself into a complex symbolic system; or whether we use some other model or current anthropology.

What is needed, therefore, is a *composite* model—an interlacing of a dominant or pivotal perspective of culture with supplementary submodels taken from current anthropological theory. What I am suggesting is that, over our preferred pivotal model, whichever we chose, we place lesser complementary models that, like transparencies, will provide the necessary supplementary details to balance off and correct our preferred dominant perspective.

[7] Luzbetak, op. cit., pp. 223-291.

[8] Luzbetak, op. cit., pp. 292-373.

My own preferred understanding of culture is that culture is a society's design for living.[9] Culture is all that we learn from our society. Culture is a society's design, plan, or code of and for behavior. Culture is, therefore, in reality a set of ideas; it does not consist of persons, things, events, or actual behavior but rather of norms, standards, notions, beliefs, and values *about* persons, things, events, and behavior. Culture is like a cabinetmaker's drawings of and for a piece of furniture, that is, it is a concept of a piece of furniture, not the actual finished product, unless the latter itself serves as a model and thereby becomes a concept. Culture is a drawing of something that exists and a drawing *for* something that does not yet exist. Because culture is a set of ideas, one can quite justifiably call culture society's body of knowledge and a people's symbolic system.

2) The Organization of Culture

Going beyond the nature of culture and entering into the second major area of cultural anthropology that will help sensitize the translator to cultural presuppositions, we come to the organization of cultures. Cultures are *systems*. They are not a heap of odds and ends; cultures are uniquely organized into subsystems and these into subsubsystem, one part uniquely interwebbed with other parts into a more or less single consistent whole. (I say "more or less" because there can be a considerable amount of inconsistency, gear grinding, and dysfunction in culture. In fact, cultures can disintegrate and die.[10])

Let us take a closer look at the organization of culture. This is important. As Blaise Pascal put it: "I find as impossible to know the parts without knowing the whole as to know the whole without specifically knowing the parts". Or as someone else put it in simpler terms: "You can never do merely one thing". That is how culture must be looked at by the translator—as an integrated whole. (You cannot, for instance, bring about a truly worthwhile economic change without dealing with the whole culture and with culture as a whole.) To be sensitized to any other type of culture is to be sensitized to something that does not exist.

At the surface level are the *forms* or "shapes" of the particular way of life, the signs or symbols minus their meanings, the building blocks of culture, the *who*, *what*, *when*, where and *what kind*. Even if these forms as forms are not unique in the strict sense of the term, they are uniquely structured at the second and third levels—at the level of immediate meanings, purposeful or logical interrelationships and presuppositions, at the level of immediate *whys*, as well as at the deepest level, that of the *starting points* of thinking, of reacting emotionally, and of motivating, that of a people's underlying premises,

---

[9] Luzbetak, op. cit., pp. 156-159; 166-172; 181-192; 223-373.

[10] Luzbetak, op. cit., pp. 316-321.

fundamental attitudes or values, and basic goals and drives—at the level of the society's unique world-view.[11]

Every normal human individual learns not one but two languages—a spoken language and a "silent language". We are "speaking" all day long even if we do not utter a single sound. How I stand, how I sit, how I walk, how and when I smile, how I close a door, how I dress, what tone of voice I use, yes, almost whatever I do, I am communicating in my silent language.[12] What is of importance to a translator is the fact that the spoken language presupposes the silent language. Most of the cultural presuppositions we have been referring to lie precisely here in the meanings of the silent language.

Let me try to explain and illustrate what I mean by the *second level* of culture, the immediate *whys* of behavior. The forms are tied to one another by purposeful, logical, and other relationships. To understand what, for instance, "clothing" means, we have to understand the linkages that a body-covering has in the particular culture. The word *clothing* does not mean the same in Alaska as it does among the Bushmen of Africa or here in New Jersey, because the relationships between clothing and the rest of culture differ from culture to culture.

To understand the meaning of clothing, we must know what in this particular culture the *reasons* are for covering the body; what the *uses* for clothing happen to be; what clothing *presupposes* (clothing presupposes for instance, money, materials, techniques, tailors, stores). To know the meaning of "clothing", we must know what *needs* clothing fills (needs like protection against the cold or the desert wind); what clothing is *associated* with, (a religion, occupation, or responsibility); what the *repercussions* are in the given society if clothing is not worn—and we might go on and on with such categories of purposeful, purely logical, and other relationships that give meaning and value to the various elements of culture.

In the United States, *clothing* means a covering for the body to deal with the inclemency of the weather; clothing is used for the purpose of modesty, and to respect others. (You recall what happened to the man in the Gospel who came to the wedding feast without his wedding garment. Something similar may happen to you if you enter certain restaurants without a coat and tie—and in most restaurants in the United States if you come in barefooted.) Clothing is used to tell everyone that I am a man or a woman. It tells everyone who understands my silent language that I am wealthy or poor, that I have good or bad taste, or that I am a hobo. By my clothing I tell everyone that my occupation is that of a bus driver, bellhop, chef, a nurse, or circus clown. It tells everyone that I am an altar boy or a member of the church choir, a girl scout, a bride or groom. My clothing, as a kind of word in my silent language, tells everyone that I have the special responsibility of a policeman, a judge, or a metermaid. But cultures

---

[11] Luzbetak, op. cit., pp. 252-263.

[12] Edward T. Hall, *The Silent Language* (Garden City, NY: Doubleday, 1959); *Beyond Culture* (Garden City, NY: Doubleday, 1976).

speak not only through *purposeful linkages* as in the examples I have just given, but through other relationships such as *repercussions*. In our culture, anyone who fails to wear clothing ends up in an insane asylum or will be locked up in the local county jail for indecent exposure. Cultural patterns, whether in the spoken or unspoken language, carry meaning also through *association*. For instance, clothing is associated with the particular occupation of a person, telling everyone that I am a termite exterminator, a chimney sweep, or a TWA flight attendant, a Culligan man or a lonely Maytag repair man, who is never called upon to repair the "breakproof" home appliance he represents. Clothing is associated with religion, as in the case of a ritual vestment or the yarmulka, or as the distinctive dress of the Amish or some other religious group. Clothing tells everyone that I am a prisoner of war, that I am a baseball player, jogger, a general, a captain of a ship, a scuba diver, or a lion trainer. Or clothing may tell everyone who understands my silent language that a couple is going to an opera, a wedding, a formal ball, or a fancy restaurant.

Cultural patterns are very much like words, sentences, and paragraphs: they are uniquely structured and carry unique meanings in both the spoken and silent language. If you put together all the prerequisites, reasons for, associations, purposes, and values of clothing, and if you bring together all that clothing is the result of, is responsible for, is the occasion for, all the needs it fills, all the tasks it performs, all that it encourages, all the roles it plays, all that it ensures, all that it triggers, all that it evokes, expresses, or suggests, or any other relationship it has in the given culture, you are on your way to understanding the meaning of the word *clothing* in a particular language and culture. If you do not bother about such cultural linkages in the given culture, you do not fully understand what the word *clothing* means here and now. Native speakers may not be able to articulate all such relationships, but they *feel* them the way one feels grammatical rules even when one is unable to articulate them.

The value of anything in a culture varies from item to item and from culture to culture. Its value depends largely on what relationships it has within the cultural system. To be sensitive to a culture means to be sensitive to the unique values of the culture. We do not understand, for instance, what *polygamy* in a particular tribe in Africa or the Pacific means unless we know how plural marriages are related here and now to such other culture patterns as prestige, tribal friendhip, interfamily obligations, wealth, family work, comfort, animal husbandry, feuding, tribal loyalty, ancestor worship, social security for widows, and possibly much much more. Selfishness and lust may not enter into the picture at all, or at most in the very last place. Polygamy is more than one husband with two wives. (That was the second level of culture; now we come to the third.)

Underlying these immediate *whys* of culture just described is *the deepest level of culture*—the inner logic, the fundamental attitudes, and basic goals and drives. Before translators can consider themselves sensitized to culture, they must appreciate the importance especially of this deepest, third level of culture, the ultimate *whys* of a way of life. This third level is responsible, perhaps more than anything else, for why, of the countless possibilities, a society chooses the particular purposeful, logical, and other relationships on the second level that I just described. The ultimate *whys* are the "soul" of the people, their basic psychology, which is revealed especially in their world-view, religion, myths and ritual.

Much has been studied and written about the world-view of some societies; of others, very little is known indeed. By *world-view* we understand the deepest questions one might possibly ask about the world and life: Who am I? Why am I in the world? What is reality? What is time and space? What about life after death? The dozens of items like these might be reduced to three or four, such as Supernature, Nature, Human Beings, and Time.

World-views as systems of knowledge are sometimes placed into one of three classes.[13] (1) the *materialistic* world-views, those that regard existence as *meaningless* for instance, the atheistic belief that the world is the result of accident; (2) the *religious* world-views, those that regard existence as *meaningful*, namely the theistic views that see a Mind behind the universe, who consider Nature as reflecting Supernature, such as are the world-views of Christians, Jews, and Mohammedans; (3) those that are *irreligious*, entirely or partly so, such as are the views of humanists and most Marxists.

A world-view has three dimensions: (1) a cognitive dimension, (2) an emotional dimension and (3) a motivational dimension.[14]

1) The Cognitive Dimension

Westerners take the world to be real, as made up of what they can experience through their senses and through the extension of their senses, the empirical sciences. In vast areas of Asia, the world is but an illusion. In the west, time is a unidirectional continuum (in fact, we find it next to impossible to picture time in any other way). However, other world-views consider time as an endless circle. The Western mind thinks empirically, that is, it forms a hypothesis and tests it; if it survives the test it is upheld, otherwise another hypothesis is set up. The Western mind proceeds from the particular to the general, emphasizing logical procedures; we look for concepts, categories, principles, and theories and hope to be able to come up with a "law", a certitude. In contrast, the Oriental mind, is largely mythological, analogical, relying heavily on feeling and intuition. The Hindu does not seek evidence as does the Westerner but hopes to arrive at truth through a mystical union with the Hindu monistic god.

[13] Hesselgrave, op. cit., pp. 126-129.

[14] Luzbetak, op. cit., pp. 253-263.

2) The Emotional Dimension

A world-view also determines how a society feels, evaluates, and reacts, for instance, the value placed on saving face by the Orientals or on loyalty by the Mafia. Such basic emotionally charged attitudes give direction to a people's idea of art, literature, music, architecture, and ritual, and determine who is a villain and who a saint.

3) The Motivational Dimension

A world-view tells the society what its priorites and ideals should be. Americans, for instance, are sometimes said to be a driven people—driven to achieve, driven toward expansiveness, and especially to the so-called pursuit of happiness, actually to individualism.[15]

Closely related to the concept of world-view is religion. In fact, one of the three categories of world-view we suggested was "religious". Religion is found especially in a people's mythology and ritual. Myth is said to be the *why* of religious life, while ritual is the how myth is lived.[16]

3. The Dynamics of Culture

The third basic requirement for cultural sensitization we said was the ability to appreciate how cultures operate.

The study of culture dynamics is a complex matter, and we will not go into the processes as such. All I wish to describe in a few paragraphs is what we mean when we say that culture is dynamic. The appreciation of this dynamism is absolutely necessary for the cultural sensitivity we are talking about.

Culture, being a kind of organic system, tends to change and adjust, sometimes successfully, sometimes not quite successfully. Like all organisms, cultures tend to persist, to remain what they are. On the other hand, new elements are constantly being added, while others are lost, substituted, or fused. Cultures are constantly changing because the individuals of society are growing in experience, are constantly adjusting according to the needs and the demands of a changing physical, social, and spiritual environment, historical events, and the growth or decline of the experience, of their particular society. Culture, as a design for living, is never a finished plan. The bearers of culture are the architects of the society's blueprint for life. These architects are constantly altering the blueprints, constantly trying to improve their plans. Innovations are

---

[15] Robert N. Bellah, et al., *Habits of the Heart: Individualism and Commitment in American Life* (Berkeley: University of California Press, 1985).

[16] John Friedl, *The Human Portrait: Introduction to Cultural Anthropology*, (Englewood Cliffs, NJ: Prentice Hall, Inc., 1976, 1981), p. 255.

introduced from within the society or borrowed from without. In any case, change always brings imbalance into the culture. Although the human mind is not perfectly logical, it nevertheless seeks harmony and consistency, usually in accord with its world-view. A change in the culture always brings an imbalance and therefore calls for a change to balance the design. Either the innovation is altered to fit the existing culture or the culture is modified to achieve the desired balance. Only then will the innovation, as a rule, be integrated into the system we call culture.

In a word, to be sensitive to culture, the translator must be aware of the fact that cultures are dynamic, acting and reacting—that they are very much alive. Culture is not a dead tradition. Culture is the here and now, with a past and most likely a future. Especially today, in our rapidly changing world, to visualize culture in any other way except in this dynamic sense would be to deal with an unreal, nonexistent way of life.

Conclusion

I realize my presentation has been quite theoretical. I remain convinced, however, that one cannot be sensitized to the cultural dimensions involved in translation work except by dealing with the broad goals I have outlined. I am also convinced that if there is any modern field that can be of assistance to translators in contextualizing their translations, that field is the Science of Culture, cultural anthropology.

DARRELL L. WHITEMAN

BIBLE TRANSLATION AND SOCIAL AND CULTURAL DEVELOPMENT

This paper explores the question of how Bible translation has contributed to people's social and cultural development. It asks the question, "Is there any empirical evidence that when a people have the Scriptures translated into their own language that it actually contributes to their development as a people, as a community, as a nation?" We will discover that although this may be an important issue to raise, it is not always an easy question to answer.

In my preliminary research on the relationship between Bible translation and social and cultural development I became intrigued and fascinated—not by what we knew, but by the paucity of empirical studies that in fact demonstrate a positive correlation between Bible translation and development. This study, therefore, does not report on numerous Bible translation success stories in development. Instead, I will construct a conceptual framework for pursuing this topic in hopes that it will stimulate research, and uncover the empirical evidence that Bible translation has contributed to development. We need to first ask the right questions in order to get the correct data, and so I will attempt to provide a "road map" whereby we can explore this fascinating area of development and discover how Bible translation and vernacular Scriptures have contributed to it.

I will begin by discussing what I mean by social and cultural development and introduce the concept of integral human development. I will elaborate on this model and discuss how Bible translation can contribute to this kind of development. I will then explore some "problem areas" where we need to be cross-culturally sensitive if translation is going to contribute rather than detract from development. Finally, I will draw on some case studies that demonstrate how in fact, translation has made a difference in development, and then I'll end with suggestions for further research on this topic.

Exploring Development

The word "development" is an explosive, emotional and often politicized term. Especially when discussing development in the Third World, it is not uncommon for the term to get hijacked by economic concerns and agendas. Nevertheless, it is a term that has undergone some important semantic shifts in the past twenty years. This has resulted in a breaking down of what I call the dominant paradigm of development which ruled intellectual definitions and discussions of development and guided national development programs following World War II.[1]

This dominant paradigm of development emphasized the rate of economic growth. Development could therefore be conveniently quantified with an empirical index such as the Gross National Product (GNP). Development, or underdevelopment as the case may be, was easily measured by the GNP and per capita income. Thus, development was perceived to be the same as modernization and this implied economic growth with a focus on technology and industrialization. The developed countries were those which were modern and industrialized. Underdeveloped countries were those which were not. Development schemes following the dominant paradigm were therefore aimed at bringing the underdeveloped countries up to the level of the developed countries in economic growth and industrialization.

We are now realizing that this model of development had a heavy Western bias, based on assumptions that are inappropriate for the rest of the world. For example, it assumed there were no limits to growth and acted as if the natural resources needed to feed industrialization were inexhaustible. Other assumptions included the belief that human beings were basically economic creatures and that they would respond rationally to economic incentives. That is, they would respond in the same way as Westerners would respond, motivated by economic concerns more than by other considerations. Another assumption of the dominant paradigm was the belief that with centralized planning, development on the national level would eventually trickle down to develop local communities. There was little or no confidence in the ability of local communities to have autonomous self-development. And, even supposing they were capable of it, it would be too slow and take too long. Development policies of the 1950s and 1960s paid little attention to the equality of development benefits. Instead the "growth-first-and-let-equality-come-later" mentality was often justified by the trickle down theory. It was believed that the poorest of the poor would eventually prosper.

This dominant paradigm of development has now been called into serious question. For one thing, it did not produce the predicted results. Those Third World countries who followed this path of development often did not reap the benefits they expected. Moreover, in recent years some of us have come to see more clearly that economic development does not automatically lead to human development. In fact the evidence of development schemes around the world indicates that there may be an *inverse* relationship; economic development often thwarts, not helps, human development.[2]

---

[1] Cf. Robert Chambers, *Rural Development: Putting the Last First,* (Ithaca NY: Rural Development Committee, 1983) and John J. Poggie, Jr. and Robert N. Lynch, eds, *Rethinking Modernization: Anthropological Perspectives,* (Westport, CT: Greenwood Press, 1974).

[2] Cf. George N. Appell, "The Pernicious Effects of Development", *Fields Without Fields* 14:31-41.

Despite the fact that this dominant paradigm of development is still a powerful force in policy arenas, there is, nevertheless, a new development paradigm in gestation that is gradually gaining legitimacy. One sign of its ascending status is that lip-service is now paid to its values even by those who still pursue strategies based on the dominant paradigm of economic growth. These alternative values include respect for cultural values, the primacy of basic needs satisfaction, the creation of jobs, and the reduction of dependency. Increasingly there is at least a tacit admission that development is essentially an ethical concern. Development policy makers are slowly realizing that man does not live by GNP alone.[3]

We see this in two recent formulations of an alternative paradigm that reveal the importance of values and ethics in any serious talk about development. In September 1986, the Marga Institute held a week-long seminar in Colombo, Sri Lanka, on "Ethical Issues in Development". Theorists and practitioners gathered there reached agreement that any adequate definition of development must include five dimensions:

1. an economic component dealing with the creation of wealth and improved conditions of material life;
2. a social ingredient measured as well-being in health, education, housing, and employment;
3. a political dimension pointing to such values as human rights, political freedom, enfranchisement, and some form of democracy;
4. a cultural dimension in recognition of the fact that cultures confer identity and self-worth to people; and
5. a fifth dimension called the full-life paradigm, which encompasses symbols and beliefs as to the ultimate meaning of life and history.[4]

Is it coincidental that a seminar held some years earlier on essential components of development in Latin America reached nearly identical conclusions? Its comprehensive definition of development centered on four areas: economic growth, distributional equity, increased participation and reduced vulnerability, and transcendental values.[5]

This change in thinking about development is reflected in the work of Everett Rogers, who has been a leading scholar of communication and development, and who has undergone a significant "paradigm shift" in his own understanding of development. For example, in 1969 in a book entitled *Modernization Among Peasants* he defined development as follows:

---

3 Denis Goulet, "Ethics in Development Theory and Practice", *Catalyst*, 17(1987):316.

4 Goulet, "Ethics", p. 317.

5 David H. Pollock, "A Latin American Strategy to the Year 2000: Can the Past Serve as a Guide to the Future?" In *Latin American Prospects for the 80s: What Kinds of Development?* (Ottawa: Norman Patterson School of International Affairs, Carleton University, Conference Proceedings, 1(1980):1-37).

Development is a type of social change in which new ideas are introduced into the social system in order to produce higher per capita incomes and levels of living through more modern production methods and improved social organization.[6]

We can see here that the focus of Rogers thinking in 1969 reflects the dominant paradigm's concern with economic growth.

In the late 1960s and through the 1970s there were four world events in particular that coalesced, causing people to call into question the credibility of the dominant paradigm. These included:

1. The ecological concern with environmental pollution in the developed nations caused people to question whether, in fact, they really did have the ideal of development made possible through high technology.
2. The world oil crisis triggered in 1974 by rapid price increases demonstrated that certain countries, in this case the OPEC nations, could make their own rules in the international development game, and suddenly produce rich developing nations.
3. The opening of international relations with China, beginning in 1972 with President Richard Nixon's visit, allowed the rest of the world to learn the details of her pathway to development. It soon became clear that within a span of two decades the largest and one of the poorest countries had created a miracle of development, accomplished with very little foreign aid. The story of China suggested that there must be workable alternatives to the dominant paradigm of development.
4. Finally, the fourth and probably most important factor was that in those countries that had followed closely the dominant paradigm, development was not going very well. In fact, in the past thirty years very little development has occurred in those nations. Instead most development efforts have brought stagnation, greater concentration of income and power in the hands of a few, high unemployment, food shortages, and huge national debts. Brazil, stands out as the leading example of a country that went this route only to end up with an overwhelming national debt and greater disparity between the rich and the poor.

These four global events brought a significant challenge to the dominant paradigm of development leading to the suspicion that there might be many alternative pathways to development. Everett Rogers, reflecting this shift, now saw development quite differently than he had in 1969. In 1975 he defined it as:

---

6 Everett M. Rogers, *Modernization Among Peasants: The Impact of Communication*, (New York: Holt, Rinehart and Winston, 1969), pp. 8-9.

A widely participatory process of social change in a society, intended to bring about social and material advancement (including greater equality, freedom, and other valued qualities) for the majority of the people through their gaining greater control over their environment.[7]

Edgar Stoesz, in his booklet entitled *Thoughts on Development*, has articulated for many of us the growing dissatisfaction with understanding and defining development from the perspective of the Western dominant paradigm.[8] Thus it is important to state what development is not:

(1) **It is not urbanization**. Although the global trend is toward increasing urbanization, especially in the Third World, it is doubtful that this is improving development. In fact, it seems to be having the opposite effect—a growing disparity between rich and poor,[9] more oppression, marginalization and dislocation of people, etc.
(2) **It is not industrialization**. The dominant paradigm held the assumption that the quickest road to development was that of industrialization. It was believed that if countries would become industrialized this would lead to their development because it would be the source for economic advancement. This has not proven to be the case.
(3) **It is not modernization**. Modernization does not guarantee social and cultural development. The growing awareness among Christians for a simplified life-style is helping us discover the faulty assumptions behind modernization.[10] We are realizing that "the throwaway, built-in-obsolescence society can not continue indefinitely in a finite world".[11]
(4) **It is not westernization**. Westernization has not lead to development in the way that we need to define and understand it today. Even if we did agree to define development in narrow, economic terms, we still have to admit that Western countries have not solved the problem of poverty in their own countries, let alone in those they have tried to assist.

In summary, before we move on to explore how Bible translation might be related to development, we need to be very clear that the model of development that I am advocating is very different from the dominant paradigm of development where urbanization, industrialization, modernization and westernization are key components. I submit that these four components do not

---

7 Everett M. Rogers, "The Anthropology of Modernization and the Modernization of Anthropology", *Reviews in Anthropology* 2 (1975:345-358), p. 358.

8 Edgar Stoesz, *Thoughts on Development*, Development Monograph Series 1. (Akron, PA: Mennonite Central Committee, 1977).

9 Cf. Mitchell A. Seligson, ed., *The Gap Between Rich and Poor: Contending Perspectives on the Political Economy of Development*, (Boulder, CO: Westview Press, 1984).

10 Wayne Bragg, "Beyond Development" In *The Church in Response to Human Need*, Tom Sine, ed., (Monrovia, CA: MARC, 1983), pp. 37-95.

11 Stoesz, *Thoughts on Development*, p. 2.

lead to development, but in fact have often had a very negative, oppressive, impact on people.

Integral Human Development

If I am going to criticize the dominant paradigm of development as inadequate for our understanding of true social and cultural development then I must be prepared to offer an alternative. The alternative I wish to suggest is what I call integral human development. I define integral human development as a process by which people gain greater control over themselves, their environment and their future in order to realize the full potential of life that God has made possible.

What are some of the characteristics of integral human development? What does a community look like when it is experiencing integral human development? Once we are clear on this description we will more readily see how Bible translation is related to furthering integral human development.

Characteristics of Integral Human Development

1. *This kind of development is integrated with the whole of life*. For example, it does not consider economic development to be more important than, say, spiritual and social development. It recognizes the importance of balance in the growth of the different components of the human community. What are some of those components? I believe the different components that must be addressed in integral human development are essentially six basic human needs: 1) physical, 2) social, 3) self-esteem, 4) purpose, 5) security, 6) spiritual. When these needs are met, then we find the kind of community I believe God intends for us. The obvious question, then, is, "can we discover how Bible translation might help people address these needs?" Wherever Bible translation enables and empowers people to address and meet these needs, then it facilitates integral human development.

Drawing on a model developed by John Roughan, who has worked for over twenty years with the Catholic Church in the Solomon Islands,[12] we can, for the sake of discussion and analysis, divide the human person and community into four major areas: personal growth, material growth, social growth and spiritual growth. Each of these four areas encompasses various components. For example, the area of personal growth includes self-respect and confidence, self-reliance, security, nutrition and health. In the category of social growth we find participation, autonomy, solidarity, education. Material growth includes those items that we normally think of when discussing development, namely transportation, communication, money, land ownership and land use. The

---

12 William Haomae, "Development Wheel of Rural Growth", *Solomon Islands News Drum*, May 8, p. 5, 1981.

category of spiritual growth contains a people's relationship with the world of the supernatural. If it is mostly negative and characterized by fear and uncertainty then this of course will inhibit their development. If on the other hand it is primarily positive and full of hope and love, as we believe it can be for all Christians, then it leads to growth.

It is always difficult to quantify the quality of life in any community, but anthropologists are now attempting to do that. If we could develop an empirical index on a scale from one to ten for each of these components, we would then be able to more clearly see how well balanced and integrated is the development in a particular community. For example, if material growth is relatively high but the components under social growth are "under nourished" then the community experiences an unbalanced, distorted "development", which actually is not development at all.

Fig. 1 Wheel of
Integral Human Development

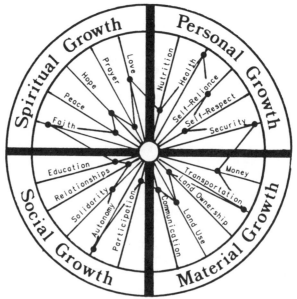

Ideally, integral human development in a community should conceptually resemble a bicycle wheel with the different components comprising the spokes of that wheel. If the different components develop together then the wheel is round and the "ride" will be rather smooth. If some components are developed while others are neglected then we get an aberration of development that is no longer conceptually like a wheel, and to continue the metaphor, people in this situation are in for a rough ride.

We in the West are having to rediscover that human beings are created to live whole lives in community, not fragmented existences as isolated and alienated individuals. We have much to learn about the integration of the secular and sacred, the critical relationship between the human and physical environments, etc. To summarize the first characteristic of integral human development, development in this mode is integrated and wholistic, relating to the totality of human existence.

2. *A second feature of integral human development is that this kind of development focuses on* **people**, *not projects*. It is concerned with the *process* by which people are developed more than the products of development such as dams, hydroelectric plants, factories, etc. A small pamphlet published by the Pacific Conference of Churches a number of years ago says it all: *Development is People*. This focus on people in development means that anything that does not promote human welfare can not be considered development. And this is precisely where so many development projects have gone wrong. With often admirable intentions they have been too narrowly conceived in economic and technological terms without carefully considering the human impact. If a project contributes to developing whole people and community life then it can legitimately be called development, but too many development schemes have failed miserably at this point. Edgar Stoesz notes that:

> Material rewards may be one of the results of development, but they should not be seen as the objective. The objective of development is people—people with the skills to compete, with purpose and determination, with a liberated attitude; people who live in a context of justice and opportunity.[13]

3. *A third characteristic of this concept of integral human development is the importance of the spiritual dimension and moral values*. Wherever social and cultural development has been attempted without careful consideration given to this area, it has fallen short.

There is a marvelous story told by Jacob Loewen that illustrates the importance of this dimension.[14] We begin with anthropologist Allan R. Holmberg who in 1949 became the director of the Vicos Project in Peru—the most ambitious program of directed culture change and applied anthropology ever undertaken by an American university. Its purpose was to bring development to 2000 *huasipongos*, "debt servants" who lived on the Vicos hacienda in the Peruvian Highlands. Its goal was to enable these people to learn how "to live as free and responsible men instead of what they had been—the animals closest to

---

13 Stoesz, *Thoughts on Development*, p. 6.

14 Jacob Loewen, "Developing Moralnets: Twenty-five Years of Culture Change Among the Choco", in *Missionaries, Anthropologists, and Cultural Change*, Darrell L. Whiteman, ed., Studies in Third World Societies, No. 25. (Williamsburg, VA: College of William and Mary, 1985), pp. 229-261.

men in the evolutionary line".[15] In 1962 when Loewen met up with Holmberg between sessions of the Congress of Americanists meeting in Mexico City, he asked him, "If you could redo Vicos, is there any one thing you did which you wouldn't do, or vice versa, which you didn't do that you would now do?" Loewen says "He looked around to make sure that we were alone and then with deep conviction said: 'I'd introduce a good dose of old-fashioned religion because without a change of value system what we really have achieved is a bigger and better beer bust'".[16] Loewen says:

> He then went on to explain how surplus potatoes had traditionally been converted into liquor. Before the Vicos project a good year might produce enough surplus potatoes for a week, or at the most two weeks of drinking. The last year, that is the year after the Vicos project terminated, had produced enough potatoes for four months supply of liquor, and the newly independent Vicos farmers missed their next planting season.[17]

The Vicos Project underscores what is evident from many attempts at "development". Namely, without the spiritual and moral dimension development efforts will go awry.

In summary, the model of integral human development which I am suggesting here, recognizes the integrated nature of human beings and communities and thus submits that development must be wholistic and balanced. This model puts people ahead of projects and says that if development attempts do not have the welfare of human beings as their first priority then they must be called into question. Call them modernization schemes, but don't call that development. And finally, the spiritual dimension of moral values is absolutely critical for any understanding of integral human development. Without this moral and spiritual dimension, we fail at the most important level of social and cultural development.

What Inhibits Development?

If, as I have argued, this is a model of development that leads to health and wholeness, what are the main forces that thwart integral human development in any community? I believe it is primarily the egocentric tendencies of individuals and the ethnocentric ones of societies, or human sinfulness and social, structural evil.

---

15 Ibid., p. 229.

16 Ibid., pp. 230-231.

17 Ibid., p. 231.

Sin has never been a favorite topic of anthropologists.[18] And yet, they have had to deal with the empirical realities of sinfulness regardless of whether they choose to call it that or something else. An axiom of anthropology is that there is always a gap between the ideal values and beliefs professed by a society and the actual behavior of people in that society. In other words, people in every society fall short of their own cultural ideals.

We see this tension reflected in the work of two well known anthropologists, Raoul Naroll and Walter Goldschmidt. In his book *The Moral Order*, the late Naroll developed a theory he called "moralnets" to show how societies need to have strong moral nets of support and stability in order to deal with plaguing social problems.[19] Christianity often reinforces existing moral nets and/or adds new ones where there were none before, or where old ones were no longer functional.[20] As we will discover later, this is an area where vernacular Scriptures can be especially helpful.

Walter Goldschmidt's *Comparative Functionalism* is a creative essay noting that one of the functions of institutions in a society is to "maintain the social system as a system, in order to prevent the society from being rent by the centrifugal tendencies of individual self-interest".[21] Despite the similarity in content, this is the anthropologist Walter Goldschmidt writing, not the words of the Apostle Paul. He goes on to note that "human society must also be seen as the means by which the egocentered psychobiological needs of the individual are both given satisfaction and held in check . . .".[22]

If egocentricism and ethnocentrism are the driving forces that thwart and even destroy the integral development of human beings, then it becomes abundantly clear that it is through God's Word that we can discover a way out of this dilemma, and find a path that leads to development of whole persons as God originally intended. The important role of vernacular Scriptures in that process cannot be overestimated.

Now, the way we approach and deal with the social and cultural impact of vernacular Scriptures that are introduced into a society will most certainly be influenced by our anthropological biases and by the models of culture and culture change that we bring to the situation. The prevailing biases and models used by

---

[18] E.E. Evans-Pritchard, *Nuer Religion*, (New York: Oxford University Press, 1974 [1956]).

[19] Raoul Naroll, *The Moral Order: An Introduction to the Human Situation*, (Beverly Hills, CA: Sage Publications, 1983).

[20] Cf. John C. Messenger, Jr., "The Christian Concept of Forgiveness and Anang Morality", *Practical Anthropology*, 6:97-103.

[21] Walter Goldschmidt, *Comparative Functionalism: An Essay in Anthropological Theory* , (Berkeley, CA: University of California Press, 1966), p. 58.

[22] Ibid., p. 59.

anthropologists to study the impact of Christianity on the non-Western world has lead to mostly negative interpretations and conclusions.[23]

This is not the place to review the tensions that have existed between anthropologists and missionaries or to lay bare the moral roots of that conflict,[24] but my research on the role of missionaries as agents of change has lead me to reject the static, functionalist, models of culture that see change, especially change introduced from outside by Christian sources, as always harmful and disruptive.[25] Such a static model is the creation of salvage anthropologists who wish that their primitive cultures could remain isolated from the influence of the rest of the world. In point of fact, this never was possible, and so the desire of anthropologists who want to preserve "their people" as fossilized relics to display as specimens in an ethnographic museum is naive and nothing short of a fanciful wish. The anthropological bias against change introduced by Christian sources is derived from an artificial abstraction from reality, designed to buttress the ideology of cultural relativism. In point of fact, cultures are changing, they are dynamic and always adjusting to new forces in the environment. When vernacular Scriptures are introduced into that environment we have the potential for growth and positive change in the lives of people who comprise that culture.

When we talk about development we need to have in our minds a model of culture that is dynamic, not static—one that sees a culture as always in transition, responding to changes in the physical, social and ideological environment.[26] With this kind of model we can better understand the role of vernacular Scriptures that are introduced into a society.

Levels of Integral Human Development

In addition to employing a dynamic model of culture when we think about social and cultural development, we must also think about human development on several levels of complexity, viz., individual, community and inter-community. Vernacular Scriptures become an important impetus and catalyst to social and cultural development precisely because the Bible provides us with a blueprint and guidelines for human interaction on each of these levels—the individual, the community and inter-community.

---

[23] Cf. Thomas O. Beidelman, *Colonial Evangelism*, (Bloomington, IN: Indiana University Press, 1982).

[24] Robert J. Priest, "Anthropologists and Missionaries: Moral Roots of Conflict", *Current Concerns of Anthropologists and Missionaries*, Karl Franklin, ed., International Museum of Cultures, Publication No. 22, (Dallas: Summer Institute of Linguistics, 1987).

[25] Darrell L. Whiteman, *Melanesians and Missionaries*, (Pasadena, CA: William Carey Library, 1983).

[26] Darrell L. Whiteman, "How Cultures Change", in *An Introduction to Melanesian Cultures*, Darrell L. Whiteman, ed., Point Series No. 5, (Goroka: The Melanesian Institute, 1984), pp. 29-55.

1. *Individual Level*. For example, if we enter the pilgrimage of having the mind of Christ (Romans 12:1-2; I Corinthians 2), we become new creatures, new creations, new human beings. Human beings, who are created in God's image, but are warped and distorted by sin, now have the potential of becoming fully functioning human beings as God intended. The bad news is that we are incapable of doing this on our own initiative. The good news is that God through Christ makes it possible to happen, for individuals to experience social and cultural development—development toward the image of Christ, as a member of the body of believers. And of course, one of the most important sources which functions as a catalyst for personal transformation is the Word of God communicated in language that human beings can understand. As individual human beings are transformed we have the basic building blocks for the social and cultural transformation of a community.

2. *Community Level*. But of course human beings do not exist in isolation, in a cultural vacuum; they are part of a physical, social and ideological context. They are people in community. Anthropological insights have helped us to better understand the power of this community context in shaping individual persons, for the thrust of anthropological investigation has nearly always been people in groups, not individual persons in isolation from others. When we think of social and cultural development it is primarily at this level of human complexity that we focus our attention. This is certainly the arena in which the bulk of anthropological research has been done. And yet it is often difficult for people from Western, industrialized countries to realize the importance of the community level of human interaction. We are so obsessed with the individual, as if he or she *did* exist in a social and cultural vacuum.

At the community level of human interaction we can readily witness the power of the gospel to transform human lives. If there is a different cultural code in the minds of people, then that influences their interaction with others, and then we can see the potential for integral human development. And, of course, the Bible, as a collection of stories or as a case book of God's interaction with human beings, has a great deal to say about human interaction at the community level. In fact the more we understand the kingdom of God, the more we see that it is a blueprint showing us how human beings should interact in community.

The Bible is full of language that instructs us in how to interact with one another. For example, in Philippians 2:1-4 Paul writes:

> Your life in Christ makes you strong, and his love comforts you. The Spirit has brought you into fellowship with one another and you have kindness and compassion for one another. I urge you, then, to make me completely happy by having the same thoughts, sharing the same love, and being one in soul and mind. Don't do anything from selfish ambition or from a cheap desire to boast, but be humble towards one another, always considering others better than yourselves. And look out for one another's interests, not just for your own.

In Ephesians 4:2 Paul also writes to Christians telling them how they should interact with one another. He says, "Be always humble, gentle, and patient. Show your love by being tolerant with one another". Later in the chapter (verses 22-24) he admonishes:

> so get rid of your old self, which made you live as you used to—the old self that was being destroyed by its deceitful desires. Your hearts and minds must be made completely new, and you must put on the new self, which is created in God's likeness and reveals itself in the true life that is upright and holy.

What a blueprint for integral human development! If communities followed these guidelines we would see integral human development occurring everywhere.

In Galatians 5, Paul gives us further insight into how God intends for us to live in community in contrast to the way we live without God's help; (Gal 5:17, 19-23):

> For what our human nature wants is opposed to what the Spirit wants, and what the Spirit wants is opposed to what our human nature wants. These two are enemies, and this means that you cannot do what you want to do. If the Spirit leads you, then you are not subject to the Law.

> What human nature does is quite plain. It shows itself in immoral, filthy, and indecent actions; in worship of idols and witchcraft. People become enemies and they fight; they become jealous, angry and ambitious. They separate into parties and groups; they are envious, get drunk, have orgies, and do other things like these. I warn you now as I have before: those who do these things will not possess the Kingdom of God.

> But the Spirit produces love, joy, peace, patience, kindness, goodness, faithfulness, humility, and self-control. There is no law against such things as these.

The kingdom of God is our biblical model for integral human development, our model of what community life can become. The fruits of the Spirit are an empirical index of behavior that should be present in this community. These characteristics are indicators of how people can and should interact with one another in community.

It is obvious that the communities of Christians in the early church were having some difficulties in this area, otherwise Paul would not have written to them with such clear, explicit guidelines of behavior expected of those people who now live in Christ, who are empowered by the spirit of God rather than enslaved by their own egotistic interests. In the same way the early Christian communities needed to hear Paul's words, so have communities in every age and in every culture needed to hear them.

3. *Inter-community Level*. Integral Human Development occurs not only within people and within communities; it also influences the nature of human interaction between communities. And of course at this level of complexity we encounter a wide range of interaction; everything from the interclan rivalry among the Chimbu in the Highlands of Papua New Guinea, armed to the teeth with bows and arrows, to the ideological battles waged between the Super Powers, armed this time with nuclear warheads. Where there is intercommunity conflict and strife it destroys integral human development.

Do we have evidence that Bible translation has contributed to development at the inter-community level? To return to Melanesia, the area of the globe I know best, we can discover that Bible translation *has* made a difference. Melanesia has more cultural and linguistic diversity than any region of the world. No doubt the isolation of groups from each other because of rugged terrain or many off-shore small islands has contributed to this diversity, but it also seems to have contributed to considerable hostility between many groups. Warfare and the threat of warfare has done much to shape Melanesian societies in the past, and is still a factor today. However the endemic warfare that was once part and parcel of Melanesian life has now greatly subsided. This is due in no small measure to the impact of Christianity, for one of its most significant contributions in these islands has been to expand the meaning of "Who is my brother?" As the light of the gospel informs traditional Melanesian societies, people are beginning to see brotherhood as more inclusive of others and not limited to only fellow kinsmen. One wishes that the result of this would be complete harmony between all the communities that have been stimulated by the gospel, but today egocentric and ethnocentric tendencies are straining the situation and tribal fighting is still occurring, although greatly reduced from the way of life Melanesians knew in the past.

Bible Translation and Integral Human Development

In this discussion I have tried to sketch briefly a model of what I have called integral human development and have argued that this is true development in contrast to efforts that focus on economic projects more than on the process of empowering people to reach the human potential God intended for them, enabling them to solve their own problems using their own available resources.

Larry and Willa Yost have given us a good definition of development that captures the essence of what I have argued is integral human development. They define development as:

> A process whereby a community is strengthened so that it can creatively
> meet its needs (spiritual, mental, physical, social) through expansion of
> awareness, increased interaction within and without the community, and
> the development of effective utilization of available resources.[27]

Given this understanding of social and cultural development what can we say
about the role of Bible translation in promoting and increasing integral human
development around the globe? It is important to caution against seeing Bible
translation as a mono-causal factor in promoting development. In other words, it
is unlikely that the translation of vernacular Scriptures is a sufficient condition
by itself to promote integral human development. In concert with other factors,
however, there is no doubt that it is a powerful catalyst.

I want to briefly list a number of areas in which I believe there is a positive
correlation between vernacular Scriptures and development, recognizing that we
need more research to uncover the case studies that illustrate the connection:

1. *Self-respect and dignity.* An important result of vernacular Scriptures is that
people often gain a new sense of who they are in relation to God through Christ;
they are loved, they are created in the image of God, they are inestimably
important as God's children. An interesting example of this phenomenon comes
from the Binumarien people of Papua New Guinea. They were a small,
dispossessed, people numbering only 114 who had been pushed around by their
stronger and more powerful neighbors. They lacked a strong sense of identity,
they had a low corporate self concept, they were miserable and oppressed.
Although they had heard stories about Jesus they assumed he was a mythological
figure like many of their own culture heroes, but, through an intensive
relationship with a Bible translator and by having the Scriptures in their own
language, they came to see themselves from a new perspective. Of particular
importance was the translation of the first chapter of Matthew's Gospel and
especially the genealogy of Jesus. This enabled them to see that Jesus was an
historical person and that Israel was a real place. Furthermore, they concluded
that if God was interested in Jesus' ancestors, he must also be interested in them
and in their ancestors. It was a significant turning point in their personal and
cultural identity. Now they saw themselves as God saw them and this brought a
new self-respect and sense of dignity to them.[28]

2. *Expansion of a people's world.* Vernacular Scriptures opens people up to a
larger world in time and space and presents them with alternatives. This is nearly
always liberating and empowering. Through the Scriptures people come to

---

[27] Larry E. Yost and Willa D. Yost, *A Philosophy of Intercultural Community Relations
and a Strategy for Preparing S.I.L. Members for Intercultural Community Work*, (Dallas:
Summer Institute of Linguistics, 1983), p. 3.

[28] Robert L. Litteral, *Community Partnership in Communications for Ministry*, (Wheaton:
The Billy Graham Center, 1988), p. 73.

realize that God starts where they are but he does not leave them there. He moves them, he challenges their culture and its assumptions and through the Scriptures enables them to move beyond the narrow confines of their own society, both diachronically (through time) and synchronically (across space). The Scriptures show people what they can become in Christ, and that must certainly be the good news of the kingdom.

3. *Literacy*. It is with some hesitancy that I include literacy as one of the contributions vernacular Scriptures make to development. This is because literacy is nearly always seen as the panacea for any development ills, when in fact the record is a mixed one.[29] In some cases it has been helpful, in other situations it has not been. The primary key to whether or not literacy contributes to development is if the vernacular literacy leads to literacy in a language that has a wider community of readers with a large volume of literature and the economic system to sustain it. The connection to development then is that people learn to read best with their own language first and then can later read a national language or lingua franca. When this happens the chances for a positive contribution to development are increased. Carol McKinney, in a helpful article that discusses why literacy is adopted or rejected, speaks of the potential power of literacy when she notes that, "As the society becomes literate, the written word becomes a very effective channel of communication. It can be used to bring about other changes in the culture such as improved health and agriculture".[30]

4. *New Sense of Identity*. Becoming new persons in Christ gives us a new personal identity. When we see this expressed on a community level we see the power of the gospel. Also, Bible translation can become a vehicle for a new identity as a people's language becomes written and the emerging literature and education provides the means for acquiring new skills. Thus, Bible translation has this dual function of both countering and challenging ethnocentrism and promoting a sense of identity. Lamin Sanneh writes that Christianity in Africa is strongest where vernacular Scriptures exist—weakest where lingua francas are dominant and vernaculars not strong.[31] This fact makes perfect sense in light of

---

29 Cf. Jack Goody, *Literacy in Traditional Societies*, (Cambridge: Cambridge University Press, 1968).

   Goody, *The Domestication of the Savage Mind*, (Cambridge: Cambridge University Press, 1977).

   Goody, *The Logic of Writing and the Oganization of Society*, (Cambridge: Cambridge University Press, 1986).

   Goody, *The Interface Between the Written and the Oral*, (Cambridge: Cambridge University Press, 1987.)

   Walter Ong, *Orality and Literacy: The Technologizing of the World*, (New York: Routledge, Chapman and Hall, 1982).

30 Carol V. McKinney, "Culture Change and its Relation to Literacy", *Missiology* 4:67.

31 Lamin Sanneh, "Christian Missions and the Western Guilt Complex", *The Christian Century*. April 8, 1987, p. 333.

the model of development we have been suggesting here. That is, with vernacular Scriptures people make the Bible their own. It becomes their book, not simply the book of the dominant culture that introduced it to them, and this enables them to understand it in their own terms. But once the Bible becomes their own and is understood in their terms they are immediately thrust beyond the narrow confines of their own time and space, their own culture and world-view, because the Bible introduces them to the activities of God in a much wider world both geographically and historically.

The development process works best when people start where they are, on their own local level, and from there expand their world. This is what can happen with the translation of Scripture into a people's language. And of course, this is the very opposite of the trickle down theory of development which has failed so miserably as a development strategy around the world.

Problem Areas in Translation and Development

If the above factors are ones that can and do contribute to integral human development when people have vernacular Scriptures, we are still faced with a disturbing fact that people have not always responded with enthusiasm or interest when the Bible has been translated into their language. Around the world stacks of translated Bibles gathering dust attest to the fact that people have not always wanted or valued vernacular Scriptures.

I believe an understanding of the development process can help us understand this phenomenon. Often times Bible translation has been done in the mode of the dominant paradigm of development. That is, it has been seen as a project done *for* a people rather than an effort that engages them in the process. This has violated an important principle of development—you don't do things for people, you empower them to do the things that will meet their needs. Julius Nyerere, the former president of Tanzania, understood this principle clearly when he argued that people cannot be developed, they can only develop themselves.[32] Loewen notes that when people are involved in translating their own Bible they are more likely to apply its truths in their daily life.[33] When we understand that the *process* of development within a community is more important than a development project, then we can better understand why some Bible translations are more readily received than others. Vernacular Scriptures that are received as a development project done by someone else will normally not have the same empowering influence of vernacular Scriptures that are created as part of a

[32] Julius K. Nyerere, "Declaration of Dar Es Salaam. Liberated Man—the Purpose of Development", *Convergence* 9(4):9-16.

[33] Jacob A. Loewen, "The Gospel: Its Content and Communication—An Anthropological Perspective", in *Down to Earth: Studies in Christianity and Culture*, John R.W. Stott and Robert Coote, eds., (Grand Rapids, MI: Eerdmans, 1980), p. 122.

development process where there is ownership by the people who have helped with the work.

Another problem that emerges with Bible translation is where people use the Bible as a fetish instead of understanding it as the Word of God. In such instances the Bible as a material artifact is used to bring good fortune, to ward off disease and illness or is used as a good luck charm. This is an example of the classic problem between form and meaning, where the form of the Bible becomes more important than the meaning it is meant to communicate to its readers. Speaking of his work among the Lumbee Indians in North Carolina, a pastor recently wrote in a personal letter, "They love their Bibles though they are relatively ignorant of its contents".

This is a problem that must be acknowledged. Once again, however, if the community is involved in the process of translation then it is more likely that the meaning of the Word of God will become more important in their lives than the form of the Bible that contains the Scripture. In this way people will be empowered by a living Word of God instead of enslaved by a static fetish.

Case Studies of Bible Translation and Development

I now want to draw on the above conceptual and theoretical discussion of Bible translation and development to briefly consider two case studies, the Hwa Lisu in China and the Tzeltals in Mexico.

Robert Litteral has researched the case of the Hwa Lisu who lived in the Yunnan Province of Southwestern China near the Burma border, and it is upon his work that we now draw.[34] In 1910 J. O. Fraser of the China Inland Mission began work among the Lisu who at the time were isolated from much outside contact as was the case with most of the other ethnic minority groups in the Yunnan Province.[35] When he went there the Lisu had had very little interaction with foreigners, but he stayed and spent many years living among them and learning to speak their language. However, after years without a response to the gospel he nearly quit to go to another group and begin work among them. Eventually, however, the Lisu showed interest in his message and work.

The Lisu had an ancient myth that explained why their language was not written. It said that their god had at one time given writing on a piece of parchment to an ancestor of the Lisu. Unfortunately, he was careless with it. A dog found it and ate it, leaving them without written language. The myth prophesied that some day the Lisu would have writing again. It would come from a person with light skin from a far country who would bring them books in the Lisu language.

---

[34] Litteral, pp. 111-113.

[35] Tseng Hsiu Li, "The Sacred Mission: An American Missionary Family in the Lahu and the Wa Districts of Yunnan, China", M.A. Thesis, Baylor University, 1987.

Working with a Karen evangelist in Burma who could speak Lisu, Fraser created a simple script for the Lisu language and then translated a catechism, a few hymns and the Gospels of Mark and John. When the books arrived, the Lisu saw it as the fulfillment of the legend of the man from a far country coming with Lisu books.

Operating on a sound principle of development, Fraser told the Lisu, as they began turning to Christ, that he had come from a distant place to tell them about God and that it was now their responsibility to go and tell others. Many people took the translated catechism, hymn book and Gospels and evangelized by reading the catechism to people. With the simple script many Lisu could learn to read in a matter of weeks. Teaching people to read was one of the responsibilities the evangelists undertook so that by the time they left a village there were Christians who could read. Conversion and literacy were adopted together.

It should not be surprising to discover that literacy among the Lisu Christians was very high. All the Christians, except the very old, learned to read. The new Christians were highly motivated to learn to read because one of the catechism questions was, "Who should learn to read?", with the answer being, "Christians". Literacy spread as the Lisu taught each other to read.

This pattern of conversion and literacy is found throughout the expansion of the Christian church. For example, in many parts of Melanesia people talk about coming into the church as "going to school". Among the Khasis in Northeast India missionaries taught that "You cannot be a Christian without reading the Bible",—so people were taught to read in schools.

The Lisu are a good example of how Bible translation has been a catalyst contributing to their development. Although the translation was started by Fraser and the Karen bilingual evangelist, other missionaries and Lisu played major roles, giving the Lisu a sense of ownership in the process. The New Testament was completed in 1939, 29 years after Fraser had begun his work with the Lisu. The Lisu Bible has been highly valued. During the Cultural Revolution in China, when many Bibles were destroyed, frequently there would be only one Bible remaining in a village. The Lisu would hide it outside their village and people would go out one at a time to read it. Today, with the more open policy toward religious freedom in China, arrangements have been made for publishing 40,000 Lisu New Testaments.[36]

From the very beginning of missionary contact, the Lisu Church was encouraged to assume responsibility instead of develop dependence. In this case development was not done for them; they were empowered to do it for themselves. The missionary served as an advisor but responsibility for leadership rested with the church. The social pattern of conversion was generally through family units and often the Christians would organize themselves into distinct villages.

Following an incarnational approach to cross-cultural ministry, missionaries were culturally sensitive, living with the people, not separate from them, in

[36] *Eternity*, October 1987, p. 14.

their villages, and in houses similar to those of the Lisu. Christianity became well integrated into their culture as a large percent of the Lisu became Christian, and the society remains so today, after nearly four decades without missionaries living among them in China.[37] The Lisu case is a good example of how Bible translation served as a catalyst to promote integral human development in a society. The Word was translated and took root, and is now growing deeply within Lisu soil.

The Tzeltals of Southern Mexico represent another example of where Bible translation has contributed to development. The story of the Tzeltals has been documented by Marianna Slocum of the Summer Institute of Linguistics.[38] At the time of her initial work among the Tzeltals in the early 1940s these descendents of the ancient Maya were a despised group, isolated, abused, oppressed and exploited, and understandably, hostile to the outside world. There was very little integral human development among them. In its place was disease caused by inadequate hygiene and nutrition, a corporate sense of inferiority, and a serious problem of drunkenness among many. Slocum notes that one seldom heard music in the Tzeltal villages and that there was a noticeable absence of joy and laughter. Such oppressive conditions of human beings have been documented through history and around the world, and the Tzeltals were simply another living example. In the terminology of Naroll's theory of moralnets, we can see that their traditional Mayan system of moralnets was no longer functional. This absence of moralnets was leading the society toward self-destruction.

Into this dismal cultural context came intervention by cross-cultural communicators of the gospel. The New Testament was translated into the highland Oxchuc dialect and the lowland Bachajon dialect. The Tzeltals began responding to the Word of God in their own language. Conversion to Christ first followed family groups along already existing kinship structures, then by communities, and then by dialect areas, with subsequent change in every aspect of their lives. Slocum says that before the Tzeltals had vernacular Scripture the factors that prohibited their development were geographical isolation, monolingualism and illiteracy, but the dominant factor was "the all-pervasive fear of witchcraft—a spiritual barrier that could only be overcome by spiritual means".[39] Those spiritual means were available in the translated Scriptures. As they responded to them, individuals and communities were transformed, for the truth did clearly make them free. Integral human development followed, bringing positive change in educational, economic, medical, social and spiritual domains.

Slocum worked with the Tzeltals from 1941 to 1964 and then moved to Colombia to take on another Bible translation project. Twenty-one years later in May, 1985, she and her partner revisited the Tzeltals,

---

37 Cf. Tseng Hsiu Li, "The Sacred Mission".

38 Marianna Slocum, *The Good Seed*, (Orange, CA: Promise Publishing Co., 1988).

39 Ibid., "Personal communication", July 9, 1988.

and were amazed at "what God hath wrought." In one generation the Tzeltal Christians have progressed in fully verifiable ways: high rate of literacy in their own language; 80+ Tzeltal paramedics caring for the medical needs of their own people in self-sustaining clinics; greatly improved standards of living; economic betterment, affecting housing, dress, educational opportunities, and lifestyle in general. They themselves repeatedly told us: "It is because of the Word of God that we have so much better lives!"[40]

The Tzeltals refer to their vernacular Scriptures as "The Good Seed". Once it was planted in their own soil it grew, and was a catalyst that stimulated growth throughout their culture. The Tzeltals are a vivid example of how the indigenizing process of translation can stimulate the process of integral human development.

Conclusion

The topic of the relationship between Bible translation and social and cultural development is a largely unexplored but nevertheless an exciting and stimulating area of research. I believe it is an unexplored arena for two reasons. First, because of the complex nature of culture change it is difficult to isolate and determine mono-causal influences on culture. In other words, we cannot construct two human laboratories (cultures) where identical conditions exist so that we can have a control group and an experimental group, and into the experimental group we insert the factor of vernacular Scriptures, and then empircally determine how they influence social and cultural development. But of course we can understand a great deal about human behavior and the role of stimulants to culture change without having to resort to "laboratory conditions". We simply have to realize the limitations of our social science models of inquiry and explanation.

The second reason this arena of Bible translation and development remains largely unexplored is because anthropologists and other social scientists have generally had such strong biases against the influence on traditional societies of the Bible, Christianity, and Christian missionaries. These biases, while frequently implicit but occasionally explicit, have tended to prevent us from seeing the positive contribution that vernacular Scriptures have made to development. It has been too easy to simply lump translation together with other mission activites and brand the whole lot as an extension of Western colonial imperialism. We are therefore grateful to Lamin Sanneh for challenging this "party line" assumption and opening up the discussion of the impact of Christianity, Western missionaries, and vernacular Scriptures on the non-western

[40] Ibid.

peoples of the world.[41] He has helped us to see "that Christian missions are better seen as a translation movement, with consequences for vernacular revitalization, religious change and social transformation, than as a vehicle for Western cultural domination".[42]

There can be no development without change. The change that occurs in persons and communities when they encounter the Word of God in their own language is a change that can be so powerful that it leads to positive growth and integral human development. This position is argued by G. Linwood Barney in discussing the development of an indigenous church and subsequent culture change among the Meo of Laos. He notes,

> Christianity, as an innovation in any culture, will cause changes, but when properly introduced and cultivated it will produce a Christian ethic within the configuration of the pre-existing culture without having caused a disintegration of that culture.[43]

It is my hope that this discussion will encourage more research that will document the positive contribution that vernacular Scriptures have made to culture change in general and to integral human development in particular.

---

41 Sanneh, "Christian Missions and the Western Guilt Complex".

Lamin Sanneh, *Translating the Message: The Missionary Impact on Culture*, (Maryknoll, NY: Orbis Books, 1989).

42 Sanneh, "Christian Missions and the Western Guilt Complex", p. 334.

43 G. Linwood Barney, "The Meo—An Incipient Church", *Practical Anthropology* 4:49-50.

BIBLIOGRAPHY

Appell, George N. 1975. "The Pernicious Effects of Development". *Fields Without Fields* 14:31-41.

Barney, G. Linwood. 1957. "The Meo—An Incipient Church". *Practical Anthropology* 4:31-50.

Beidelman, Thomas O. 1982. *Colonial Evangelism*. Bloomington: Indiana University Press.

Bragg, Wayne. 1983. "Beyond Development". In *The Church in Response to Human Need*. Tom Sine, ed. Pp. 37-95. Monrovia, CA: MARC.

Chambers, Robert. 1983. *Rural Development: Putting the Last First*. Ithaca: Rural Development Committee.

Evans-Pritchard, E.E. 1974 [1956]. *Nuer Religion*. New York: Oxford University Press.

Goldschmidt, Walter. 1966. *Comparative Functionalism: An Essay in Anthropological Theory*. Berkeley: University of California Press.

Goody, Jack. 1977. *The Domestication of the Savage Mind*. Cambridge: Cambridge University Press.

————. 1986. *The Logic of Writing and the Organization of Society*. Cambridge: Cambridge University Press.

————. 1987. *The Interface Between the Written and the Oral*. Cambridge: Cambridge University Press.

————, ed. 1968. *Literacy in Traditional Societies*. Cambridge: Cambridge University Press.

Goulet, Denis. 1987. "Ethics in Development Theory and Practice". *Catalyst* 17:314-330.

Haomae, William. 1981. "Development Wheel of Rural Growth". *Solomon Islands News Drum*. May 8, p. 5.

Litteral, Robert L. 1988. *Community Partnership in Communications for Ministry*. Wheaton: The Billy Graham Center.

Loewen, Jacob A. 1980. "The Gospel: Its Content and Communication--An Anthropological Perspective". In *Down to Earth: Studies in Christianity and Culture*. John R. W. Stott and Robert Coote, eds. Grand Rapids: Eerdmans, pp. 115-130.

————. 1985. "Developing Moralnets: Twenty-five Years of Culture Change Among the Choco". In *Missionaries, Anthropologists, and Cultural Change*. Darrell L. Whiteman, ed. Studies in Third World Societies, No. 25. Williamsburg, VA: College of William and Mary, pp. 229-261.

McKinney, Carol V. 1976. "Culture Change and its Relation to Literacy". *Missiology* 4:65-74.

Messenger, John C. Jr. 1959. "The Christian Concept of Forgiveness and Anang Morality". *Practical Anthropology* 6:97-103.

Naroll, Raoul. 1983. *The Moral Order: An Introduction to the Human Situation*. Beverly Hills, CA: SAGE Publications.

Nyerere, Julius K. 1976. "Declaration of Dar Es Salaam. Liberated Man--the Purpose of Development". *Convergence* 9(4):9-16.

Ong, Walter. 1982. *Orality and Literacy: The Technologizing of the World*. New York: Routledge, Chapman and Hall.

Poggie, John J. Jr. and Robert N. Lynch, eds. 1974. *Rethinking Modernization: Anthropological Perspectives*. Westport, CT: Greenwood Press.

Pollock, David H. 1980. "A Latin American Strategy to the Year 2000: Can the Past Serve as a Guide to the Future?" In *Latin American Prospects for the 80s: What Kinds of Development?* Ottawa: Norman Patterson School of International Affairs, Carleton Univeristy, Conference Proceedings, Vol. 1, November 1980, pp. 1-37.

Priest, Robert J. 1987. "Anthropologists and Missionaries: Moral Roots of Conflict". In *Current Concerns of Anthropologists and Missionaries*. Karl Franklin, ed. International Museum of Cultures Publication No. 22. Dallas: Summer Institute of Linguistics, pp. 13-40.

Rogers, Everett M. 1969. *Modernization Among Peasants: The Impact of Communication*. New York: Holt, Rinehart and Winston.

————. 1975. "The Anthropology of Modernization and the Modernization of Anthropology". *Reviews in Anthropology* 2:345-358.

Sanneh, Lamin. 1987. "Christian Missions and the Western Guilt Complex". *The Christian Century*, April 8, 1987, pp. 330-334.

————. 1989. *Translating the Message: The Missionary Impact on Culture*. Maryknoll, NY: Orbis Books.

Seligson, Mitchell A. ed. 1984. *The Gap Between Rich and Poor: Contending Perspectives on the Political Economy of Development*. Boulder, CO: Westview Press.

Slocum, Marianna. 1988a. *The Good Seed*. Orange, CA: Promise Publishing Co.

————. 1988b. "Personal communication". July 9, 1988.

Stoesz, Edgar. 1977. *Thoughts on Development*. Development Monograph Series 1. Akron, PA: Mennonite Central Committee.

Tseng Hsiu Li. 1987. "The Sacred Mission: An American Missionary Family in the Lahu and the Wa Districts of Yunnan, China". M.A. thesis, Baylor University.

Whiteman, Darrell L. 1983. *Melanesians and Missionaries*. Pasadena, CA: William Carey Library.

————. 1984. "How Cultures Change". In *An Introduction to Melanesian Cultures*. Darrell L. Whiteman, ed, pp. 29-55. Point Series No. 5. Goroka: The Melanesian Institute.

————, ed. 1985. *Missionaries, Anthropologists and Cultural Change*. Studies in Third World Societies, No. 25. Williamsburg, VA: College of William and Mary.

Yost, Larry E. and Willa D. Yost. 1983. *A Philosophy of Intercultural Community Relations and a Strategy for Preparing S.I.L. Members for Intercultural Community Work*. Dallas: Summer Institute of Linguistics.

ULRICH FICK

FUTURE BIBLE TRANSLATION
AND THE FUTURE OF THE CHURCH

Introduction

From a person who was shaped by a German academic tradition you would surely expect a number of prolegomena—some of you might even be disappointed if these introductory remarks do not form the main part of my presentation.

I will limit my remarks to two predictable points.

First, you all realize that it gives me a special advantage and disadvantage to present the last paper in this series of lectures.

The real advantage is that I was able to listen and partially absorb what was said over these past two days. I did constantly add to or modify my own set of notes as our symposium proceeded.

The disadvantage is similarly obvious: what I have here now is a highly provisional mixture of what I had thought and written in advance, and of the new highlights and aspects which this encounter has brought to our attention. So, rather than giving you a well balanced and pre-fabricated view on future Bible translation and the future of the Church, I am here with a number of preliminary responses to our discussions, and with an attempt at drawing some conclusions which, I assume, will ask for further work, further defining, refining, and redefining.

Prolegomenon Beta: From a speaker who comes from Stuttgart, where Hegel was born, you can expect that all material—his own as well as what he picked up during the meeting—will automatically organize itself in three parts ("Er sagt es klar und angenehm, dass erstens, zweitens, drittens käm . . "). I am under the impression that there were indeed three major areas of topics—or "Themenfelder"—which emerged time and again during our discussions. Namely first: what is the character of the Bible and its effect on those who meet and read it? To me this is a phenomenological consideration: how does the Scripture by the very way it is structured state conditions for its study and understanding? What about its diversity and its unity? "De natura Scripturae" might a speaker have called this chapter some centuries ago.

The second major cluster of topics centers around current forecasts on the growth of the church into the next millennium. Which role will the translation of the Bible, from what we can see in the past two centuries, most likely play in the development of the Church in the future? To me, this is a missiological consideration.

These two aspects, taken together, lead to a third field of questions: we are challenged by the symposium to understand better the correlation between Bible translation and the growth of the Church in order to outline a number of concrete tasks which arise from the fact that we are about to move on to a new and basically different situation. What can we do, what are we supposed to do? This is a consideration of strategy.

Part 1

The Character of the Bible and Its Implications

1.1. The character of the Bible

We all agreed that the book that we translated has a distinct character. Let me illustrate it by saying what the Bible is not: not a systematic presentation of Christian doctrine, a "summa theologiae" (which the Fathers of the Church could well have sifted out of all parts of Scripture in order to make this systematical, topical presentation the fundamental statement of faith). The Bible is not a harmony of Christian teaching, nor a historical outline, a "history of salvation".

Just remember the many illustrations which were presented here in all papers for the diversity of the material which we encounter in the Bible. "Not a book, but a library". The ancient Church, when deciding on the canon, wanted people to have four Gospels, not a "life of Christ", but a collection of four different presentations of the teaching and the person of Jesus, the Christ, each written for a different audience and under a different main aspect of the message. And the second main section in the New Testament is a collection of letters, again with a variety of recipients, a variety of authors responding to a variety of situations and challenges. Add to this the Old Testament, which has the same literary character of a collection of heterogeneous materials combined only by the common theme of reflecting God's actions to reveal himself, and human responses to this revelation. All of this gives us a highly complex compendium of texts with a variety of theologies, all interrelated, all part of a whole, but with various layers and emphases.

So any person who opens the Bible will encounter a complex collection of statements by various human speakers and writers, all of which, like a symphony, are but one voice in a tapestry of sound.

The history of the world and of faith in this world is reflected in the Bible and cannot be ignored. On the contrary: the better we understand a message in its own historical and cultural context, the better we understand its meaning within the entirety of the biblical message, and so its meaning for today. Far from darkening or even destroying the substance of the Bible, scholarly historical analysis of the setting from which the biblical texts originated illuminates their meaning.

This is not a deficiency of the Bible. It is the consequence of an act of God without which we would be ignorant of him: it is a consequence of his incarnation, his readiness to let human beings speak about him. The Bible is the result of God's decision to enter his own creation in order to be met by his creatures.

I am sure you all realized how often during these days we used the categories and the terminology of Christology in our attempts to describe the nature of the Bible: it is "fully human and fully divine". No monophysite thought pattern when it comes to the Bible! The two natures of Christ are mirrored also in the Bible: the diversity of the Bible is the human dimension—God revealing himself in human history—while the unity of the Bible, the fact that all of it is part of a consistent revelation of God, can be grasped only with the eyes and ears of faith—like humans confessing the Lordship of Christ are led to do so not by the convincing logic of an intellectual exercise but by the power of the Holy Spirit. Like Christ who was true man and true God, the Bible is fully human and fully holy.

So we just cannot take the Bible for a book which fell from heaven. No, it grew over centuries out of the human experience of encountering God in this world, in their own personal history and in history at large, and over the centuries readers and hearers did in faith grasp its unity as a consistent message of salvation, addressed to all, and so including themselves.

1.2. Fundamentalism does not recognize the specific character of the Bible

Only a fundamentalism which is blind to the historical origins and the specific kerygma of the many parts of the Bible can claim that there is no difference in accentuation, no reference to and dependence on various historical contexts and cultural patterns, no shifts of emphasis, no difference in importance, no tension between various theologies in the Bible. Those who are involved in the discussion about the inerrancy of the Bible—on either side: those defending as well as those attacking—can continue only as long as they ignore the character of the Bible as a multi-layered composition, as a multi-voiced concert of many instruments to the glory of God. It takes some effort, it seems to me, to overlook the fact that fundamentalism starts by taking the Bible for what it does not want to be taken.

Bible translators cannot do their work without recognizing this character of the Bible whenever and wherever they work. One simply cannot focus on the meaning of a biblical text in order to find an adequate expression of it in the languages and words of today without becoming acutely aware of the implications of language and words at the time when this text was first formulated. No one is more aware of the historical context of the text than a person whose aim is to translate that text. So what I am saying here is daily fare for our translators. It is not so well understood, however, by some parts of the church and some teachers of the church, thus my emphasis here. Nor do I find sufficient consideration at all places of the tasks which the Bible presents to its readers by being what it is.

1.3. The Bible gives concrete tasks to its readers

There was also consensus among us that the way the Bible was formed and is presented to us does, on the other hand, contain a number of tasks which all readers have to be prepared to face.

Readers cannot understand anything without an effort to differentiate and to compare. They have to distinguish not only between the skopus and the historical terminology of a text, but also between various skopoi, stated in various settings. In other words: the Bible, because of not coming to us as a composite text which would systematize and harmonize the messages which it carries, asks for an exegetical analysis and a theological effort towards systematization on the side of each reader.

Here the history of biblical interpretation—which exists in various degrees everywhere as part of the cultural tradition of each reader—can both help and hinder. People put what they read in the Bible into a system of understanding without being fully aware of what they are doing. Dr. Nida spoke about an "informed or un-informed reading".

There is the milieu of traditional interpretation of a text by the Church which inevitably flavours the understanding of the individual who reads the Bible. This, I think, can help and hinder: it can assist people in putting messages which they hear when reading at the place where they belong. It can on the other side be an obstacle for a real, existential encounter with the Bible because "we have heard that before, we know it all". Biblical messages can be neutralized and domesticated by a neutralizing and domesticating interpretation by the Church.

Here a task for Bible translators in signalled. With increasing urgency they are asked by the churches to assist the readers in their difficult task of finding their own access to the center of this book. This signal ought to be seen by the Bible Societies in their function as publishers of Bibles: what helps can they give which would enable the readers to find their own ways into this book? Not by pushing a particular doctrine—that is, the understanding of Scripture held by a particular church. This was the purpose of adding note and comment to Scripture texts at the time the Bible Societies were founded: notes at that time were as a rule highly polemical and apologetical, anti-Catholic in Protestant Bibles, anti-Protestant in Catholic Bibles . . . If the Bible Societies wanted to produce Scriptures which could be used by all, they had to reach the conclusion that they would publish the text "without note and comment".

Today, the Bible Societies have good reasons to make it their policy to include a different, non-controversial kind of notes. This is possible because the area in which exegetical consensus exists has widened dramatically, and similarly the opinions held in theological faculties on which historical information is needed to understand a text are quite alike. So at the present time several teams are at work formulating interconfessional notes which are to go with interconfessional translations, and the results of the work done so far are highly encouraging. The purpose of this exercise is not to make one church grow but to make the Church grow.

I hasten to add that sometimes an encounter between a person and a text can be so hot, so strong that the fuses of all "Vorverständnisse" as well as everything which "helps" would offer are burned through, and so an immediacy results which is in no need of notes or explanations. Such an experience of a new discovery has to prove itself against the traditional interpretation. Many mission and re-awakening movements have started like that. The traditional interpretation of the Bible is no safeguard against God's spirit moving people, nor is scholarly assistance with notes an indispensable help towards discovering the meaning of the text. By the power of the Word, which is beyond explanation, people have been, are, and will be led to say and do new things, as God wants it.

1.4. No chance for a Biblical theology without access to the whole Bible

Such a discovery, however, could remain an isolated and thus misleading message if it is based on a text taken out of context. People can form a sound biblical theology only on the basis of having access to the whole Bible.

If we understand Christian theology as the intellectual effort to find and formulate the essence of God's revelation that is documented in the Bible in the context of a given life situation of the church, then it cannot be based on a limited number of pre-selected biblical texts but needs, as a starting point, access to the whole Bible.

The reason for this is simple. All selections of Bible passages follow a given theological concept of what is "central" and what is "ephemeral". Anyone editing a "shorter Bible" has to determine what should be included and what should be excluded, and this can only be done following the pattern of a theological system which has already been decided.

This is why the Bible Societies listen so carefully to churches who tell them they need the whole Bible. We just cannot be satisfied by distributing the New Testament alone (as is the main emphasis placed by the Gideons in their extension programs), nor would we want to offer, as a final format, Bibles which only contain "the important sections". Important to whom?

Christians in the Third World who so far had access only to very limited parts of the Bible will only be able to develop their indigenous theologies once they can see these texts in the entire biblical perspective.

At this point, I would like to take a look together with you at the forecasts on world Christianity.

Part 2

The Future of the Church

2.1. Where does the Church grow?

It is a known fact that within a few years we will have a distribution of Christians around the world which will be dramatically different from the picture one could see at the beginning of this century.

Statisticians predict that the number of Christians in the western world will decrease. The white-skinned populations of the globe will become an even smaller minority anyway. Among them, the number of Christians will further diminish. Nominally Christian countries have no social pressure any more to maintain membership in a church even without conviction. At the same time, populations in Africa, Asia, and Latin America will grow, and within these populations also the number of Christians will increase at a rate which in Africa is significantly above the population growth rate. Already since mid-1987, more than half of the Christian world population is non-white. This trend will accelerate. We move towards a time when the majority of Christians will live in developing, poor, third world countries, no longer in industrialized, affluent European/North American countries.

Surprises are in store, of course.

It is possible that the erosion of churches with only nominal membership can be arrested by a genuine re-awakening, a re-commitment of large numbers of people who now are Christian only by name. Also the socialist countries may have some surprises in the making. Such developments can happen by God's power, and are known to him alone.

But present trends visible to us today indicate that the overwhelming number of Christians will be in African, Asian, and Latin American churches, in churches, however, which are far from being fully equipped with Bibles in their own languages.

The present figures from translations reports are known:

The whole Bible has been translated into 303 languages,
the New Testament into 670,
single biblical books into 911 languages,
which gives a total of 1,884 languages.

Bible Society have reasons to hesitate, however, when too much emphasis is put on these figures. They know that a quite few of these translations have become obsolete—either by having never been very accurate, or due to the passage of time and the process of change. Some of our translation consultants say that the majority of the translations which are at present on the market are unsatisfactory from one point of view or another. Proof of this are newly published versions which are not accepted by the people for whom they were produced, while on the other hand sometimes publications are snatched up in no time, but due to timid planning people then have to wait for months for a reprint to become available.

It seems that with the changing picture of world Christianity, Bible translation will have to face a challenge of new magnitude.

2.2. UBS translation forecast

In a working plan for the eighties, the 1980 UBS Council meeting in Chiang Mai, Thailand—a gathering representative of all member societies around the world—has given its translation staff a distinct direction.

The Bible Societies accepted the goal of producing common language translations of the Bible—plus a full series of graded Scripture materials for beginning readers—in 227 identified major languages of the world, namely national or official languages, by 1990. With a few exceptions, these translations will be finished by the end of the decade.

We have to look, however, at the function of these major languages. They are eminently important for trade and communication, of course. What about the smaller languages which people use in their homes? Would they want or not want to worship and pray in these languages?

We hear that an estimated 47 percent of Nigerians today understand and read English (that is more than 40 million people). Can we be satisfied with supplying English Bibles to Nigeria, French Bibles to Madagascar and Zaire, Portuguese to Mozambique and Angola? While the lingua franca is essential in professional life for many, is it similarly essential in their religious life? And how deep down do national languages reach? Hindi did not, after all, become the national language of India, as planned by the Nehru administration.

Research done on indigenous churches in Africa indicates that the ethnic identity of these churches is very important. Reports from Bolivia and Ecuador tell us that with the publication of the whole Bible in Quechua and Aymara new life could be seen in the churches of these large Indian populations.

The Bible Societies have on their own added to their work in national and official languages the production of a full range of New Reader materials as a translation priority. I would like to suggest that the UBS put time and energy into the study of the use of languages in various levels of life—home, school, market, office, police, military, government, etc.—and decide on the basis of a constant observation of language use which languages are the most important and promising as carriers of new translations. Readings of the situation will change as the distribution of Christians around the world changes.

Part 3

The Correlation Between Bible Translation and the Growth of the Church

3.1. Growth is not merely a numerical aspect

We were asked by several speakers not to think of church growth only in terms of figures. The number of church members, of course, is an indicator of the size of a church, and changes in size deserve to be watched, be they positive or negative.

Figures, however, do not indicate the reason for change.

In the past church membership could well be the result of a sociological consideration—it could be part of a political change and the cultural adaptation which followed from this change. In ancient times the armies of the victorious nation brought with them their gods, built temples for them in occupied territories, and those of the occupied nation who wanted to cooperate decided to worship these gods. I personally remember the surprising success of Mormon missions in post World War II Germany: becoming Mormon at that time meant a ticket to the glorious United States and the promise of a better life.

Today at many—certainly not most—places of the world there exists, at least in theory, a religious pluralism. This is why countries which base citizenship on identifying with a state religion in general have a hard time. Even socialist countries of the world are in the process of moving from a single state ideology—example: the Stalin era in the USSR—which is protected against any new interpretation, let alone against any opposing views, to a new phase where the dominance of this sole correct ideology is weakened and allows a variety of views.

3.2. Growth of the Church in a pluralistic society

In the context of other religions which are all permitted and socially accepted, instead of social pressure or political supervision there can be only personal reasons for people to be Christian. I take this for an advantage. Growth of the church under these circumstances can only be the result of a convincing encounter with God—either in his word in the Scriptures, or in the life of a Christian community which represents the power and love of God in this world in a convincing way.

Rather than seeking certain privileges—which in the past were often open only to Christians—or than giving in to the expectation of the society, people may join a church and live with the Bible out of personal motivation.

Such a motivation, as we all know, is a complex chemistry of internal and external experience: the desire for God, the search for meaning, the longing for salvation, the invitation of a community which lives a different life, the compulsion to draw practical consequences of spiritual experiences, and all of this enhanced or contradicted, clarified or dimmed by environmental, economic, social, or political factors. Christianity in the past could spread along trade routes or from cell to cell in a prison, it could grow in an open society or under severe restriction. What happened in the People's Republic of China before and after the cultural revolution—and what amazingly came to light after it—is but one lesson about the mystery of faith.

One thing is sure: there cannot be a convincing contemporary Christian witness without the Bible.

3.3. The Bible and Christian witness as motor of growth

"Indigeneous theology", properly understood, is much more than a mere intellectual exercise. The intellect is only the instrument applied. The result is an existential interpretation of faith by means of action in a given context.

Churches will usually grow once this process has been brought to such a result. All of it needs the Bible as a standard and measure, as well as a motivation.

You see this when you look at the present range of radical theologies and their reference to the Bible. Black theology, liberation theology and feminist theology all wage their individual battles with biblical texts, and all have their particular problems with certain elements which they find in the Bible. Liberation theology is at war with those voices of the Bible which seem to support quietistic acceptance of the status quo. Black theology has to fight against what they see as a white interpretation of the Bible. Feminist theologians have the worst battle of all, because they find the patriarchal society of ancient times mirrored in the Bible, they hear in the original text "exclusive language", and, most ominous, there are the figures of God Father and Son . . .

Still, they all want to demonstrate biblical confirmation for their main focus and thrust, and go to the Bible for support. All will depend on how much they are able to listen even to those voices in the Bible which resist being used and which even oppose their theology.

Spiritual growth can only come from a patient and day-by-day readiness to listen particularly to those messages from the Bible which do not support what we always said and what we always wanted to do.

It is the persistent application of the Bible—by reading, praying, explaining, sharing, doing—in a context in which we find ourselves which adds spiritual depth and an increasing awareness of the presence and power of God to mere numbers which are added to church statistics.

3.3. To translate the Bible means doing groundwork for the church of tomorrow

There is a clear correlation between having access to the entire Bible in a certain language and the spiritual identity and determination of those who read it.

It is only the message of the Bible which, after all, can break the inherent egocentricity or—if taken in a corporative way—the ethnocentrism which are part of our human nature.

If there is hope that the Church of tomorrow will not fall apart and be fragmentized in the form of thousands and thousands of egocentric or ethnocentric little kingdoms, but will become, beyond our present separations, a church universal—this hope can only be fulfilled once all have access to the Bible.

For the world of tomorrow, a church shaped by the message of the Bible could be an important challenge. It could show people that, with the pressure of a growing world population, we can afford not to withdraw into our individual corners and defend what we have, against all the others. In tomorrow's world—where people will no longer fight one another with spears and arrows, but with weapons accessible to all which could be fatal for all—the church can show that it is possible to exercise unselfishness, to exercise self-control, to accept others and to extend love.

The world does not necessarily have to become a battle ground, devastated by ever escalating conflict. There is a chance that people see the chance for survival and communal life by tolerating, accepting, and even appreciating each other.

I see a world picture in the future in which world Christianity can play an essential role—just by demonstrating an alternative. The Christian task for being different, even tomorrow, can be essentially supported by the Bible Societies who can make accessible to all people that message which tells them why they can be different.